TRANSCENDENCE
AND IMMANENCE

D0989453

TRANSCENDENCE AND IMMANENCE

A Study in Catholic Modernism and Integralism

BY

GABRIEL DALY, O.S.A.

CLARENDON PRESS · OXFORD

1980

Oxford University Press, Walton Street, Oxford OX2 6DP

OXFORD LONDON GLASGOW
NEW YORK TORONTO MELBOURNE WELLINGTON
KUALA LUMPUR SINGAPORE JAKARTA HONG KONG TOKYO
DELHI BOMBAY CALCUTTA MADRAS KARACHI
NAIROBI DAR ES SALAAM CAPE TOWN

*Published in the United States
by Oxford University Press, New York*

British Library Cataloguing in Publication Data

Daly, Gabriel
    Transcendence and immanence.
    1. Immanence of God — History of doctrines
    2. Transcendence of God — History of doctrines
    3. Theology, Catholic — History
    I. Title
    231'.4   BT124   79-42790

ISBN 0-19-826652-9

*Typeset by Anne Joshua Associates, Oxford
and printed in Great Britain by
Billing & Sons Ltd.,
London, Guildford and Worcester*

Sic ergo quaeramus tanquam inventuri; et sic inveniamus tanquam quaesituri. 'Cum' enim 'consummaverit homo, tunc incipit' (Eccles. 18:6).

(Augustine, *De Trinitate*, ix,1)

Acknowledgements

My gratitude is due in the first instance to the Reverend Professor A. T. Hanson, who has been a source of constant stimulation and encouragement to me. I profited greatly from his advice at every stage of my research and especially from his comments on the completed manuscript. Professor N. Lash also read the manuscript and made many helpful comments. I am grateful for the interest and encouragement I received from the Reverend M. Nolan, O.S.A., the Reverend Professor F. X. Martin, O.S.A., the Reverend M. Hurley, S.J., and Dr J. Coulson. Through the good offices of Professor J. P. Mackey I was able to read Dr Mary Buckley's unpublished thesis on von Hügel, *Experience and Transcendence*.

The Reverend D. Power, O.M.I. did much to facilitate my work on the Lemius papers in the archives of the General House of the Oblates of Mary Immaculate in Rome. He was unsparing of his time and interest, and I am most grateful to him and to the General Archivist of the Oblates for enabling me to consult these documents in such friendly and hospitable surroundings.

I am indebted to many librarians; but my particular thanks are due to the Reverend D. Fleury, S.J., Librarian of the Milltown Institute of Theology and Philosophy, Dublin, and to the Milltown Park Jesuit Community for putting their library so fully at my disposal.

Many confrères and friends helped with such tasks as photocopying and proof-reading. The Reverend L. O'Sullivan, O.S.A., gave me much practical assistance at every stage of my work. Mrs E. Sides typed the manuscript with skill and patience. Finally I wish to thank the staff of the Oxford University Press, who gave me much helpful advice.

Exculpation of all the above from any complicity in, or approval of, the judgements expressed in this book should, in view of the inescapably controversial nature of the material covered, be taken as perhaps more than conventional.

June 1979   GABRIEL DALY

Contents

Acknowledgements   vii

Abbreviations   x

Introduction   1

1. ROMAN FUNDAMENTAL THEOLOGY IN THE LAST QUARTER
   OF THE NINETEENTH CENTURY   7

2. THE BLONDELIAN CHALLENGE   26

3. ALFRED LOISY AND THE RADICALIZATION OF THE
   MODERNIST MOVEMENT   51

4. HISTORY AND DOGMA: THE DEBATE BETWEEN ALFRED
   LOISY AND MAURICE BLONDEL   69

5. LUCIEN LABERTHONNIÈRE'S 'CRITICAL MYSTICISM'   91

6. FRIEDRICH VON HÜGEL: EXPERIENCE AND
   TRANSCENDENCE   117

7. GEORGE TYRRELL: REVELATION AS EXPERIENCE   140

8. THE INTEGRALIST RESPONSE (1): PRELUDE TO THE
   ROMAN CONDEMNATION OF MODERNISM   165

9. THE INTEGRALIST RESPONSE (2): *PASCENDI* AND AFTER   190

10. MODERNISM IN RETROSPECT   218

Appendix 1. Joseph Lemius (1860–1923), Draughtsman of *Pascendi*   232

Appendix 2. The Anti-Modernist Oath   235

Bibliography   237

Index   247

Abbreviations

A.A.S.	*Acta Apostolicae Sedis.*
A.P.C.	*Annales de philosophie chrétienne.*
A.S.S.	*Acta Sanctae Sedis.*
Aspects	R. Aubert, 'Aspects divers du néo-thomisme sous le pontificat de Léon XIII', in *Aspetti della cultura cattolica nell'età di Leone XIII* (Rome, 1961).
Au cœur	R. Marlé, *Au cœur de la crise moderniste* (Paris, 1960).
Autour	A. Loisy, *Autour d'un petit livre* (Paris, 1903).
B.L.	C. Tresmontant (ed.), *Maurice Blondel–Lucien Laberthonnière: Correspondance philosophique* (Paris, 1961).
B.L.E.	*Bulletin de littérature ecclésiastique.*
B.V.	H. de Lubac (ed.), *Maurice Blondel et Auguste Valensin: Correspondance, 1899–1947*, 3 vols. (Paris, 1957–65).
C.C.	G. Tyrrell, *Christianity at the Cross-Roads* (London, 1909).
Civ. Cat.	*La Civiltà Cattolica.*
Crisi	P. Scoppola, *Crisi modernista e rinnovamento cattolico in Italia* (Bologna, 1961).
D.C.	E. Le Roy, *Dogme et critique* (Paris, 1907).
Dru	A. Dru and I. Trethowan (eds.), *Maurice Blondel: The Letter on Apologetics and History and Dogma* (London, 1964).
E.A.	F. von Hügel, *Essays and Addresses on the Philosophy of Religion* (1st Series, London, 1921; 2nd Series, London, 1926).
E.F.I.	G. Tyrrell, *Essays on Faith and Immortality* (London, 1914).
E.L.	F. von Hügel, *Eternal Life: A Study of Its Implications and Applications* (Edinburgh, 1912).
E.P.R.	L. Laberthonnière, *Essais de philosophie religieuse*, in C. Tresmontant (ed.), Lucien Laberthonnière, *Le Réalisme chrétien: précédé de: Essais de philosophie religieuse* (Paris, 1966).
E.T.	F. von Hügel, 'Experience and Transcendence', in *The Dublin Review*, 138 (1906).

F.M.	G. Tyrrell, *The Faith of the Millions. A Selection of Past Essays* (1st Series, 2nd edn., London, 1902; 2nd Series, London, 1901).
G.T.L.	M. D. Petre (ed.), *George Tyrrell's Letters* (London, 1920).
H.D.	M. Blondel, 'Histoire et dogme: Les lacunes philosophiques de l'exégèse moderne', in *Les Premiers Écrits de Maurice Blondel*, vol. ii (Paris, 1956).
Histoire	E. Poulat, *Histoire, dogme et critique dans la crise moderniste* (Paris, 1962).
H.J.	*Heythrop Journal.*
I.P.Q.	M. Nédoncelle, 'A Recently Discovered Study of von Hügel on God', in *International Philosophical Quarterly*, 2 (1962).
Lettre	M. Blondel, 'Lettre sur les exigences de la pensée contemporaine en matière d'apologétique et sur la méthode de la philosophie dans l'étude du problème religieux', in *Les Premiers Écrits de Maurice Blondel*, vol. ii (Paris, 1956).
Life	M. D. Petre (ed.), *Autobiography and Life of George Tyrrell* (London, 1912).
L.N.	F. von Hügel, *Letters from Baron von Hügel to a Niece* (London, 1928).
M.E.	F. von Hügel, *The Mystical Element of Religion: As Studied in Saint Catherine of Genoa and Her Friends*, 2 vols. (2nd edn., London, 1923).
Mémoires	A. Loisy, *Mémoires pour servir à l'histoire religieuse de notre temps*, 3 vols. (Paris, 1930–1).
Outlines	A. Sabatier, *Outlines of a Philosophy of Religion Based on Psychology and History* (London and New York, 1902).
P.C.	F. von Hügel, 'Petite consultation sur les difficultés concernant Dieu', in P. Scoppola, *Crisi modernista e rinnovamento cattolico in Italia* (Bologna, 1961).
Programme	A. L. Lilley (ed.), *The Programme of Modernism: A Reply to the Encyclical of Pius X 'Pascendi Dominici Gregis'* (London, 1908).
R.C.F.	*Revue du clergé français.*
R.C.I.G.	L. Laberthonnière, *Le Réalisme chrétien et l'idéalisme grec*, in C. Tresmontant, Lucien Laberthonnière, *Le Réalisme chrétien, précédé de: Essais de philosophie religieuse* (Paris, 1966).
R.E.	G. Tyrrell, 'Revelation as Experience', in *Heythrop Journal*, 12 (1971).

R.S.R.	*Recherches de science religieuse.*
S.C.	G. Tyrrell, *Through Scylla and Charybdis; Or, The Old Theology and the New* (London, 1907).
S.L.	B. Holland (ed.), *Baron Friedrich von Hügel: Selected Letters, 1896–1924* (London, 1928).
S.R.	A. Loisy, *Simples réflexions sur le décret du saint-office 'Lamentabili sane exitu' et sur l'encyclique 'Pascendi dominici gregis'* (Ceffonds, 1908).
Variety	A. R. Vidler, *A Variety of Catholic Modernists* (Cambridge, 1970).

Introduction

In 1962, the year in which the Second Vatican Council opened, there appeared the fifth English edition of Ludwig Ott's *Fundamentals of Catholic Dogma*, a book which may go down in history as the last of the widely used neo-scholastic 'manuals'.[1] It is a masterpiece of compression, containing within its 500 pages the essential elements of the four-year course in dogmatic theology formerly taken by students for the Roman Catholic priesthood. On modernism Ott has this to say:

> The cognitional theoretical basis of Modernism is agnosticism, according to which human rational cognition is limited to the world of experience. Religion, according to this theory, develops from the principle of vital immanence (immanentism) that is, from the need for God which dwells in the human soul. The truths of religion are, according to the general progress of culture, caught up in a constant substantial development (evolutionism).[2]

It would be hard to better this passage as a summary, pared down to absolute essentials, of the teaching of Pope Pius X's Encyclical Letter, *Pascendi dominici gregis*, which was published on 8 September 1907 and which condemned 'the doctrine of the Modernists'. The encyclical, of course, specified many issues not included in Ott's passage (he mentions several of them elsewhere in his book); but in these words we have the gist of what the encyclical regarded as the basic errors of modernism, namely, agnosticism and the doctrine of vital immanence.

The present study is an investigation into the substance of this charge. Anti-modernist writings employ the term

---

[1] L. Ott, *Fundamentals of Catholic Dogma*. English edn. by James Canon Bastible D.D. Trans. from German by Patrick Lynch Ph.D. (Cork, 1962), German original, *Grundriss der Katholischen Dogmatik* first pub. 1952. Anyone lacking first-hand experience of the neo-scholastic tradition will find in Dr Ott's book a useful conspectus of its content and method.

[2] Ibid., pp. 16 f.

'agnosticism' in a specialized sense. The opening chapter will therefore indicate the normative elements in the philosophico-theological system against which the modernists reacted and for which reaction they were judged to be 'agnostic'. The terms 'transcendence' and 'immanence' received theological and philosophical prominence as a result of the Kantian critique of metaphysics. Since the Kantian critique was regarded as totally incompatible with Catholic theology, these terms did not normally feature in that theology and were in fact described by one prominent anti-modernist as 'barbarous'. The central chapters will attempt to discover why and how the modernists chose to use them as a means of bringing Roman Catholic theology into alignment with developments in contemporary critical thought. The last three chapters will examine respectively the build-up of the anti-modernist campaign, its culmination in the condemnation of 1907, and the subsequent effect of that condemnation upon Roman Catholic theology.

Much time, space, and energy has been devoted to deciding who was and who was not a modernist. Since the condemnation of modernism resulted in ecclesiastical obloquy for certain important Catholic theologians at the dawn of the present century and in the sequestration of their writings from active influence in Catholic theological life, it became incumbent on students of the thought of such men as Maurice Blondel and Friedrich von Hügel to show that their subjects had not been struck by the Roman thunderbolts but were, at the worst estimate, merely singed. It is the contention of this book that these exercises in beleaguered discipleship, never seemly, are now unnecessary in the changed atmosphere of the Roman Catholic Church after Vatican II. The anti-modernist documents have been rendered obsolete as canons of orthodoxy by the Roman Catholic magisterium itself.

Catholic theologians in recent times have begun to make some rather cautious concessions to the theological importance of what the modernists were saying. However, the thinking of normally precise theologians has been remarkably slipshod in this matter. Modernism 'proposed wrong solutions to many problems it had grasped aright'.[3] This sort of cosy simplification is nothing less than tendentious and misleading. The 'solutions' proposed by the modernists retain their theological importance today, especially after one has made the necessary discriminations: what solutions, to what problems, by which modernist? In no matter more than the central one of transcendence and immanence does it become so necessary to make these discriminations. The present study is intended as a contribution towards this task. It is high time for Roman Catholic theologians to cease making ritual obeisances towards the myth of a concerted modernist threat to the unity, orthodoxy, and stability of the Church.

To invoke the term myth in this context is not to imply that there was no substance to the charges brought against modernism by the Roman authorities. It is simply to claim that the assumptions made by the anti-modernists — for example, that modernism was an internally coherent system expressing itself in a carefully concerted movement — were so wide of the mark, that the understanding of modernism to be found in the Roman documents should be taken as symbolic of an attitude rather than as an accurate assessment of a factual situation. More than that, the historical theologian today may well find himself compelled by the evidence to see those documents as contributing to the very problems they were proposing to settle. One can quite reasonably argue that the Roman condemnation of modernism did far more harm to Catholic theology than did the writings of any modernist. 'Modernism', then, may best be regarded as a term of convenience employed by one school of thought in the Catholic Church to describe certain ideas, tendencies, and attitudes which that school saw as incompatible with its own tenets.

In 1907, and for many years thereafter, those tenets were quite simply identified with Catholic orthodoxy. There are therefore some good theological reasons for jettisoning the term modernism altogether. Attractive as this proposal is from a theological standpoint, it is not historically feasible.

[3] K. Rahner and H. Vorgrimler, *Concise Theological Dictionary*, ed. C. Ernst, trans. R. Strachan (London, 1965), p. 290.

The term came into existence during the period in question, was employed as a pejorative label, but was not seriously contested by Loisy, Tyrrell, or the Roman radicals. Tyrrell was forthright: 'Clear naming is essential to clear thinking; a spade is not a shovel.'[4] He therefore accepted the label and proceeded to define the contents of the package. 'By a Modernist, I mean a churchman, of any sort, who believes in the possibility of a synthesis between the essential truth of his religion and the essential truth of modernity.'[5] Émile Poulat's definition of modernism reflects Tyrrell's diagnosis: 'En son sens le plus général, le modernisme peut se définir comme la rencontre et la confrontation actuelles d'un passé religieux depuis longtemps fixé, avec un présent qui a trouvé ailleurs qu'en lui les sources vives de son inspiration.'[6] Tyrrell, however, went still further when he remarked of *Pascendi* that whereas the encyclical 'tries to show the Modernist that he is no Catholic, it mostly succeeds only in showing him that he is no scholastic'.[7] There is enough truth in this judgement to allow one to demand of any theologian who refers to 'modernism' that he show the provenance of his understanding of the term. If he accepts the definition of modernism provided by *Pascendi*, let him say so without equivocation and we shall know where we stand with him. If he does not accept that definition, it is incumbent upon him to show what view of *Pascendi* he does take, and from what other sources, theological or historical, he derives his definition and understanding of modernism. If one does not take one's definition and understanding of modernism from *Pascendi*, it is my contention that there remains no convincing reason for distinguishing between 'modernism' and 'liberal Catholicism' or between the 'modernism' of Tyrrell, Blondel, or von Hügel *in respect of neo-scholastic orthodoxy as it was then understood and practised.*[8] Any distinctions

---

[4] G. Tyrrell, *Christianity at the Cross-Roads* (London, 1909), p. xvii.

[5] Ibid., p. 5.

[6] Poulat, *Histoire*, p. 15. Poulat repeats this definition verbatim seven years later in his article ' "Modernisme" et "Intégrisme". Du concept polémique à l'irénisme critique', in *Archives de sociologie des religions*, 27 (1969), p. 5.

[7] M. D. Petre, *Life*, vol. ii, p. 337.

[8] See, however, W. J. Schoenl, 'George Tyrrell and the English Liberal Catholic Crisis, 1900–1901', in *Downside Review*, 92 (1974), pp. 171–84. Schoenl draws a clear and unconvincing distinction between modernism and liberal Catholicism.

we make between the leading modernists will need to be made on the basis of what each wrote (as we should do with theologians in any other age) and not on the basis of their alleged conformity or lack of conformity with a concept of orthodoxy which has been substantially changed by the official magisterium of the Roman Catholic Church itself.

The following are some of the assumptions, limitations, and definitions which control the subject-matter of, and its presentation in, this book.

(1) The period under review extends approximately from 1869 (the meeting of the First Vatican Council) to 1910 (the completion of the Roman condemnation of modernism). The core of the crisis can be found in the three years from 1904 (when the term 'modernism' probably appeared for the first time in its pejorative sense) to 1907 (when the decree, *Lamentabili*, and the encyclical, *Pascendi*, were issued).

(2) No assumptions about orthodoxy or heterodoxy are made, if for no other reason than that the canons of ortho-doxy which governed the Roman Catholic Church during the modernist period have been, both explicitly and im-plicitly, revised by the formal conciliar magisterium of the Roman Catholic Church itself in the last fifteen years.

(3) It is therefore unnecessary, except as an academic historical exercise, to distinguish between those who were modernists in the full sense, those who were 'fellow-travellers', and those who were not personally envisaged in the Roman condemnation. This condemnation (for which only a bold few, of whom the most notable was Arthur Vermeersch, would claim infallibility) is as open to theological and histori-cal investigation and reassessment as are the views of the modernists themselves.

(4) The term 'modernist' is thus inescapably imprecise. It is taken here to apply to any Roman Catholic writer whose thinking and methodology led him to challenge the over-all philosophico-theological *schema*, or any significant element therein, of the then prevailing neo-scholastic conception and method of doing philosophy and theology.

(5) Since the topic of this book is transcendence and immanence, and since the short description of modernism offered here is 'any Roman Catholic challenge to the received

neo-scholasticism of the period', I shall take the publication of Maurice Blondel's doctoral thesis, *L'Action*, in 1893 as the point at which the modernist challenge can be reasonably said to have begun.

I have made these few discriminations so that my position will be clear to the reader, who, if he prefers a different perspective, will be able to make the necessary allowances and consequent adjustment of interpretation. References to Blondel, von Hügel, and Laberthonnière as 'modernist' may jar on the susceptibilities of some of their Roman Catholic admirers. This introduction should have made it plain that no pejorative connotation is implied. The chapters which follow are intended to show why.

I Roman Fundamental Theology in the Last Quarter of the Nineteenth Century

The conception of theological orthodoxy which triumphed over modernism by *force majeure* rather than by free and open debate was described appositely by some of its defenders as 'integralism'. In their minds it stood or fell *as a whole*, and a divinely guaranteed whole at that. It comprised certain clearly defined philosophical foundations together with a systematic superstructure the various elements of which were each seen as indispensable to the whole. Its defenders became convinced during the first decade of the twentieth century that both foundations and superstructure were under insidious and radical attack from the inside. The present chapter will attempt to indicate those areas in Roman[1] theology and philosophy which had particular structural importance in the over-all system and which were felt to be under greatest threat from modernist views on transcendence and immanence. The system was designed to demonstrate and defend an objective order of divine facts and teachings the evidence for which was believed to be open in principle to verification by any right-minded person. Most Roman Catholic theologians were convinced that this firm and methodological objectivization constituted the characteristic strength of Catholicism as constrasted with what they saw as the vacillations and unpredictabilities of Protestant subjectivism. When the modernists were accused, as they frequently were, of capitulating to Protestantism, their accusers had in mind not this or that doctrine of the Reformers but the general drive towards individual, personalized, subjective response which seemed to the scholastic mind to be so erratic and capricious as to be incapable of receiving the stamp of certifiably divine authority.

---

[1] It should be noted that the word 'Roman' is used throughout this book in its strictly geographical sense and not as an ecclesiological adjective.

Since it was the philosophy of Immanuel Kant which seemed to give strongest critical support to the drive towards 'subjectivism' implicit in Luther's doctrine of faith, Kant rapidly became the *bête noire* of Roman Catholic apologetic. This is not to imply that the challenge of Kantianism was recognized for the first time during the modernist period. The bishops and theologians of the [First] Vatican Council were already aware of the generally unsettling effect upon theology of the Kantian critique; but they did not focus their attention on Kant as later Catholic apologists would do. Instead they carried out their deliberations in the light of a generalized awareness of, and hostility to, eighteenth- and nineteenth-century 'rationalism'. In the Dogmatic Constitution, *Dei Filius*, on revelation and faith, they set about charting a course between rationalism and fideism. The problem for them was not how one could speak about a transcendent being and that being's relationship with historically situated man; rather they were concerned so to construe the act of faith as not to call in question its basic rationality on the one hand or its supernatural origin and character on the other. The distinction between 'rational' and 'supernatural' was not intended to imply an antithesis, but it survived into the modernist period to be expressed in ways which did in fact often suggest such an antithesis. Time and again those who advocated the new Blondelian apologetic were accused of denying the supernatural character of faith because they postulated, as inherent in human nature itself, an 'exigence' for the supernatural. On the whole, the anti-modernist preoccupation with the gratuitousness of supernature served to cloud the main issues under debate, while the appeal to the teaching of the Vatican Council often lacked cogency, precisely because the conciliar Fathers had not directed their attention towards an apologetic of immanence. The necessity, which neo-scholastic theologians experienced, of holding a balance between the 'natural' claims of reason on the one hand and the 'supernatural' character of the act of faith on the other, ensured that increasing attention would be given to the distinction between the preliminaries to faith (*preambula fidei*) and the act of faith itself. This distinction would in turn widen the gap between 'fundamental'[2] theology and 'dogmatic' theology proper, giving the former an apologetical character which Blondel was to stigmatize as 'extrinsicism'.

The deliberations of the Vatican Council had focused attention on two major theological issues. The first of these was ecclesiology restrictively considered as the theology of the *teaching* Church, and especially of the role of the Pope in that teaching. This issue concerns us only indirectly here. One simply notes that a reinforced theology of papal primacy facilitated centralization not only of Church government but also of the theological elaboration and defence of Roman Catholic beliefs. The second issue, the theology of faith and reason, is crucial to an understanding of the conflict over transcendence and immanence.

How was 'reason' to be understood and then related to faith? The question was philosophical, and it posed the further and inescapable question: which philosophy? The philosophical eclecticism which then prevailed in Roman Catholic academic life did not appear capable of producing the ringing summons that many Catholics felt to be necessary. Gioacchino Pecci, elected Pope Leo XIII in 1878, was one of those who were convinced that Catholic theology needed more secure philosophical moorings. Able to draw on the enhanced authority and mystique which the recent Council had bestowed on his office, Leo set about making the philosophy of Thomas Aquinas mandatory for the whole Church. He expressed his grand design in an encyclical letter, *Aeterni Patris* (4 August 1879).[3]

Aeterni Patris is occasionally and inaccurately described as a call to return to scholastic philosophy *in general*, St. Thomas being seen as a symbolic representative of the whole

---

[2] Fundamental theology is described by Hurter, one of the leading textbook authors of the period, as concerning itself with 'the very fact of revelation, which is the foundation (*fundamentum*) of special [i.e. dogmatic] theology'. Hurter adds: 'Ea si proprie loqui velimus non est theologia, sed propaedeutica philosophica ad theologiam.' (H. Hurter, *Theologiae dogmaticae compendium in usum studiosorum theologiae*, vol. i (12th edn., Innsbruck, 1909), p. 9 and note.)

[3] Text in *Acta Sanctae Sedis* [*A.S.S.*], 12 (1879-80), pp. 97-115. R. Aubert provides a useful summary in his important article, 'Aspects divers du néothomisme sous le pontificat de Léon XIII', in *Aspetti della cultura cattolica nell'età di Leone XIII* (Rome, 1961) [*Aspects*], pp. 140-8.

scholastic tradition.[4] The fact is that Leo's encyclical is unambiguously a summons to return to the philosophy of Aquinas *simpliciter*. Aubert has pointed out that since it was Leo who initiated the movement which only later issued in a truly critical study of medieval philosophy, he himself can hardly be expected to have appreciated the diversity, indeed pluralism, of that philosophy,[5] and he may have supposed that the differences between Thomism and Augustinianism were less significant than they in fact were. The encyclical also makes it plain that the Pope had principally in mind the training of students for the priesthood. Thomism would protect them, he felt, not only from the dangerous vagaries of secular philosophy, but also from the fideistic tendencies to be found in nineteenth-century French Catholic thought. The Vatican Council had directed the mainstream of its teaching towards the harmony which exists *de jure* between faith and reason. Leo proclaimed that that harmony could be found *de facto* in the doctrine of St. Thomas, who had constructed his philosophical system in the light of Christian faith without destroying its rational autonomy.

The Pope backed his manifesto with vigorous action. He instructed the Gregorian University in Rome to teach only Thomism. It was an instruction which placed a severe strain on Jesuit 'obedience of the intellect', since many of the Gregorian's staff were disciples of Suarez and even, to some extent, of Descartes.[6] Leo also brought pressure to bear on the other Roman colleges and on the Catholic University of Louvain. In the latter case the eventual and somewhat reluctant outcome was the appointment of Désiré Mercier as 'Professor of Philosophy according to St. Thomas'.[7]

It would be idle to suppose that on the morrow of the publication of *Aeterni Patris* the whole Catholic Church

---

[4] For example Jean Rivière, in his *Le Modernisme dans l'Église* (p. 69) wrote that *Aeterni Patris* 'restaurait le culte de la philosophie médiévale'.

[5] Aubert, *Aspects*, pp. 148–9.

[6] See the official history of the Gregorian, *L'Università Gregoriana del Collegio Romana nel primo secolo dalla restituzione* (Rome [1925]), p. 34.

[7] G. Van Riet, *Thomistic Epistemology: Studies Concerning the Problem of Cognition in the Contemporary Thomistic School*, vol. i (St. Louis and London, 1963), pp. 124–63, gives an account of Mercier's work at Louvain.

woke up, groaning or exulting as the case might be, to find itself Thomist. As Laberthonnière was to remark many years later: 'An intellectual movement of the kind which Leo XIII wanted to inaugurate cannot be improvised or brought to instant success simply by command.'[8] Even where the response was unforced, the manner of its implementation could be strikingly varied. The Roman method was to return *tout court* to the thirteenth century, embrace the cultural and scientific limitations implicit in this return, and present the Christian faith in a manner which recognized no pressing need to differentiate between the cultural setting for theology in the thirteenth century and that of the nineteenth century. Louvain under Mercier responded to Leo's programme in a way which was more critical and more historically informed. Mercier and his colleagues were genuinely concerned to recover the spirit of Aquinas and to draw inspiration from it to meet the challenge of their own age. They believed that Thomism had first of all to be mastered at its source and in its own right before it could be vindicated by measuring itself unashamedly against all contemporary philosophies. 'St. Thomas must be for us a beacon not a barrier' became Louvain's slogan.[9]

Closely associated with the Roman colleges as instruments of theological and philosophical centralization were the Roman textbooks, or 'manuals', as they are commonly called, which standardized both the material content and the

[8] R. P. Lecanuet, *La Vie de l'Église sous Léon XIII* (Paris, 1930), p. 472. As a consequence of the Leonine programme Procrustean tactics were resorted to in efforts to show how one could be, say, a Scotist or a Saurezian and yet be faithful to the mind of the Pope. See Aubert, *Aspects*, p. 139. See also von Hügel's comments in a letter to Ward cited in L. F. Barmann, *Baron Friedrich von Hügel and the Modernist Crisis in England* (Cambridge, 1972), p. 140n. Conformity to Leo's injunctions probably put a greater strain upon *pietas* than upon intellectual integrity. Tyrrell was hardly exaggerating when he wrote: 'In the gross, all ecclesiastics agree in their philosophical conclusions; and as to minor differences, all Jesuits in the gross agree with Suarez, all Dominicans with St Thomas, all Franciscans with Scotus. Obviously the existence of such extrinsically produced uniformity is incompatible with that independence of thought which it is the very aim of a philosophical education to foster.' (M. D. Petre (ed.), *Autobiography and Life of George Tyrrell*, vol. i (London, 1912), pp. 271 f.)

[9] Aubert, *Aspects*, p. 185. Mercier outlined the aims of the new School of Philosophy at Louvain in an article, 'La philosophie néo-scholastique', in *Revue néo-scholastique*, 1 (1894), pp. 5–18.

method of its presentation. The existence, content, and form of the typical manual constitute a phenomenon of considerable theological, pedagogical, and sociological significance. It is to the manuals one must go if one is to determine the character, quality, and, particularly, the limitations of Catholic theology between the two Vatican Councils. Given a propositional view of revelation, deductive method in theology, and an ever-increasing concern to identify and label doctrinal assertions according to the degree of their ecclesiastical authority, the method employed by the manuals was both theologically consistent and pedagogically effective. The principal manuals were written in Latin.[10] Those which were written in modern languages followed the Latin exemplars closely (often with baneful effect on their prose style). The fact that the most influential manuals were always written in Latin ensured that their influence would not be restricted to the native countries of their authors. Roman theology was ultramontane not merely in its ecclesiology and church discipline but also in its cultural assumptions (a fact which is not always fully appreciated in accounting for the Italianization of the Roman Catholic Church in the late nineteenth and early twentieth centuries); and as it gradually permeated the seminaries of the world, it filtered out almost all regional variations. Such variations as did occur in theological interpretation were governed by subscription to one or other of the schools of thought which were eventually permitted within the over-all neo-scholastic framework. It is an eloquent comment on the situation as it was then that today these variations have simply vanished or retain merely archaic interest.

The manuals can be roughly classified into two types. The first consisted of seminal works such as Franzelin on

---

[10] Perrone gives as a reason for this that Latin is a universal language and therefore specially fitted to enshrine the truths of the Catholic faith. In Perrone's view there were considerable dangers in translating Christian dogmas into the vernacular. The process of translation would expose them to subtle changes, subjective interpretations, and all the ambiguities possible to one who writes in a living language. In an age when seductively erroneous philosophies abound, he remarks, it behoves the Catholic theologian to employ a linguistic medium which is not subject to these vagaries. In short, his argument is that an immutable theology demands a dead language. (J. Perrone, *Praelectiones theologicae*, vol. iv, *De locis theologicis* (Paris, 1883), pp. 683 f.)

Tradition and Billot on the analysis of the act of faith. The second, and far larger, type included the works of synoptists who provided a complete course in dogmatic and fundamental theology specifically designed to meet the needs of students for the Roman Catholic priesthood anywhere in the world.[11] The degree of uniformity achieved in these manuals is striking and should not be neglected by anyone seeking to appreciate the nature and temper of·Roman Catholic theology between the two Vatican Councils. The condemnation of modernism had the effect of reinforcing this uniformity spectacularly. The manuals mapped out with precise and inflexible lines the terrain within which Catholic theology and philosophy were to be studied and taught. They decreed the material to be treated and the terminology with which to treat it. 'Transcendence' and 'immanence' (as ordinarily understood in theological parlance) were not included in the terminological canon, except where they had to be referred to in the refutation of 'adversarii'.

Giovanni Perrone, who taught at the Collegio Romano for three spells between 1824 and 1853 and was regarded as the foremost Roman theologian of his age, was the one who first gave to the relationship between faith and reason the prominence it would retain in the manuals for more than a century to come.[12] It was Perrone who worked out the triple proof, 'ex Scriptura, ex Traditione, ex ratione', which was still being employed in the manuals well into the second half of the twentieth century.[13]

In the cluster of questions associated with transcendence and immanence Perrone set more than one precedent which

[11] Neo-scholastic theology was clerical *de facto* rather than *de jure*. Rome, while not explicitly approving of Mgr. Talbot's view that the laity should stick to hunting, shooting, and entertaining, was undoubtedly happier when they did so. 'Lay' theology was apt to be a trifle adventurous and its practitioners insufficiently moulded by the methods of the Schools. Furthermore — and this became very clear during the modernist crisis — clerics like Tyrrell and Laberthonnière who got out of line could be reached anonymously through the ecclesiastical chain of command, while laymen like von Hügel, Le Roy, and Blondel could be dealt with only by open confrontation, which the Vatican strove to avoid if at all possible.

[12] J. Bellamy, *La Théologie catholique au XIXe siècle* (3rd edn., Paris, 1904), p. 43.

[13] Y. M.-J. Congar, *A History of Theology* (New York, 1968), p. 189.

was affected neither by the Vatican Council nor by the introduction of stricter Thomism after 1879. In the first treatise
of his *Praelectiones, Tractatus de vera religione*, Perrone lays
down a logical sequence which was, with minor variations,
to dominate the presentation of revelation theology down to
the Second Vatican Council's Dogmatic Constitution, *Dei
Verbum*. Perhaps the most characteristic feature of Perrone's
treatise is the weight it places on *a priori* argumentation. At
the risk of repeating a cliché of post-Vatican II theology we
must note the fact that revelation is conceived proposition-
ally by Perrone and his successors throughout the period
under review. No Roman theologian will qualify in any essential respect Perrone's definition of revelation as the
manifestation of some truth or truths which is supernatural
both in origin and in the mode of its communication.[14]

Perrone and his manualist successors deployed their
argument forensically and in strict logical sequence: Revelation is possible; its occurrence can be demonstrated by signs
of indisputably supernatural provenance; these signs are by
common consent miracles and prophecies (which in turn are
proved to be possible). Up to this point the argument has
been dealing in a prioristic abstractions. Now it moves to the
plane of what it claims to be historically verifiable fact. Jesus
Christ by his miracles, especially by his resurrection, has
proved the authenticity of his claim to be sent by God. It
should be noted that neo-scholastic fundamental theology
was not concerned to demonstrate the divinity of Christ.
That task would be undertaken in theology proper by the
treatise, *De Verbo Incarnato*. The apologetical argument bore
merely upon the authenticity of Christ's claim to speak with
divine authority. This authority he in turn can be proved to
have delegated to the Church which he founded, handing
over to its custody the divine truths which he had taught, and
promising to it the assistance of the Holy Spirit in the carrying out of its mission through the ages to come.

The Thomistic revival which took place during the last
quarter of the nineteenth century tightened the argument at
several points, without however altering its structure in any

---

[14] J. Perrone, *Praelectiones theologicae*, vol. i, *De vera religione* (Paris, 1883),
p. 2.

essential respect. In 1888 Louis Billot, S.J., was, at the specific behest of Leo XIII, brought to Rome from his native France to lecture at the Gregorian University, where he remained until he was created a cardinal in 1911. Billot was a Thomist by conviction rather than by conscription. He had an unconcealed contempt for any theological or apologetical method which made an appeal, however nuanced, to experience, desire, or the affections. Theological impressionism, such as, for instance, the role assigned by men like von Hügel, Tyrrell, and Loisy, to intuition in the epistemology of religion, faith, and prayer, Billot simply regarded as weakmindedness. True religion and faith were about certainties, and one could not in his view be certain about any matter which one could not expound with absolute cognitive clarity. It is no accident that one of his major problems in theology and apologetics was to defend the *obscuritas* of faith. The 'aliquam intelligentiam' sanctioned by the Vatican Council was for him a more than sufficient warrant for a conceptual system of the utmost clarity and rigidity. At the time of the modernist crisis Billot was the leading exponent of a theological perspective which saw revelation as assertion, faith as intellectual assent, and theology as a mainly deductive procedure.

Louis Billot was to become the guardian *par excellence* of what Tyrrell liked to describe as 'the new theology'.[15] Much of Billot's work in fundamental theology centred on a strictly logical, indeed surgical, analysis of the act of faith. His major aim was to chart a course through the narrow straits between rationalism and fideism which Roman Catholic theology in that period saw as one of the most hazardous of theological journeys. His argument rests on a careful distinction between the preamble to faith and the act of faith itself. The authority of the God who reveals is apprehended

[15] Meaning by the term 'new' the theology which came into being after the Vatican Council. Ironically, when Tyrrell first heard of Billot, probably in 1895, he expressed a strong wish to read him. 'Though Ours [sc. the English Jesuits] hate him, I hear great accounts of him from outsiders. He seems to realise my ideal of a critical and independent treatment of S. Thomas regardless of the results.' (Tyrrell to Thurston, in J. H. Crehan, 'Tyrrell in His Workshop', in *The Month*, 231 (1971), p. 111.) Tyrrell, it should be remembered, was removed from Stonyhurst partly at least for his enthusiastic championing of Aquinas (see M. D. Petre, *Life*, vol. ii, pp. 40–7).

('attingitur') both in the *preambula fidei* and in the *actus fidei*, but in a different manner. In the preambulatory stage it is apprehended not directly but mediately through 'argumenta seu signa' which are of varying degrees of cogency and thus productive of varying degrees of certainty. At this stage all that needs to be achieved is the removal of 'prudent doubt'. In the act of faith itself, however, God's authority is apprehended as the reason for belief, 'hoc est, non ut quod creditur, sed ut propter quod aliquid creditur'.[16] Billot is here rejecting both Suarez's opinion that the authority of God revealing is itself an object of faith, and the opinion of Lugo and Franzelin that the believer has immediate *knowledge* or intuition of the fact of revelation. Instead Billot affirms one single act of faith embracing revealed truth as its material object and divine authority as its formal object. The act of faith itself is not the outcome of logical argumentation, for such argumentation belongs to the preambulatory stage where alone scientific method is in order; it is, in the ontological sense, a simple and reverential[17] adherence of the mind to what God has revealed, because he has revealed it.

Billot assumed without question the hegemony of dogmatic theology over both biblical studies and philosophy. The dogmatic theologian, as Billot saw it, told the apologist not only what he had to find and demonstrate but also *how* he was to do so. Billot was an implacable foe to any arguments based on man's appetitive or affective side. Reason and will are the only faculties directly involved in the act of faith and in the steps preparatory to it. These preparatory steps constitute the matter of apologetics or fundamental theology. Credibility, he stated quite bluntly, is the *extrinsic* condition which precedes the act of faith.[18] This is precisely the 'extrinsicism' which we shall find Blondel attacking. One

---

[16] Billot, *De ecclesia Christi* (2nd edn., Rome, 1903), p. 44.

[17] The Vatican Council had described faith as an 'obsequium'. In Billot's distinction between 'foi scientifique' and 'foi d'hommage' only the latter term conveys what the Council meant by 'obsequium' (cf. R. Aubert, *Le Problème de l'acte de foi: Données traditionnelles et résultats des controverses récentes* (4th edn., Louvain and Paris, 1969), pp. 241–55).

[18] Billot, *De ecclesia*, p. 47: 'Credibilitas in praesenti dicit extrinsecam illam obiecti cuiuspiam seu doctrinae conditionem, ex qua habet ut possit terminare prudentem actum credendi.'

might describe it (somewhat maliciously) in Billot's own native categories as a kind of *a priori* agnosticism about the nature and content of revelation and an *a posteriori* fideism in its appeal to *signa* (miracles and fulfilled prophecies) which give extrinsic guarantee of credibility.

Billot's argument can be outlined as follows. Because of my *a posteriori* conviction about the empirically observable *signa*, I am prepared to believe *a priori* what may appear to me at present to be not merely difficult but even irrational. By faith I sign a blank cheque the detailed sum of which is to be filled in by the issuing bank, which is utterly trustworthy. I do not need to postulate any intrinsic relationship between *what* is revealed, on the one hand, and the sort of being I am, on the other. Thus the evidence which prepares me to believe must of necessity be miraculous (by definition *praeter naturam*) precisely because I lack the sort of *interior*, sheerly human, preparation for what God reveals to me.

One would scarcely be caricaturing this approach if one were to describe it as robotic apologetics. Man, given the appropriate external circumstances, is a machine programmed to believe. Billot simply has no problems about the transcendent Being who is himself the motive for belief in what he reveals. Nor — beyond the darkened intellect and enfeebled will of man — has Billot any problems about the psychological and social constitution of human existence. His entire conception of faith and its cognitive structure rests firmly on what Aubert has called 'a very strict parallelism between religious faith and human faith'.[19] It was precisely this lack of an *internal* personal and moral dimension in Billot's treatment of religious faith which Laberthonnière assailed with such vehemence. And it was in turn precisely Laberthonnière's postulation of such a dimension which Billot stigmatized with no less vehemence as vacillation and the febrile cult of subjectivity at the expense of objective clarity and strength.

In the neo-scholastic apologetic of that age we look in vain for any recognition of the problems posed for Christian

---

[19] Aubert, *Le problème de l'acte de foi*, p. 252. 'Cette conception', Aubert asks, 'ne sacrifie-t-elle pas trop la saveur proprement religieuse de la foi divine?' Today one might be inclined to put the question less gently than Aubert could do in 1945.

theology by the course taken by philosophy since Hume and Kant. As we shall see in later chapters, the very terms transcendence and immanence were treated by the neo-scholastics sometimes with incomprehension, usually with distaste, and always with discomfort, as a foreign intellectual coinage. The philosophical situation for which they were the appropriate currency was simply not taken seriously in the neo-scholastic manuals. More than that, it was apprehended as radically dangerous to faith. The neo-scholastic system was constructed on the conviction that God's existence can be demonstrated by speculative reason through the principle of causality; that the essential characteristics of the divine nature can be discerned by the same means, through the medium of the doctrine of the analogy of being; that the possibility of revelation has first to be vindicated by pure reason and its actual occurrence demonstrated by historical investigation; that the content of revelation is expressed, not symbolically, but analogically; and that this content is guaranteed as authentically divine in origin by empirically verifiable facts. Not merely did the system stand or fall as a whole; it was fatally vulnerable to any suggestion that causality does not operate in the same manner in the transcendent as in the historical realm. The modernists, responding in varying ways and degrees to the Kantian critique and to the general advance of critical studies in many cognate fields, attempted to break out of a pre-critical mode of thought and in doing so came up against a refurbished Aristotelianism supported by a reinforced ecclesiastical authority. This is why the work done by Leo XIII must be seen as crucial in motivating and sustaining the anti-modernist campaign.

Leo's pontificate lasted a quarter of a century, and it witnessed a large-scale counter-revolution in Roman Catholic patterns of thought. It is not easy to assess the merits and demerits of what actually happened. That a stimulus to higher philosophical and theological studies had been given is undeniable. Those studies, however, pointed backwards rather than forwards. The newly-centralized Catholic Church looked out upon the world of its time and found it more of a threat than a challenge. The campaign of retrenchment initiated by Pius IX was prosecuted with vigour under Leo. Part of that campaign consisted in the abandonment of a somewhat untidy philosophical eclecticism and the attempted substitution for it of a strict fidelity to the theological and philosophical system of St. Thomas Aquinas. Implementation of the new programme was uneven and often inept. Many of the neo-Thomists were simply inadequate as scholars, intolerant as churchmen, and intemperate as controversialists. They saw things too clearly to see them well, as Blondel remarked.[20] They frequently and seriously underrated the intellectual cogency of the case they were attacking.

The system they promoted, though grounded in a thoroughly transcendentalist and supernaturalist conception of revelation and faith, was paradoxically both rationalist and positivist in its theological methods. It treated the supernatural 'content' of divine revelation as divine truth crystallized into assertions formulated in Scripture and in the documents of Tradition. These assertions, their supernatural provenance having first been demonstrated by appeal to divine 'facts', became the object of logical manœuvres and speculative development in isolation from the lived reality of which they were the conceptual and linguistic representation. Deductive reasoning, brought to bear on revealed assertions, was deemed to be the process eminently suited to the theological enterprise. This process might be described, not unfairly, as supernatural rationalism. It avoided the substance of rationalism, in that it saw itself as deriving its data not from autonomous reason but from supernatural revelation; but its mode of thought was rationalist, in that it neglected, and, after 1907, repudiated, any experiential, affective, or intuitive mode of thought. It was positivist in that it approached its sources, namely, the text of Scripture and the documents of the ecclesiastical magisterium, as simple data whose givenness and transcendent meaning were there for all to see. The *facta externa* were there to be observed and registered by the senses just as any pikestaff might be.

---

[20] M. Blondel, 'Lettre sur les exigences de la pensée contemporaine', in *Les Premiers écrits de Maurice Blondel*, vol. ii (Paris, 1956), p. 9.

The interpretative element was given a minimal role as something 'subjective' and therefore by definition open to error and waywardness. The would-be believer had merely to observe, register, and respond with his mind and will. He brought nothing of his own to the process beyond the *tabula rasa* so conveniently underwritten by Aristotelian epistemology. History was what really happened, and the documents which bore witness to these happenings shared in their objective givenness. Thus eternity was expressed in time, and the absolute in historical contingency, without stress or strain. The truths revealed were eternal and immutable but they subsisted in the flux of history untouched by its vagaries and particularities. The massive objectivity of this system reduced the role of the historian to one of simple communicator. Whatever interpretation was needed would be provided by a divinely guided magisterium. The theologian, whose task it was to deal speculatively with revealed truths, needed no historical skills or training for the adequate performance of that task. Dogma, not history, provided him with the material necessary for the pursuit of his craft; and a stern magisterium was there to see that he reached the correct conclusions.

The purpose of this chapter has been to give a brief indication of the character and structure of neo-scholastic fundamental theology as it was conceived and practised at the time of the modernist controversy. The modernists took issue not merely with many of the elements which went to make it up, such as its notion of revelation, doctrine, and the role of miracle, but with its over-all conception of the apologetical task.

Before turning to Maurice Blondel's challenge to neo-scholastic apologetics, we shall advert briefly to certain precedents for that challenge to be found in earlier French religious thought, specifically to the provenance and significance of the terms *fait intérieur* and *fait extérieur* which occur frequently in the writings of Blondel and his school and which have a particular relevance to the debate over immanence.[21]

---

[21] See B. Reardon, *Liberalism and Tradition: Aspects of Catholic Thought in Nineteenth-Century France* (Cambridge, 1975). Dr Reardon deals informatively with such figures as Augustin Bonnetty, Louis Bautain, and Alphonse Gratry,

The Vatican Council had addressed itself in the main to the challenge of 'rationalism' and 'semi-rationalism'. Its glance was directed more towards Germany than towards France. In view, however, of the common integralist allegation that the Council had ruled out all possibility of an immanence apologetic, it is important to note that one of the more prominent theologians in the ranks of the episcopate at the Council, Archbishop Victor Dechamps,[22] had, in his own right as a theologian, propounded a view of apologetics which was deeply sensitive to the interior and personal dimension of the act of faith and, more significantly, of the preliminaries to faith. Maurice Blondel was delighted to discover in Dechamps's work striking similarities to his own approach.[23]

One of the most respected figures at the Council, Dechamps was leader of the party which sought the definition of papal infallibility.[24] This fact might lead one to suppose that his view of faith and apologetics would be predominantly intellectualist. Not so, however. As a theologian Dechamps had given considerable attention to the apologetical question and was particularly concerned that apologetics should not be restricted in scope to the supposed needs and abilities of the learned. Apologetics must, he held, rest on facts rather than on abstract arguments. 'There are only two facts to be verified: the one within you, the other outside you; they seek each other out so that they can be united, and you yourself are the witness of both of them.'[25] He later together with the characteristically French intellectual movements of Traditionalism and Ontologism.

[22] On Dechamps see *Dictionnaire de théologie catholique* (Paris, 1924), vol. iv, cols. 178–82; E. Hocedez, *Histoire de la théologie au XIXe siècle*, vol. ii, *Épanouissement de la théologie, 1831–1870* (Brussels and Paris, 1952), pp. 280–2; R. Aubert, *Le problème de l'acte de foi*, pp. 142–5 (with further references given there). Of particular importance in the present context is F. Rodé, *Le Miracle dans la controverse moderniste* (Paris, 1965), pp. 166–72.

[23] Blondel, writing over the signature of his friend Canon F. Mallet, published a series of articles on Dechamps's apologetic in the *Annales de philosophie chrétienne* between 1905 and 1907. He later republished these articles with some modifications in *Le Problème de la philosophie catholique* (Paris, 1932), pp. 59–123.

[24] See C. Butler, *The Vatican Council, 1869–1870* (Fontana Library, London, 1962), p. 108.

[25] *Œuvres complètes du Cardinal Dechamps* (Malines, 1874) as cited by F. Rodé, *Le miracle dans la controverse moderniste*, p. 168.

described the 'interior fact' as 'le besoin qu'éprouve incon-
testablement la raison d'une authorité divine enseignante en
matière de religion'.[26] The *fait intérieur* is incarnated in the
living organism of the Church. The subjective dispositions of
the believer are an essential element in the process by which
men come to faith.[27]

It is important to take note of Dechamps's teaching on the
fait intérieur for two reasons. First, it suggests that the
Vatican Council did not intend to rule out an immanent
dimension in the preparation for faith; and, second, because
of the discomfort that neo-scholastic orthodoxy experienced
with this dimension, the theology of the *fait intérieur* was
lost to general sight in the period between the two Vatican
Councils. Whether Dechamps can be credited with all that
Blondel attributed to him is doubtful.[28] The point is significant mainly where we find neo-scholastic theologians like
Schwalm and Gayraud attempting to discredit immanence
apologetics by an appeal to the authority of the Vatican
Council.

Concern for the *fait intérieur* in French theology has its
origin in the thought of Pascal.[29] Now, Pascal's power to
divide men in their estimation of him remains one of the
most fascinating phenomena in the history of religious
thought. One expects Voltaire and the *Philosophes* to exe-
crate him, for he has no time for the passionless and unin-
volved God of the Deists. Pascal is in the Augustinian tradition of redeemed pessimism. It was not, however, for this
that so many of the neo-scholastics described him as 'le
funeste Pascal'. They deprecated his anti-rationalism. As a
mathematician of genius Pascal had won the right to speak
with authority on the limitations of *l'esprit de géométrie*;
but to them it seemed nothing less than treason for such a

---

[26] Op. cit., p. 168.   [27]Ibid., pp. 169–171.

[28] Aubert, *Le Problème de l'acte de foi*, p. 342. It has sometimes been supposed that Dechamps's view of the Church as 'fait extérieur' influenced the First
Vatican Council's teaching on the Church as moral miracle. In the light of recent
research, however, it would appear more likely that Franzelin was the principal
author of this line of thought at the Council. See A. Dulles, *A History of Apologetics* (London, 1971), p. 192.

[29] See D. M. Eastwood, *The Revival of Pascal: A Study of His Relation to
Modern French Thought* (Oxford, 1936); see esp. Ch. 5, pp. 48–71, for a concise and penetrating account of Pascal's intellectual method.

one to refer so slightingly to the role of reason in man's approach to God. They believed in *l'esprit de géométrie* as an instrument for analysing the preliminary steps towards faith. Pascal offered instead *l'esprit de finesse* and the logic of the heart. Like Newman after him, Pascal was more interested in principles than in reasons. The *cœur* of Pascal's epistemology, both religious and scientific, shares with Newman's 'illative sense' the ability to call forth either an answering resonance or dismay and incomprehension from his readers. 'We know the truth not only through our reason but also through our heart. It is through the latter that we know first principles, and reason, which has nothing to do with it, tries in vain to refute them.'[30] To someone like Louis Billot these were the words of a visionary and a dreamer who had abdicated from his intellectual responsibilities; while to Lucien Laberthonnière they were evidence of a religious philosophy which penetrated to the depths of man as a religious being. To be sure, Billot could define what he meant by 'intellect' and 'truth' with far greater precision than Pascal and his disciples could have defined what they meant by 'heart'; but the latter would have regarded Billot's clarity as being not merely in excess of the facts but also religiously inept and spiritually sterile. Only intuition, with its wide lens and soft focus, could in their view do justice to the magnitude, mystery, and grandeur of God's word to man. Precision could come later, when the mind set itself the task of analysing, synthesizing, and structuring the data of religious experience; and even then precision itself would demand a recognition of the impressionistic character of the data. This was why Laberthonnière could describe Pascal as a 'positivist of interior reality'.

Pascal's 'positivism' takes man as he is, wretched in the awareness he has of his divided self, but blessed in being able to know that he is wretched. Some of Pascal's critics have tended to see in this existential awareness little more than an expression of his alleged Jansenism. There is, however, no need to appeal to the much-tortured word 'Jansenism' in order to account for Pascal's sensitivity to man's dark side.

[30] Pascal, *Pensées*, fr. 282. The edited translation referred to here is A. J. Krailsheimer, *Pascal: Pensées* (Penguin Books, Harmondsworth, 1966), p. 58.

In this, as in so much else, Pascal was a faithful disciple of
St. Augustine. His apprehension of the divided self is based
on introspection and social observation, and he put it
forward as an apologetic which would be recognizable in
principle by any observer, believer or unbeliever, of the *fait
intérieur*.[31] It is the divided self which makes nonsense of the
claim that discursive reason can reach God. Pascal was
supremely aware of the ambiguity of the verb 'to know'. He
does not deny that God can be 'known' by discursive reason;
he simply observes that this use of 'know' is of no religious
significance. 'That is what faith is: God perceived by the
heart, not by the reason.'[32] Those who would charge Pascal
with fideism and sentimentalism overlook the fact that his
ordre du cœur is quite clearly an intellectual one. Man is a
reed, but a thinking reed. It was not an irrationalist who
wrote: 'Thus all our dignity consists in thought. It is on
thought that we must depend for our recovery, not on space
and time, which we could never fill. Let us strive to think
well; that is the basic principle of morality.'[33]

Laberthonnière would attack Platonic idealism and
contrast it with Christian realism; but he would never reject
the Platonic ideal of virtue as knowledge. Virtue can be
rightly said to begin and end in knowledge, when knowledge
is conceived not in restrictively discursive terms, but as an
expression of the whole man who thinks and acts in accord-
ance with his principles. Pascal's doctrine that it is the heart
which recognizes and responds to principles is central to that
stream of thought which stems from Augustine, which was
driven underground mainly by the pressure of Christian
Aristotelianism, but which surfaced again in the writings of
Pascal, Kierkegaard, Coleridge, Newman, Maurice, and the
modernists.[34] In this way of thinking, reason may supply

---

[31] The French draughtsmen of Vatican II's Pastoral Constitution, *Gaudium et
Spes*, on the Church in the Modern World, were at several points clearly influenced by Pascal. See J. Ratzinger's informative chapter in H. Vorgrimler (ed.),
Commentary on the Documents of Vatican II, vol. V (New York and London,
1969), pp. 115–63, esp. pp. 120–34.

[32] *Pensées*, fr. 278, Krailsheimer, p. 154.

[33] Ibid., fr. 347, Krailsheimer, p. 95.

[34] See J. Coulson, *Newman and the Common Tradition* (Oxford, 1970), for an
illuminating discussion of this alternative mode of Christian thought.

supportive 'proofs' for various religious claims, but it is the heart which 'grasps their significance, and effects their synthesis'.[35] The decisive element, the one which supplies the absolutely necessary moral and existential dimension of any transcendentally significant act, is intuition. Scholastic philosophy had no real interest in the phenomenon of intuition, and no categories within which to consider it. Scholasticism therefore relinquished it to the 'mystics', those saintly eccentrics whom it saw as living an ethereal existence in the upper reaches of contemplative prayer, but whom it excluded by promotion from the strictly theological arena. The mystics could be allowed their preoccupation with the apophatic as long as they kept away from dogmatic theology. Pascal could raise theological eyebrows by his doctrine of the heart, but since Pascal was not a 'philosopher' and still less a 'theologian', he need not be seriously treated by either. (It was an attitude not altogether dissimilar from that taken by hardline linguistic philosophers towards the 'nonsense' of existentialist philosophy.)

The modernists in general, and the Blondelians in particular, insisted on trying to reintroduce the Pascalian vision into the mainstream of Catholic theology. For doing so they were condemned as 'immanentists'. Blondel's strictures on 'extrinsicism' were in effect a rejection of the *esprit géométrique* as an instrument of approach to faith. Laberthonnière's 'dogmatisme moral' was a recognition of the *esprit de finesse* as a necessary instrument in both the preparation for, and the actual practice of, faith. Integralist theology was soon to show its invincible distrust of all appeals to Pascal's *cœur*. Maurice Blondel's 'method of immanence' was a clear pointer to the reforms which Roman Catholic fundamental theology would have eventually to undertake.

---

[35] J. Chevalier, *Pascal* (London, 1930), pp. 272-3.

2 The Blondelian Challenge

> To hold obstinately to the idea that one can restore,
> by means of a dead rationalism, something which is
> dead in the old School is inevitably to fall again
> before the assaults of the two-fold critique which has
> [already] destroyed both Christian pseudo-philosophy
> by the metaphysics of transcendence and rationalist
> pseudo-philosophy by the doctrine of immanence,
> itself now outdated.[1]

In this characteristically dense sentence Maurice Blondel, a
thirty-five-year-old lay Catholic philosopher from Dijon,
summarized his critique of the sort of apologetic for Catholic
belief which was to continue its domination of official
Church teaching during the next sixty years. In 1896, when
the *Letter on Apologetics* first appeared, it was still possible
to hope that Catholic fundamental theology would take
cognizance of critical thought from the time of Kant onwards
and would consequently see the need to make, if not large-
scale modifications, at least some sort of hermeneutical
adjustment to a thirteenth-century perspective on faith and
knowledge. The defenders of the status quo were not slow
to pronounce the incantation 'Kantianism', which, in
scholastic circles, normally had the force of an automatic
condemnation. The casual Kant-watcher of the period might
easily have overlooked the last phrase of the sentence just
quoted which declared that the doctrine of immanence was
now itself obsolete. In place of a *doctrine* of immanence
the writer was proposing a *method* of immanence. The

[1] 'S'opiniâtrer à restaurer ce qui dans l'ancienne École est mort, au moyen
d'un rationalisme mort, c'est retomber d'avance sous les coups de la double
critique qui a tué la pseudo-philosophie chrétienne par la métaphysique de la
transcendance, et qui a tué la pseudo-philosophie rationaliste par la doctrine de
l'immanence, elle-même dépassée.' M. Blondel, 'Lettre sur les exigences de la
pensée contemporaine en matière d'apologétique et sur la méthode de la philosophie dans l'étude du problème religieux', in *Les Premiers Écrits de Maurice
Blondel*, vol. ii (Paris, 1956) [Lettre], p. 92.

terminology was strange to scholastic ears. The very term 'immanence' belonged to a foreign vocabulary derived from German philosophy and lent itself to diagnosis as a structural support for Protestant subjectivism. At no stage in the ensuing debate was Blondel's distinction between 'doctrine' and 'method' accepted by his Catholic opponents as having any substantive bearing on the case at issue. In their eyes an objective doctrine demanded an objective method. They saw no reason at all for adopting a programme such as that mentioned by Blondel to a friend in 1893. 'I have tried to accomplish for the Catholic form of religious thought what Germany has done long ago and continues to do for the Protestant form . . .'[2] That was the crucial difference between Blondel and his Catholic critics: he saw that there was a case to answer; they did not. In the event, their viewpoint was to prevail in the Roman Catholic Church down to the 1960s.

Since we are here concerned with the problem of transcendence and immanence at a specified period in the history of Christian thought, some clear limitations must be carefully noted. No attempt will be made to give a comprehensive account of Blondel's over-all contribution to philosophy and Christian thought. A complete appraisal of Blondel's thought would involve a study of the so-called 'Tetralogy', published after its author had passed his seventieth year.[3] We are here concerned with what Blondel scholars generally refer to as his 'first period', which closed with the *Letter* of 1896, to which we must add some writings of his middle period, notably *Histoire et dogme* (1904), together with relevant letters from his edited correspondence.[4]

Blondel's commentators have been sensitive to the misunderstandings and misrepresentations which have afflicted their subject. Blondel emerged from the modernist crisis battered, bruised, but uncondemned. As we shall see later, he was clearly envisaged in the anti-modernist literature and in *Pascendi* itself, but Church opinion, even in that Draconian

---

[2] M. Blondel, *Lettres philosophiques* (Paris, 1961), p. 34.

[3] *La Pensée, L'Être, L'Action* (a two-volume revision of the original *L'Action*), and *La philosophie et l'esprit chrétien*, all of which appeared between 1934 and 1946.

[4] See J. Lacroix, *Maurice Blondel: An Introduction to the Man and His Philosophy* (New York, 1968), p. 18.

age, accepted a distinction between disapproval and out-right condemnation. But disapproval is disapproval none the less; and from 1907 onwards Blondel's disciples have worn *Pascendi* like an albatross around their necks. To the obscurities and tactical ambiguities of the master they have added their own in a tortured crusade designed to clear him of the charge of 'modernism'. In the greatly changed atmosphere of post-conciliar Roman Catholicism the work of these men tends to look like a large-scale exercise in needlessly beleaguered discipleship. We should not forget, however, that they were victims of a loyalty torn between their admiration of a great religious thinker and their membership of a Church which made neo-scholasticism the touchstone of orthodoxy. It is, however, no longer necessary even for the most ecclesiologically anxious of Roman Catholics to engage in a paralysingly cautious exegesis of Blondel's early writings.

There can be no doubt that it was as a philosopher and only as a philosopher that Blondel wished to be judged. His special conception of the role of philosopher, however, enabled him to maintain this *persona* even when he entered into matters of history, psychology, and especially theology. It is impossible to accept his own self-evaluation as a practitioner of philosophy and of nothing else. The fact is that he made several excursions, some of them not very successful, into history. (His debate with Loisy showed, as we shall see, some inability to recognize the nature of the historian's task.) While not a professional psychologist, he nevertheless displayed a flair for psychological insight which, at least to the untrained observer of psychological matters, seems apposite and penetrating. Both he himself and his critics claimed that he was not a theologian. One should be slow to accept this judgement. Today we are rather more hesitant in our attempts to define theology than were the men of Blondel's age. There is something faintly absurd about Eugène Portalié's admonitory remarks to Blondel in a letter dated 29 April 1904 which complimented the philosopher on his courage in standing out against a philosophy hostile to Christianity but which observed in a highly patronizing manner that the non-theologian, even with the best will in the world, is almost certain to fall into errors of the most serious kind.[5] What does not seem to have struck Portalié is that if it was easy for someone like Blondel to fall into grave theological error, that was as much a judgement on the received idea of theological orthodoxy as it was on Blondel's supposed tendency to deviate from it. Portalié was a good scholar within the limits set by neo-scholasticism, but he was neither equipped nor disposed to appreciate what Blondel was trying to say. Blondel's conception of the philosophical enterprise was foreign to the neo-scholastic *theological* conception of that enterprise. One can only regret that Blondel was so ready to acquiesce in his gratuitous and arrogant exclusion from the theological field of play. Since it was the theologians who wrote the script for the philosophers in the neo-scholastic system, one must resolutely point out that any attempt to re-define the role of philosophy in that system must of necessity have a theological dimension of crucial importance, no matter how one chooses to define theology.[6] Blondel had not passed through a course in seminary theology; but he was (partly in consequence) a far better theologian than many of his critics who had. Today's Roman Catholic theology of revelation and tradition owes infinitely more to Blondel than to Billot and his disciples.

The man who in 1893 defended his doctoral thesis on 'Action' did so as a philosopher. Having had the greatest difficulty in persuading the Faculty of Philosophy at the Sorbonne that action was a suitable topic for philosophical investigation, he proceeded to shock them still further by arguing at great length and with notable originality that philosophy, without in any way losing its autonomy as philosophy, could demonstrate man's need ('exigence') for the supernatural. It was magnificent, but was it philosophy? The Sorbonne had its doubts. The task that Blondel set himself still looks daunting. In the 1890s it was academic suicide. He was given his doctorate, but for two years he found it

[5] *B.V.*, vol. i, pp. 160 f. Portalié was at this time professor of theology at the Institut Catholique of Toulouse.

[6] The relationship between theology and philosophy in the light of Blondel's thought is discussed in H. Duméry, *Blondel et la religion* (Paris, 1954), and in H. Bouillard, *Blondel et le christianisme* (Paris, 1961). See also A. Dru and I. Trethowan (eds.), *Maurice Blondel: The Letter on Apologetics and History and Dogma* (London, 1964) [*Dru*], pp. 105–12.

impossible to secure a university teaching post for no other reason than that he had allowed revealed religion to invade an area considered to be secular by definition. His thesis was in fact a sustained argument against some fundamental assumptions of the French philosophical establishment. The Catholic establishment, as it was to do ten years later when Loisy challenged Harnack, looked on with slightly puzzled pleasure until it realized that any successful Christian challenge to the forces of darkness seemed to have the effect of draining the batteries which powered the forces of light.

Before setting out to write his thesis Blondel gave a succinct statement of his aim to Émile Boutroux, professor at the Sorbonne and the *rapporteur* of his thesis.

Between Aristotelianism which devalues and subordinates practice to thought, and Kantianism which segregates them and exalts the practical order to the detriment of the other, there is something needing definition, and it is in a very concrete manner, by the analysis of action, that I should like to establish what that something is.[7]

A good case deserves good pleading, Blondel later remarked, and we must recognize that 'there is a wrong way of defending the truth'.[8] Aristotle was not the man to do the pleading in the late nineteenth century. In isolating the intellect from other life-forces Aristotle had placed an inadequate weapon in the hands of Christian apologists. Kant had demonstrated the vulnerability of a predominantly intellectualist approach to God. Kant, however, had gone too far; and Blondel now proposed to reopen the cognitive road to transcendence while taking account of Kant's legitimate criticism of traditional metaphysics. Blondel therefore accepted the methodological implications of the Kantian critique. The point of departure on the road to transcendence must be human experience. Kant must be released from the prison of finitude he had built for himself and his followers when he sealed off pure from practical reason and thus had 'broken the highest faculty in man'.[9] Blondel proposed to heal the breach created by Kant and to dissolve the pessimism which had resulted from it. Analysis of human action, the dynamic force-field

---

[7] M. Blondel, *Lettres philosophiques*, p. 10.   [8] *Lettre*, p. 8.
[9] M. Blondel, *Carnets intimes, 1883–1894* (Paris, 1961), pp. 223 f.

of man's existence, would, Blondel claimed, show that what begins as an exploration of immanence points inexorably towards a transcendent term.

It has been said that Blondel's method of doing philosophy is to hold a dialogue with his philosophical mentors, often without naming them, and always with total self-assurance. He fussed and fretted about being misunderstood, but he never lost sight of his main objective: to demonstrate at once the autonomy and the insufficiency of philosophy in the prolegomena to religious faith. Philosophical inquiry, taking immanence as its base, conducts the inquirer to a vision of the limitless, horizonless perspective of eternity and bids him make his choice: either remain immured in the daily round of penultimate choices, in themselves necessary and good but devoid of transcendent reference and therefore ultimately trivial, or, by the interior dynamic of action commit oneself to the transcendent possibilities offered by revelation. To present this vision on a large enough philosophical canvas was the problem Blondel set himself in *L'Action*. Philosophical investigation must on this view be an affair of the whole man.[10] The investigation must generate its own motivating power without looking for it outside itself.[11] Action is the highway leading from immanent experience to transcendent Being. The quest for truth is all; but neither Aristotle nor Descartes must be allowed to provide the definition of truth.

Well before writing *L'Action* Blondel had rejected as impoverished the epistemological methodology of Aristotle and Descartes, the two philosophers then dominating Catholic philosophy. 'Truth is no longer *adequatio rei et intellectus* and one no longer lives on "clear ideas". But there remains the truth, and the truth which remains is living and active; it is: *adequatio mentis et vitae*.'[12] Blondel finds Aristotelian intellectualism to be quite simply incompetent before the challenge to commitment envisaged by his conception of the philosophical enterprise.[13] As for clear ideas, he

---

[10] *L'Action*, p. xxiii.   [11] *L'Action*, p. xxii.
[12] *Carnets intimes, 1883–1894*, p. 86.
[13] See J. J. McNeill, *The Blondelian Synthesis: A Study of the Influence of German Philosophical Sources on the Formation of Blondel's Method and Thought* (Leiden, 1966), pp. 38 f. Dr McNeill suggests that Blondel was reacting

expresses in the *Letter* a distaste for people 'qui voient trop clair pour bien voir'.[14] Scholastic thought has normally been impeccably clear, but the clarity has often seemed to be well in excess of the facts.

Roger Aubert has pointed out that there was in France at the turn of the century a lively interest in the phenomenon of belief.[15] This interest was characterized to a great extent by reaction against Thomistic intellectualism, a conception of faith, that is, which located its centre in the intellect while relegating will and feeling to the periphery. Scholasticism did indeed give the will a role in the believing process, but that role was an extrinsic one, what Ollé-Laprune called 'une sorte de mécanisme logique'.[16] Feeling and imagination were seen not merely as peripheral but also as a possible hindrance. Since the condemnation of Quietism and the onset of Catholic apprehensions about the theology of Schleiermacher, the whole idea of 'religious feeling' was viewed with deep suspicion which, after 1907, hardened into rank hostility. This suspicion, however, ran counter to the very strong current of French thought extending back to the early Traditionalists and ultimately to Pascal and the *fait intérieur*. It is not without significance that the scholastics of the period often referred to 'le funeste Pascal'. The difficulty for Christians who thought instinctively with Pascal and the early nineteenth-century theological romantics was how to secure their position from the charge, and possibly the reality, of fideism. The French 'Spiritualist'[17] tradition in philosophy, deriving from Maine de Biran, gave some academic support to those Catholics who were unhappy with scholasticism's desiccated intellectualism. The Spiritualist school reacted against materialism, determinism, and Enlightenment

---

more against Spinoza's realism than Aristotle's. McNeill goes on to make a shrewd observation: 'What is surprising is not the confusion on the part of Blondel of Scholastic realism with Spinoza's doctrine; what is surprising is the fact that his Scholastic correspondents seem to accept Blondel's definition of their position without protesting.' (Ibid., p. 39 n.)   [14] *Lettre*, p. 9.

[15] R. Aubert, *Le Problème de l'acte de foi: Données traditionelles et résultats des controverses récentes* (4th edn., Louvain and Paris, 1969), p. 270.

[16] Cited in Aubert, op. cit., p. 269.

[17] Blondel made a plea that the term 'Spiritualist' be dropped (*Lettre*, pp. 31-2).

rationalism in general. It sought to humanize philosophical anthropology by emphasizing the role of the will and of human aspirations in philosophical inquiry. The spirit of man, wrote Maine de Biran, 'always aspires to the absolute and the unconditional'.[18] Though Maine de Biran's remark was made in a strictly philosophical context, Christian thinkers were quick to see its relevance to that stream of Christian thought which stretched back through Pascal and the medieval mystics to Augustine whose 'cor inquietum' was given its 'reasons' by Pascal.

Taking Maine de Biran's 'aspirations to the absolute and unconditional' as his controlling thesis, Blondel set out to show that human aspiration has a logic of its own which can be examined by the light of pure philosophy, independently of revelation and Church doctrine.[19] It is from his analysis of action that Blondel derives what he later described as his method of immanence. Action is the 'perpetual point of junction between [religious] belief and knowledge'. In the language of Aristotelian teleology, action is the link between the efficient cause and the final cause; it is the means whereby the transcendent interpenetrates the immanent by supplying a dynamic thrust to life which is never exhausted by life's concrete choices.[20] Here we meet the celebrated Blondelian distinction between the *volonté voulante* and the *volonté voulue*. The 'will willed' is the succession of actual concrete choices we make from moment to moment. These concrete choices always fall short of human potentiality in that they always point beyond themselves to a further and higher possibiility. To rest in them at any stage as an ultimate goal is to be guilty of superstition. The 'will willing' is the dynamic force immanent in man's nature inexorably driving him on towards self-transcendence. With a neat dialectical twist Blondel utilizes his thesis to make an interesting com-

---

[18] P. Tisserand and H. Grouhier (eds.), *Œuvres de Maine de Biran*, vol. x, p. 95n., as cited in F. Copleston, *A History of Philosophy*, vol. ix, *Maine de Biran to Sartre* (London, 1975), p. 29.

[19] It was a claim which committed Blondel to a contest on two diametrically opposite fronts. Victory on one front would simply intensify hostilities on the other. In the event, it was his difficulties with his fellow believers which helped to have him recognized by the secular philosophical establishment.

[20] See *L'Action*, pp. 467–70, and *Lettres philosophiques*, pp. 35 f.

ment on the paradox of freedom and determinism. The dynamic thrust of the 'will willing' is an ontological as well as a psychological necessity. The determinism consists in having to make choices, and Blondel goes on to point out that the refusal to choose is itself a choice. Freedom is preserved only by its constant exercise in the quest for further self-transcendence. In man the determination of nature expresses itself in free choice. Man is condemned to freedom. Blondel's position differs from that of atheistic existentialism in that he believes that the determinism leads ultimately to God.[21]

From the very first moment of conceiving his project Blondel refused to smooth his academic path by restricting his analysis to the *notion* of action. In his view the philosopher could make an authentic analysis of action only by handing himself over to the transcendental dynamic of the 'will willing'. There could be no question of standing back from the process in pretended detachment. Action could be authentically described and analysed only from the inside. (The reduction of philosophy to linguistic analysis would have struck him as the very grammar of inauthenticity and triviality.)

Although *L'Action* is a long and dense exercise in the practice of the 'method of immanence', it nowhere mentions the phrase explicitly.[22] It is only in the *Letter on Apologetics*, where Blondel addresses himself specifically to the problem of apologetics, that we find the phrase expressly employed and discussed. The occasion of the *Letter* is significant. In

---

[21] 'En posant le déterminisme, on en tire la liberté. En voulant la liberté, on exige le devoir. En concevant la loi morale, c'est une necessité de la produire dans l'action pour la connaître et la déterminer en la pratiquant.' (*L'Action*, p. 143. See pp. 138–43 for the whole argument.)

[22] Blondel was later to claim that circumstances forced it on him. 'Qu'il me soit permis de noter que je ne suis pas responsable de l'emploi qui a été fait des mots *immanence, méthode d'immanence*: ils ne figurent pas dans *l'Action*; je ne m'en suis servi qu'après coup et pour protester contre des méprises qui m'attribuaient, également à tort, ou une doctrine de pure transcendance ou une doctrine toute immanentiste.' (*Études blondéliennes* (Paris, 1951), vol. i, p. 22.) There are occasions — and this is surely one of them — when one tends to lose patience with Blondel in his defensive wrigglings. If he had not adopted the phrase 'method of immanence', he would have had to employ some other, presumably equally unsatisfactory, phrase. His troubles came not from terminology but from the nature of the problem he had chosen to tackle.

1895 the Abbé Charles Denis, a priest of the Beauvais diocese, bought and took over the editorship of the *Annales de
philosophie chrétienne*. He signalized the event by an article
on the need for a new apologetic. Metaphysical apologetic
had, he claimed, lost its point. Instead, what was needed was
an apologetic rooted in moral experience and psychological
observation. Denis (whom von Hügel stigmatized in a letter to
Tyrrell as 'a quick-witted Philistine'),[23] referred by name in his
article to Fonsegrive and Ollé-Laprune, and with these he
coupled Blondel. The controlling idea of these philosophers,
Denis claimed, was to get Christian apologetics on to the psychological plane. 'This was the aim of M. Blondel's celebrated
thesis on Action.'[24] It was precisely the sort of remark which
was apt to give Blondel sleepless nights. Although he admired
both Fonsegrive and Ollé-Laprune, he distanced himself from
their positions, especially on the role of moral and psychological consciousness in the apologetical position implied
throughout *L'Action*. He did not want his argument to be
mistaken for one of psychological introspection.[25] While
Blondel was pondering how to reply, Denis wrote to ask him
for his collaboration in the *Annales*.[26] Blondel thereupon
decided to accept the invitation for two reasons. First, he
wished to show that his approach to apologetics was not
psychologically-based but was philosophically controlled
throughout. Second, he had been warned by Laberthonnière
that in neo-scholastic circles he was likely to be criticized for
affirming that there was a continuity between the natural
and supernatural orders,[27] and this seemed a useful occasion
for elucidating his position on the question. His intentions,
as always, were pacific. He believed that it would be an
excellent thing if believers were to become aware of the situation in secular philosophical thought. He did not foresee the
storm which his views on traditional apologetics would raise.

Blondel scholars are anxious to point out that the *Letter*

---

[23] B. Holland (ed.), *Baron Friedrich von Hügel: Selected Letters, 1896–1924*
(London, 1928), p. 98.   [24] *A.P.C.*, vol. 130 (1895), p. 656.
[25] This point was to become especially significant when the Italian modernists responded and reacted to Blondel's thought during the first decade of the
twentieth century.
[26] R. Saint-Jean, *L'Apologétique philosophique: Blondel 1893–1913* (Paris,
1966), pp. 29 f.   [27] *B.L.*, p. 79.

is not a finished statement of Blondel's position and that one must read it in the light of his later work, *Le problème de la philosophie catholique*,[28] in which he criticizes and modifies the position he took in 1896. It is, however, his original position which concerns us here. Blondel's commentators have tended to play down his contribution to the modernist crisis, a tactic which, however understandable in an ecclesiastically straitened age, is hardly defensible from the standpoint of critical history.

The *Letter on Apologetics* has been described as Blondel's masterpiece.[29] What is quite certain is that, together with *L'Action*, which it made explicit on several crucial and theologically neuralgic points, it initiated the philosophico-apologetical debate which was to continue into, and become a part of, the modernist challenge to the accepted notion of Catholic orthodoxy. The *Letter* is arranged in three sections. The first section discusses various apologetical methods. In it Blondel dismisses the possibility of an apologetic based on science, which he sees as limited to phenomena and therefore as uninterested in transcendent meaning or reference.[30] He then turns to traditional Catholic apologetic of the sort we considered in Chapter 1. His criticism of it, though commonplace today, was original and explosively radical for French Catholicism in 1896. He attacks the methodological distinction made by traditional apologetics between the *a priori* defence of the possibility of revelation and the *a posteriori* treatment of Christianity as fact like any other fact. It is not enough to demonstrate separately the possibility and actuality of the supernatural, 'we must show *the necessity for us* of adhering to this reality of the supernatural'.[31] Without this demonstration there is no genuinely philosophical case to be made for Christian faith. It is not the province of philosophy to pronounce on the facts but merely to 'determine the mental dispositions which prepare for the understanding of facts and for the practical discrimination of truths the provenance of which is to be found elsewhere.[32]

[28] M. Blondel, *Le problème de la philosophie catholique* (Paris, 1932).

[29] H. Duméry, *Blondel et la religion*, p. 1.

[30] *Lettre*, p. 11. The physical sciences 'n'ont point à s'inquieter d'atteindre ou de révéler le fond des choses . . .'.

[31] Ibid., p. 13, Blondel's italics.   [32] Ibid., p. 14.

Philosophy cannot produce faith but it can show that man is not morally free to reject with impunity the possibility of faith and a supernatural order.[33] If philosophy is not competent to pronounce on the facts, where and how do proofs fit into a philosophical apologetic? And since to mention proof in this context is to mention miracle, what about the latter? When one considers that Blondel was here touching on an issue at the very heart of traditional apologetics, one can only marvel at the sang-froid with which he disposes of miracles as proofs of transcendent presence in history. Miracles, he writes,

are truly miraculous only for those who are already prepared to recognize the divine action in the most usual events. And it follows that philosophy, which would offend against its own nature by denying them, is no less incompetent to affirm them, and that they are a witness written in a language other than that of which it is the judge.[34]

Rarely can a theological war have been declared so casually. We have already seen how in traditional apologetics miracles provided the principal cognitive method for diagnosing the presence of the transcendent in history; yet here was Blondel disposing of their empirically probative value, not as rationalism had done, or as positivism continued to do, viz., by a blunt denial of their possibility or actuality, but rather by caging them in brackets and then walking nonchalantly past. The argument as deployed by Blondel out-Husserls Husserl, and from a scholastic standpoint could only have seemed utterly destructive of the foundations of faith.

Leaving the traditionalists no time to recover, Blondel immediately delivers another major assault on one of the most cherished of received positions. 'If the [revelatory] fact is to be accepted by our minds and even imposed upon our reason, an interior need and, as it were, an ineluctable appetite must prepare us for it.[35] This sentence could be paralleled by many others from the *Letter*. The conviction

---

[33] Ibid., p. 13 '... que l'homme ne peut se passer impunément...'. Blondel's continual use of the verbs 'se passer' and 'se dépasser' manifests his central concern with the dynamism of man's relationship with God. Faith has 'a logic' which is not extrinsically imposed on it but is interiorly generated by the dynamism of action.

[34] Ibid., p. 14. For a full documentation of the debate on miracle see F. Rodé, *Le Miracle dans la controverse moderniste* (Paris, 1965), esp. pp. 53–89, which deal with Blondel's *Letter on Apologetics*.   [35] *Lettre*, p. 15.

it expresses is fundamental to Blondel's approach to apologetics. Laberthonnière made it the focal point of an article written for the *Annales* in the following year.[36]

As the anti-modernist campaign intensified in France and Italy over the next ten years, the words 'necessity', 'need', and 'appetite' were made the object of incessant attack. They were deemed to be suggestive of 'fideism', 'voluntarism', and 'naturalism'. In the context of miracle Blondel's approach stood out in sharp opposition to what he was soon to describe as 'extrinsicism'. Man cannot encounter the transcendent in history merely by contemplating miraculous events and allowing them to authenticate an externally delivered revelation. There is no point, he remarks, in offering an argument one regards as *objectively* compelling to a subject who is not disposed to listen to it.[37] Here we have a practical psychological application of the method of immanence which, it cannot be sufficiently emphasized, Blondel always regards as first and foremost a metaphysical procedure.

The second section of the *Letter*, assessed in retrospect by Blondel as having a more enduring importance than the rest of the essay, discusses the mutual relationship of religion and philosophy. The problem quite simply is how to preserve the autonomy of both while allowing each to interpenetrate the other. The following passage is a compendium of the whole *Letter*.

In a phrase which must be explained but which immediately indicates the seriousness of the conflict, modern thought, with jealous susceptibility, takes the notion of *immanence* to be the very condition of [doing] philosophy; that is to say, if there is among [its] controlling ideas an issue which it sponsors as a decided advance, it is the idea, basically quite correct, that nothing can enter into man which does not emerge from him and correspond in some way to a developmental need, and that there is nothing, whether it be historical fact, traditional teaching, or an obligation imposed from without, no compelling truth or admissable precept, which is not in some way autonomous and autochthonous. On the other hand, however, nothing is Catholic which is

---

[36] *A.P.C.*, vol. 133 (1896-1987), pp. 497-511, 615-32. Laberthonnière reprinted it with some explanatory additions as Chapter 4 of his *Essais de philosophie religeuse*.

[37] *Lettre*, p. 28. See *Dru*, pp. 94-7, for a helpful clarification of Blondel's rather idiosyncratic use of the terms 'subjective' and 'objective'.

not *supernatural* — not only transcendent in the simple metaphysical sense of the word (for it is possible to think of truths and beings superior to ourselves which we could, from the depths of our own being, affirm immanently) but supernatural in the fullest sense. In short, man cannot draw out from his own resources [truths and obligations] which are nevertheless laid upon his mind and will as a charge.[38]

This is one of the strongest statements Blondel ever made on the subject of transcendence and man's relationship with the transcendent. It would appear virtually to commit him to an acceptance not only of the *method* but also of the *principle* of immanence.[39] Christian revelation is not merely transcendent but supernatural, that is, beyond the power of man to discover for himself, yet imposed on man's thought and will. The transcendent and the supernatural are not the same thing. The transcendent is in principle open to *natural* human discovery and affirmation. The supernatural is inaccessible to man until made the subject of God's free gift.

Philosophy refuses to find in man anything which does not proceed from man himself. Yet revealed religion has its source outside man (transcendence) and is inaccessible to man's natural powers (supernature). Leaving the question of supernature till later, we may note how Blondel has set the problem in a way which will command attention from his fellow philosophers. He has accepted their terms of reference; more, he shares their conviction about the necessity for an immanent *point de départ* for all philosophical inquiry. In turn he asks them to remain open at least to the possibility of discovering signs of transcendence in the human dynamic revealed by immanent analysis. Action is the key. Thomistic stasis has proved inept. Thomism *starts* from principles

---

[38] *Lettre*, p. 34.

[39] In a letter to Le Roy (16 November 1905) Blondel distinguished between (1) the *doctrine* of immanence, which denies all possibility of knowing the transcendent, (2) the *principle* of immanence, which affirms that all human thought is centrifugal and that God cannot bypass this fact of human nature, and (3) the *method* of immanence, which 'consiste à chercher comment les apports réellement transcendants *quoad originem, quoad rem, quoad modum doni*, sont composables avec nous, comment en un mot le mouvement centripète ne refoule pas, mais sublime le mouvement centrifuge'. Cited in R. Virgoulay, 'La Méthode d'immanence et l'encyclique Pascendi: Incidences de la crise moderniste sur la pensée Blondélienne', in *Recherches de science religieuse*, vol. 58 (1970), pp. 434 f.

which are nowadays called in question — a fact which dis-
credits it in advance as an effective apologetic.[40]

Scholastic theology superimposed the supernatural upon
the natural.[41] The relationship was seen as an extrinsic one.
There was, however, an area of overlap resulting in point of
fact in three zones: reason looked after the lowest zone, faith
looked after the highest, while the middle zone was occupied
by truths accessible to both reason and faith. Protestantism,
remarks Blondel, attacked this dualism as an Aristotelian
corruption and rejected the idea of a rational preparation for
faith.[42] As a result the middle zone was suppressed, since
Protestantism saw it not as a 'terrain de la concorde' but as
an area more likely to be a 'champ des conflits et de la
guerre'.[43] Reason and faith were thus divorced so radically
that they no longer shared any common ground whatever.
Philosophy after Kant thus achieved complete autonomy,
but at a ruinous cost to man's spiritual unity. If, however,
philosophy and Christianity are to meet, there must be some
common ground. To discover what this ground might be was
Blondel's major preoccupation.[44] He found it in the insatiable
demands of the *volonté voulante*, always pointing beyond
every choice of the *volonté voulue* and thus committing man,
willy-nilly, to a journey towards the absolute which, he
claimed, is, objectively considered, nothing less than the
supernatural revelation given in Christ and made available to
us in Christian tradition.[45]

Christian apologetic, according to Blondel, rests on a
recognition that human action produces a sickness which has
to be diagnosed before man can ask the right questions.[46]

---

[40] *Lettre*, pp. 27 f. Time and again in the literature on Blondel we are reminded that when he refers to Thomism he has in mind, not the thought of
Aquinas (with which, it is alleged, he was not very familiar), but that of his own
Thomistic contemporaries. While there is some truth in this observation, it should
not lead us lightly to suppose that once one has disentangled Aquinas from the
corruptions of his latter-day commentators, there is no problem in harmonizing
his thought with Blondel's.

[41] *Lettre*, p. 29.   [42] Ibid., p. 30.   [43] Ibid.

[44] 'Trouver un terrain commun où croyants et incroyants soient également
à l'aise pour traiter, sans passion, des grands intérêts qui les passionnent, c'est là
mon dessein.' (*Études blondéliennes*, vol. ii, p. 104.)

[45] I have here completed the Blondelian case by implicit reference to the conclusion of *Histoire et dogme*.   [46] *Lettre*, p. 36.

If Christianity were a way of life simply added to nature, one could justly refuse it, since there would be no intelligible connection between the natural and the supernatural. But there *is* a connection. Revelation seeks us out and confronts us with an inescapable choice. It makes neutrality impossible: not to rise becomes a positive backsliding ('déchéance').[47] In short, philosophy delivers man at a point where he has to make a decision about revelation.[48] This sort of approach to philosophy makes detachment not only impossible but undesirable. Blondel prescribed for the philosopher nothing less than the moral and spiritual conversion demanded by the authentic practice of his craft. This fact alone would debar Blondel from a serious hearing at many philosophical conferences.[49]

According to Blondel, philosophical apologetics has for its main purpose the demonstration of man's *intrinsic* need for the transcendent and the supernatural. The need is present whether man chooses to recognize it or not; and the task of the method of immanence is to confront each individual man with it and ask what he proposes to do about it. Before pronouncing on the meaning of what we are thinking, we have to establish what we are in fact thinking.[50] In effect Blondel is saying to the unbeliever: let us agree that this is how man experiences the dynamic and ultimately transcendent drive of his choices, all of which point beyond themselves to a further goal. Whether there exists in transcendent reality a goal which will satisfy man's will is a separate question.

---

[47] *Lettre*, p. 37.

[48] This was of course the major conclusion of *L'Action*. '. . . il est impossible de ne pas reconnaître l'insuffisance de tout l'ordre naturel et de ne point éprouver un besoin ultérieur; il est impossible de trouver en soi de quoi consenter ce besoin religieux. *C'est nécessaire*; et *c'est impracticable*. Voilà, toutes brutes, les conclusions du determinisme de l'action humaine.' (*L'Action*, p. 319.)

[49] In 1902 the *Societé Française de Philosophie* had to decide whether to admit the word 'action' into the *Vocabulaire technique et critique de la philosophie*. Léon Brunschvicg (whose own philosophy ruled out all questions of a transcendent God) put his finger on the crux of the problem when he said 'En acceptant le mot de M. Blondel, nous le suivons sur son terrain, et nous donnons une sorte de consécration à une doctrine qu'en réalité nous n'admettons pas.' (Cited in R. Saint-Jean, *L'Apologétique philosophique*, p. 26.) In its own way this was a backhanded compliment to the unity existing between Blondel's thought and his philosophical method.   [50] *Lettre*, p. 39.

Blondel emphasizes the moral — indeed even the ascetical — dimension of the dynamic force he is analysing. To 'act', in his sense of the word, is to take part in a drama which cannot reach its denouement until the decisive question has been faced.[51] Faith begins as a willingness to say 'yes' to the possible, Blondel adding the Pascalian remark that 'le *oui* procure infiniment plus que le contraire du *non*.'[52] Of course evasion of the decisive question remains a genuine option, but 'to turn away from one's destiny does not mean escaping from it.'[53] Jean Lacroix has described Blondel as the philosopher of man's 'natural and incurable inachievability'.[54] 'This philosophy of insufficiency leads up in fact to an insufficiency of philosophy.'[55]

Blondel completes the second section of the *Letter* with a reaffirmation of the autonomy of philosophy. He denies that there is a specifically 'Christian philosophy' any more than there is a 'Christian physics'.[56] This view was later contradicted by both Jacques Maritain and Étienne Gilson, but Blondel (who was by then, much to the disgust of Laberthonnière, seeking a *rapprochement* with Thomism) stuck to his guns on this issue and was grateful for de Lubac's interpretation of his conception of philosophy as 'open to Christianity'.[57]

The third and last section of the *Letter* is less satisfactory than the other two. It contains a historical excursus which Blondel later described as cavalier and artificial.[58] He takes scholasticism to task for employing a concept of reason and philosophy which was in fact responsible for all the attacks made on it. These attacks were, in his view, justified and beneficial both for philosophy and for Christianity in that they made possible the discovery by both philosophy and Christianity of each other's proper autonomy. Hence Blondel saw neo-scholasticism's call for a return to the pre-critical stance of medieval philosophy as a particularly regrettable

---

[51] *Lettre*, p. 44.
[52] Ibid., p. 45.
[53] Ibid.
[54] Lacroix, *Maurice Blondel*, p. 35.
[55] Ibid., p. 23.
[56] *Lettre*, p. 47.
[57] H. de Lubac, 'Sur la philosophie chrétienne: Réflexions à la suite d'un débat', in *Nouvelle revue théologique*, 63 (1936), p. 245. The question is discussed in *Dru*, pp. 105–12.
[58] *Dru*, p. 171.

putting back of the clock. Christianity must realize that it needs the help of a completely autonomous philosophy if it is to commend itself to the modern unbeliever.

Sixteen years later, writing to Auguste Valensin, Blondel averred that the *Letter on Apologetics* was addressed not to theologians but to the philosophers who had disqualified him in the name of reason and to the university authorities who had shown him the door.[59] While it is difficult to accept that he had given no thought to the theologians (Laberthonnière's warning had already alerted him to possible theological difficulties), it was the theologians who took umbrage at the *Letter*. Although we shall examine the anti-modernist campaign at length in Chapters 8 and 9, it will help our appreciation of Blondel's contribution if we here consider the main lines of the attack on the *Letter* which occurred before Loisy's *L'Évangile et l'Église* had radicalized the situation by introducing the problem of biblical criticism and the nature of dogma. Many of the points made against Blondel survived through the heart of the modernist crisis to be used against other 'modernists'.

The attack on Blondel in the 1890s was Thomist-inspired and was initiated by the Dominican M. B. Schwalm in the pages of the *Revue thomiste*.[60] Schwalm centred his attack on two charges: (1) that Blondel had fallen completely for neo-Kantian subjectivism and that, together with Renouvier, Lachelier, and Boutroux, he had helped to propagate in France the maleficent notions which had been prevalent in Germany twenty-five years earlier. Schwalm claimed that Blondel's method pushed Kantianism to its last phenomenalist consequences. Speculative reason takes cognizance of the fact that we have ideas, but it is declared incompetent to judge whether

---

[59] *B.V.*, vol. ii, p. 338.

[60] In a little over two years Schwalm wrote four articles for the Dominican journal: 'Les Illusions de l'idéalisme et leurs dangers pour la foi', *Revue thomiste*, 4 (1896), pp. 413–41; 'L'Apologétique contemporaine: Doit-elle adopter une méthode nouvelle?', ibid., 5 (1897), pp. 62–94; 'La Crise de l'apologétique', ibid., 5 (1897), pp. 338–70; 'Le Dogmatisme du cœur et celui de l'esprit', ibid., 6 (1898), pp. 578–619. The first of Schwalm's articles is summarized in R. Saint-Jean, *L'Apologétique philosophique*, pp. 55–60. In 1909 Blondel said of this article that it was 'la méprise initiale qui a donné le diapason à *toute* la controverse ultérieure contre mon prétendu subjectivisme et mon prétendu immanentisme', *B.V.*, vol. ii, p. 183.

these ideas correspond to what is outside us;[61] (2) that Blondel robbed miracles ('ces signes évidents et nécessaires de la présence du surnaturel dans l'Église') of their probative value, thus destroying the rational basis for belief.[62]

In December of the same year, 1896, Blondel was attacked in the *Annales de philosophie chrétienne* by the Abbé Hippolyte Gayraud (who had left the Dominicans in 1893 in order to devote himself to 'a missionary apostolate' of social and political character). Gayraud's attack was academically more light-weight than Schwalm's, and it covered more or less the same ground on miracles; but it introduced another, and theologically sensitive, issue into the debate. Gayraud accused Blondel of 'naturalism', on the grounds that the latter had written of the *necessity* of the supernatural. The supernatural, Gayraud remarked, is by definition gratuitous. To describe it as necessary is to destroy its character as freely given by God.

Schwalm and Gayraud agree in their claim that Blondel's method of immanence ran contrary to the teaching of the Vatican Council on the role of miracles in Christian apologetics. As Laberthonnière was shortly to point out, Schwalm and Gayraud both sought to convict Blondel of heresy, but the heresies suggested by each contradicted the other.[63] Schwalm accused him of fideism, Gayraud of naturalism. 'One or other of the two', remarked Laberthonnière dryly, 'has to be wrong. And the fact that they contradict one another ought to make them ask whether they are not both wrong.'[64]

It is instructive to advert to the year these charges were levelled against Blondel, namely the autumn and winter of 1896 to 1897. In these months Loisy, rusticated to Neuilly from the Institut Catholique of Paris, was spending his retreat in intensive study and was still engaged in writing his *Livre inédit*, the unpublished work from which he was

[61] 'C'est la pratique, l'action, qui lui apprend la vérité objective de ce qu'elle pense', Schwalm, *Revue thomiste*, 4 (1896), p. 413.

[62] Ibid., p. 433.

[63] L. Laberthonnière, 'Le problème religieux à propos de la question apologetique', in *A.P.C.*, vol. 133 (1896-7), pp. 497-511.

[64] Laberthonnière, art. cit., as reprinted in *Le réalisme chrétien: précédé de: Essais de philosophie religieuse* (Paris, 1966), pp. 136-7n.

shortly to quarry the articles he wrote under the pseudonym 'Firmin'. Tyrrell was on the staff of the Jesuit journal, *The Month*, and was much in demand for retreats and conferences. Buonaiuti, a young, enthusiastic, and pious clerical student, had just begun his studies for the priesthood. Von Hügel, drawn momentarily away from the study of Eucken, was pondering with approval the message of *L'Action* and the *Letter on Apologetics*. In the midst of this peaceful and palpably unsubversive atmosphere Marie-Benoît Schwalm and Hippolyte Gayraud were already intoning the key phrases of the anti-modernist campaign which would reach full orchestration in Pius X's encyclical letter, *Pascendi dominici gregis*, a decade later: Kantian subjectivism, fideism, voluntarism, anti-intellectualism, and naturalism. The object of their attack, the Professor of Philosophy at the University of Aix, refused to go into print to defend his theories but went instead to Lourdes to examine his conscience.

As we shall see, the charge of Kantianism was soon to become stock-in-trade in the anti-modernist arsenal. Since Blondel was the philosopher most closely associated with the 'new apologetic', and since the new apologetic was eventually to be condemned as Kantian, this is an appropriate point at which to examine the charge. Neo-scholastic theologians and philosophers frequently used the term 'Kantian' as a pejorative label much as McCarthyite Americans used the word 'communist'. Henri de Lubac provides a full and informative note on Kantianism in his edition of Blondel's correspondence with Auguste Valensin.[65] Kantianism had, says de Lubac, become an obsession in some theological circles. In these circles Blondel was regarded as the leader of a school which would, precisely by its adoption and dissemination of Kant's philosophy, destroy the rational foundations of Catholic belief. Just as Marsiglio Ficino tried to Platonize his century, wrote the Abbé Gombault in a prize-winning essay submitted to the Institut Catholique of Paris, and published in 1902 to 1903, so M. Blondel is trying to Kantianize ours.[66] The metaphors resorted to by the scholastics paint a vivid picture of how they represented Kantian thought to

[65] *B.V.*, vol. i, pp. 60–5. [66] Ibid., vol. i, p. 61.

themselves and to others. Gayraud, in an article published in the *Revue du clergé français* in 1902, argued that miracles are the *facta divina* placed before man's reason as testimony to divine revelation.[67] If, however, reason has been 'enfeebled' 'under the debilitating and toxic influence of positivism, of sensualism, and of the Kantian criticism', it may simply fail to register the significance of the facts.[68] The metaphor of toxicity was soon to cross the Alps where it would appear as 'il veleno kantiano'. Gayraud had been arguing since 1896 that a Christian could not be a Kantian,[69] because Kantianism by its 'transcendental scepticism' and epistemological relativism had opened up a chasm between itself and Christian belief.[70] This chasm M. Blondel has signally failed to bridge by his method of immanence. M. Blondel is therefore a danger to Catholic faith because he offers us an illusory bridge across an impassable chasm. Christianity is objective and absolute, while Kantianism is subjective and relativistic.

The antinomy 'objective/subjective' was deployed and dilated upon at every turn in the scholastic argument. Already in 1902 Albert Leclère, a professor in the University of Berne, writing as an impartial observer of the French philosophical scene, claimed that the scholastic rejection of Kant was based on a fundamental misunderstanding of the Kantian position.[71] In trying to fit Kant's critique into their own categories, Leclère claims, the scholastics seriously misconstrue what Kant meant by 'objective reality'. 'They forget that he [Kant] puts forward numerous objections to Berkeleyan idealism.'[72] The 'object' of which Kant speaks is not the 'object' of Aristotelian epistemology but rather the relationship existing between Aristotle's object and the mind of the knower. This fundamental misunderstanding renders the scholastics incapable of seeing in the philosophy of

[67] H. Gayraud, 'Le problème de la certitude religieuse', in *R.C.F.* 30 (1902), pp. 113-30.

[68] Ibid., pp. 122-3.   [69] *P.V.*, vol. i, p. 60.

[70] H. Gayraud, 'Une nouvelle apologétique chrétienne', in *A.P.C.*, vol. 133 (1896-7), pp. 253-73, 400-8.

[71] A. Leclère, 'Le Mouvement catholique kantien en France à l'heure présente', in *Kantstudien*, 7 (1902), pp. 300-63.

[72] Ibid., p. 339.

immanence anything but pure subjectivism. Although Leclère can hardly be regarded as the impartial observer he represents himself to be, he is here making a point of real relevance and importance. His description of scholastic thought as 'metaphysical empiricism'[73] neatly complements Laberthonnière's description of Pascal as 'a positivist for whom interior reality, living reality, is the essential and primordial fact'.[74]

The scholastics, according to Leclère, place full reliance on speculative reason in matters of transcendent reference; indeed they seem to know of no other kind of reason and to have no conception of what Kant meant by practical reason. They thus represent the 'Novateurs' (i.e. the followers of Blondel and Bergson) as Catholics seduced by Protestantism, metaphysicians seduced by agnosticism, and Christian apologists who resort to Kantian faith in duty 'in order to remain what they are'.[75] Though Leclère's article was dismissed by Blondel as superficial and mischievous,[76] and though it comprises an assembly of very large generalizations, it remains an interesting and informative survey of the French philosophical scene at the turn of the century. Blondel's tetchy dismissal of it seems to have been prompted by two factors. First, it associated him too closely with the Catholic Bergsonians, especially Le Roy, from whom Blondel was trying to distance himself. But, more significantly, it associated him with Kant's philosophy, and on this topic Blondel's ambivalence was a source of torture to himself and of irritation to others. Leclère had conceded that the Blondelians and Bergsonians differed significantly from each other, but he claimed that they shared a common inspiration: 'the method of their religious philosophy is that of Kant, adjusted to the demands of their faith.'[77]

Leaving aside for the present the fears, hostility, and misunderstandings of the scholastic camp, we may reasonably

---

[73] Leclère, p. 362n.
[74] L. Laberthonnière, 'L'Apologétique et la méthode de Pascal', in *E.P.R.*, p. 195.
[75] Leclère, art. cit., p. 337.
[76] *B.V.*, vol. i, p. 374. Laberthonnière took a more favourable view of Leclère's article than Blondel did. (See L. Laberthonnière, *Essais de philosophie religieuse* (Paris, 1903), Appendix 3, pp. 322-3.) [77] Leclère, art. cit., p. 330.

inquire into the extent to which Blondel's thought was in
fact influenced by Kant. Blondel himself is unfortunately
an unreliable guide in the inquiry. He told A. Gardeil, a
disciple of Schwalm, in 1912 that no system of thought was
more repugnant to him than that of Kant. 'I wrote *L'Action*
before having read him. What I was in fact reading while
working on *L'Action* was St Bernard.'[78] To put it as mildly
as possible, this was a serious overstatement. He may have
been reading St. Bernard while he worked on *L'Action*; he
was unquestionably antipathetic to some aspects of Kant's
thought; but, as McNeill's research has clearly shown, from
internal evidence it is quite certain that Blondel 'did have an
extensive and profound knowledge of Kant's moral philosophy at the time he wrote *Action*'.[79] 'There is no room,
then, for legitimate doubt that Kantian critical philosophy
was one of the most important influences on the formation
of Blondel's method in *Action*. But that influence takes the
form of a subtle mixture of acceptance, rejection and transformation.'[80]

No philosopher working in the mainstream of French
philosophy at that time could have escaped the influence of
Kant. Blondel put up a much better defence for himself when
he remarked that he sought to transcend Kantianism by the
use of its own logic. Before writing *L'Action*, he asked in his
diary: 'Is it impossible to destroy the magic spell of Kantian
thought, as Kant did in the case of Cartesianism, as Descartes
did in the case of peripatetic thought? Can one create a
Catholic Kantianism?'[81] These are not the reflections of a
mind untouched by Kant. Blondel, however, liked to claim
that there was more of Spinoza than Kant in his method of
immanence.[82] What he took from Spinoza above all was the
latter's concern for the totality, the unity, of philosophical
inquiry. Blondel was one of the leading French authorities on
Spinoza. In an article on the latter he wrote: 'The essence
of immanent criticism, the idea which is its foundation, is
that every act, every work of man or nature, has its value as

---

[78] *B. V.*, vol. ii, p. 183.   [79] McNeill, *The Blondelian Synthesis*, p. 46.
[80] Ibid., p. 47.   [81] M. Blondel, *Carnets intimes, 1883–1894,* p. 105.
[82] See *L'Action*, p. 475, where Blondel sites his own position somewhere
between Kant and Spinoza.

well as its reality determined by the whole of which it is a part.'[83] Blondel was clearly influenced by Spinoza's concep-tion of life as a drama in which man comes to spiritual maturity by reflecting upon and acquiescing in the presence of the infinite in each state of mind.[84] But Blondel resolutely refuses to reduce the perfect life to speculative knowledge, however important in itself that knowledge may be. He applauds Spinoza for seeing that morality involves meta-physics but condemns him for converting morality into metaphysics. Blondel shows none of the instinctive attraction towards pantheism which is apparent in von Hügel.

In view of the fact that immanentism was one of the major charges brought against modernism, it is, on the face of it, curious that Blondel's admitted interest in Spinoza was scarcely commented upon by his Catholic critics. Kant remained the villain behind the scenes throughout the modernist period. Yet Spinoza's God is immanent in nature to the point of total identification, while Kant's God is transcendent to the point of inaccessibility. This fact alone should alert one to the vagaries of both terms, 'transcen-dence' and 'immanence', as used in the modernist debate. In spite of their adverse comment on the dangers of immanentism, the neo-scholastics were not really disturbed by its prospect, for they were supremely confident of their ability to refute it. What they did genuinely fear was a system of philosophical inquiry which placed the knowing and willing subject at the core of man's approach to God. Subjec-tivity as the controlling perspective in the inquiry suggested relativity in the interpretation of the findings; and this was radically unacceptable to them. When the crisis began in earnest in 1902 with the publication of Loisy's *L'Évangile et L'Église*, there could be no doubt what the crucial issue was going to be: is Catholic dogma an objective, coherent, and perennially valid statement of transcendent facts, or is it a conflation of time-bound and space-bound responses to situations and challenges which are of their nature ephemeral?

---

[83] B. Aimant [sc. Blondel], 'Une des sources de la pensée moderne: l'Evolution du Spinozisme', in *A.P.C.*, 64 (1894), pp. 332 f.
[84] Ibid., p. 334. See McNeill, op. cit., pp. 16–41.

With the arrival of Loisy, Tyrrell, and Le Roy, Blondel was, to his great relief, upstaged until the draughtsmen of *Pascendi* sought an underlying philosophy to account for the mortal threat which they saw facing the Church. The 'method of immanence' could, with a little ingenuity, be made to fit the bill, especially if labelled 'Kantian'.

The charge initiated by Gayraud and taken up by others, namely, that Blondel's method of immanence denied the gratuitous character of supernature is perhaps best considered in connection with the contribution made to the modernist debate by Lucien Laberthonnière, Blondel's friend and closest disciple, who had warned him of the likelihood that he would indeed be attacked by the theologians precisely on this point, and who set about defending him with clarity and vigour.

3 Alfred Loisy and the Radicalization of the Modernist Movement

Alfred Loisy claimed to detect in Friedrich von Hügel an obsession with the problem of transcendence and immanence.[1] He himself asks us to believe that the whole question left him unmoved. While for von Hügel the question of God as a personality independent of the universe was 'un cauchemar angoissant',[2] 'ni la personnalité de Dieu, ni l'immortalité de l'homme n'ont été ni ne sont objet d'inquiétude pour mon esprit.'[3] Although there is an abundance of evidence that Loisy was passionless to the point of frigidity, it is not easy to accept his claim that his speculations on the question of God and immortality were carried out merely to appease others and never for his own peace of mind.[4]

There are two views of Loisy which go back to the modernists themselves. The first is Loisy's self-portrait supplemented by Henri Bremond. The second, and diametrically opposite, view is given by Albert Houtin and Félix Sartiaux, Loisy's erstwhile friends and disciples. The first portrait gives us a man tragically caught up in the events of his time, broken on the wheel of ecclesiastical obscurantism and left to live out his life in lonely isolation and proud integrity at Garnay and Ceffonds. The second portrait is of a supercilious egotist, vain, querulous and — most damaging of all — a thoroughgoing sceptic who maintained a front of religious belief and practice, in short, a hypocritical tactician.

In a theological matter as profound and pervasive as divine transcendence one can hardly dismiss as irrelevant and impertinent the question of personal faith. Yet such a personal inquiry can seem out of place in the context of academic discussion. There are, after all, no scientific criteria for

[1] A. Loisy, *Mémoires pour servir à l'histoire religieuse de notre temps*, 3 vols. (Paris, 1930–1) [*Mémoires*], vol. ii, p. 449; vol. iii, pp. 24, 107, 141, 153–68 (*passim*).

[2] *Mémoires*, vol. iii, p. 24.   [3] Ibid., p. 23.   [4] Ibid., pp. 23 f.

diagnosing the presence or quality of religious faith. It is quite apparent that by 1906, at the latest, Loisy was no longer a Roman Catholic in any sense remotely acceptable to the Catholic magisterium of the period. Like most of the modernists, however, he appealed to the Church of the future. Perhaps the most celebrated attempt to defend Loisy's stance was that put forward by Henri Bremond, who made a distinction between 'dogmatic faith' and 'mystical faith', and conceded that while Loisy clearly lacked the former, he retained the latter.[5] At best the term 'mystical' is a notoriously imprecise one. The modernists tended to employ it as a serviceable antonym for 'scholastic'. Rejecting scholastic rationalism and extrinsicism, they were forced to appeal to a pre-conceptual, intuitive, generalized opening of both heart and mind towards the absolute. Thus Raymond de Boyer de Sainte Suzanne writes of Loisy: 'Like Edward Le Roy and Henri Bremond, and with his customary vigour, he sited the source of religion in the sort of intuitive thought which is devoid of concepts, anterior to worship, and anterior, a fortiori, to theological speculation.'[6] The trouble is, however, that the terms 'transcendence' and 'immanence' are not pre-conceptual or anterior to theological speculation. They are philosophically precise attempts to define the nature of the absolute in relation to man and his history.

The question that faces us here is one of deciding where Alfred Loisy stood in the matter of divine transcendence *during the modernist period*. This temporal limitation is important, because in referring to the writings of the later Loisy, especially to the *Mémoires*, we need to remain

[5] E. Poulat, *Une œuvre clandestine d'Henri Bremond: Sylvain Leblanc: Un clerc qui n'a pas trahi: Alfred Loisy d'après ses Mémoires, 1931* (Rome, 1972), pp. 97, 148. A. R. Vidler shares this view: 'Loisy's dogmatic faith had been sapped by 1886, but until 1904 he retained a sincere mystical faith.' (*A Variety of Catholic Modernists* (Cambridge, 1970), p. 45.) Dr Vidler later remarks that Pius X's rejection of Loisy's appeal 'more than anything else, snapped the mystical bond that still held Loisy to the Church' (ibid., p. 48). Poulat believes that in making a distinction between Loisy's 'foi dogmatique' and his 'foi mystique', Bremond was reflecting his own personal difficulties (Poulat, op. cit., p. 97). Again one is forced to note how idiosyncratically the word 'mystical' is used during the modernist period. Here it seems to mean simply 'extra-ecclesiastical'.

[6] R. de Boyer de Sainte Suzanne, *Alfred Loisy: Entre la foi et l'incroyance* (Paris, 1968), p. 61.

constantly on the alert for instances of anachronistic retro-jection of later interpretations on to earlier situations. In 1908 Loisy announced that he wished to be judged by his publications only, and not by conversations, letters, or interviews.[7] According to Félix Sartiaux, Loisy, under the express influence of Bergson's *L'Évolution créatrice* and the unrecognized influence of Hébert's doctrine of symbolism, returned in his last period to an explicit if highly idiosyn-cratic theism.[8]

That Loisy was a thoroughgoing immanentist in the years which followed the condemnation of modernism is hardly open to question (except by those who would deny him even his 'mystical' monism and would regard him as an atheist playing around aesthetically with pseudo-mystical ideas). For present purposes, however, he must be judged on those of his writings which preceded the condemnation of modern-ism. Whether he had in fact lost his faith (dogmatic or mystical) in 1886, or at any time between then and 1908, has no *verifiable* bearing on his contribution to the modernist movement. Our concern here is with his challenge to the accepted scholastic statement of Catholic orthodoxy on those matters directly or indirectly referable to the transcen-dence/immanence category.

Loisy was in the habit of claiming to be a historian and exegete as distinct from a philosopher or theologian. Inside many historians, however, there is a philosopher trying to get out; in Loisy's case he escaped successfully, but only at the price of being disowned whenever he became a forensic

---

[7] E. Poulat (ed.), A. Houtin and F. Sartiaux, *Alfred Loisy: Sa vie — son œuvre* Paris, 1960), p. 150. The notice which Loisy instructed Houtin to insert in *Le Siècle* (21 Feb. 1908) read: 'C'est à ces livres, et *à ces livres seulement*, parce que ces livres seuls contiennent l'expression exacte et complète de sa pensée, qu'il se permet de renvoyer tous ceux qui veulent connaître ses conclusions sur la vie de Jésus, les origines chrétiennes et les thèses fondamentales de la théologie catholique.' Presumably, however, he did not intend to exclude his articles from the canon.

[8] Sartiaux quotes this sentence from Loisy's *La Crise morale du temps présent et l'éducation humaine* (Paris, 1937), p. 242: '*Dieu existe*, c'est à dire un Etre *au-dessus* de tous les êtres, une Puissance au-dessus de toutes les puissances, un Esprit au-dessus de tous les esprits, qui est le principe et la source de toute vie dans l'ordre sensible et dans l'ordre insensible, dans l'ordre éternel des mondes.' (Cited in Poulat, *Alfred Loisy*, pp. 252 f.)

embarrassment. Thus Loisy, in correspondence with Wehrlé over his dispute with Bondel in 1903, wrote: 'Je ne suis qu'un pauvre déchiffreur de textes, et la haute philosophie n'est pas mon fait: que les philosophes m'apportent des lumières!'[9] Wehrlé seems to have missed the irony of Loisy's appeal for philosophical illumination, for we find him writing immediately to Blondel asking him to supply the needed light. Blondel was not taken in by Loisy's ironic disingenuousness.

M. Loisy declares modestly that he is 'only a poor decipherer of texts'. He thus appears to make a systematic renunciation of any incursion into the diverse areas of metaphysics and theology. To what extent is this claim to be an historian and only an historian possible or legitimate?[10]

This was to remain Blondel's controlling conviction throughout his debate with Loisy. In *Histoire et dogme* he remarks that 'when someone lacks an explicit philosophy he normally has an uncritical philosophy. And what he takes to be straightforward matters of fact are often mere hypotheses ('constructions').[11] Blondel can be accused of failing to appreciate Loisy's case in many important respects, but in this one he was not merely right, he anticipated the later hermeneutical move away from nineteenth-century positivism. Loisy was indeed a philosopher of religion and gloried in it. He later told his friend Raymond de Boyer de Sainte Suzanne that he attached more importance to his philosophical than to his exegetical work.[12] The matter is put beyond doubt by the series of articles he wrote for the *Revue du clergé français* between 1898 and 1900. In these articles we

[9] *B.V.*, vol. i, p. 112. Marlé (*Au cœur*, p. 72) omits the 'haute', an adjective which clearly has an ironic purpose. (Loisy told Blondel that he – Blondel – was cut out to write encyclicals.)

[10] Blondel to Wehrlé, cited in Marlé, op. cit., p. 75.

[11] M. Blondel, 'Histoire et dogme', in *Les Premiers Écrits de Maurice Blondel*, vol. ii (Paris, 1956), p. 168.

[12] R. de Boyer de Sainte Suzanne, *Alfred Loisy*, p. 26. In Rome, Genocchi, commenting in a letter on the probable condemnation of *L'Évangile et l'Église* and *Autour d'un petit livre*, remarked that he hoped the Biblical Commission would not get involved: 'I due ultimi libri non sono di esegesi né, a propriamente parlare, di critica biblica. É un sistema complesso di filosofia religiosa.' (F. Turvasi, *Giovanni Genocchi e la controversia modernista* (Rome, 1974), pp. 188 f.)

have his basic ideas, many of which were later to be clarified, organized and developed in *L'Évangile et l'Église* and *Autour d'un petit livre*.[13]

Writing to Maude Petre, Tyrrell once remarked that though 'impatient of German fogginess', he was quite conscious that his 'besetting mental sin' was 'clearness'.[14] Loisy, if he had had Tyrrell's unsparing self-critical awareness, might with profit and with more reason have reached a similar conclusion about himself. Gallic clarity is there; but it is a deceptive clarity, achieved by a frequent shifting of perspective which robs us of a central point of reference. A contemporary critic, T.-M. Pégues, put it bluntly when he remarked that 'la pensée de M. Loisy se nuance et va et revient sans qu'il soit possible, semble-t-il, de la saisir ou de la fixer.'[15] That judgement suggests something more than the frustration of a mystified scholastic looking for fixed essences in a sea of constantly shifting meanings. Pégues was referring specifically to *L'Évangile et l'Église*, a book which mystified many, including Harnack[16] and Batiffol,[17] and which still fascinates both by the elegance of its style and by a dexterity which verges on sleight-of-hand. The reader has a persistent feeling of 'now you see it, now you don't'. The book is fatally flawed by the ambiguity of its target. In order to understand Loisy one must first of all forget Harnack, says M. Poulat;[18] but can one genuinely do this, even as a methodological expedient? Loisy's book was offered to the Catholic reading public as a refutation of Liberal Protestant

---

[13] Of the Firmin articles Poulat (*Histoire*, p. 74) writes: 'Ces articles témoign-ent d'une pensée en possession d'elle-même mais encore à la recherche se son expression.'

[14] British Library Add. MS. 52367, T. to M.D.P., 16.11.1900.

[15] T.-M. Pégues, 'Le Livre de M. l'abbé Loisy', in *Revue thomiste*, 11 (1903), p. 85.

[16] 'I am frequently unable to recognize my thought in the form he gives it . . . Is it a case of a Latin unable to understand a German or a Catholic unable to understand a Protestant?' (cited in Poulat, *Histoire*, p. 93n).

[17] Poulat, *Alfred Loisy*, p. 109.

[18] 'Il faut d'abord oublier Harnack pour comprendre Loisy, avant d'y revenir pour les confronter l'un et l'autre, car, bien que le second ne cesse de se référer au premier, c'est la façon dont il l'a interprété qui nous importe avant tout.' (*Histoire*, p. 61.) Writing to Houtin in 1906, Loisy speaks of giving the impression that he was further from Harnack than he really was (*Mémoires*, vol. ii, p. 270). See Poulat, op. cit., p. 93.

individualism. It would seem, however, that Loisy contrived a deliberately ambiguous method of approach in several respects. First, he deliberately placed the 'Catholic' and Liberal Protestant conceptions of the Kingdom in excessively sharp opposition to each other. Second, he went out of his way to minimize the ground he held in common with Harnack. Third, he played down his debt to, and basic agreement with, Weiss's consistent eschatology. Finally, he allowed a strong measure of equivocation to pervade his conception of Catholicism. When he places 'Catholicism' in opposition to (Liberal) Protestantism, he is using the former term in a totally idiosyncratic manner. His 'Catholicism' is basically a recognition of the social dimension of religion. He sees the Church as a natural stage in that evolutionary process which itself gave rise to Jesus' preaching of the apocalyptic Kingdom. He wrote to Blondel: 'My book contains only one thesis: the Church is the Gospel continued. Christian development is not extrinsic or foreign to the Gospel.'[19]

His book may have contained, as he claimed, only one *explicit* thesis, namely, the evolving continuity between Gospel and Church, but it also contained at least one *implicit* thesis which Loisy knew to be in full conflict with current orthodoxy, both Catholic and Protestant. Harnack had diagnosed a moral discontinuity between the Gospel message and the Hellenized Church. Loisy, with Weiss and Schweitzer, diagnosed a historical and eschatological break between Jesus and the Kerygma. Roman Catholic orthodoxy of the period accepted no break whatever, either between Jesus and the Kerygma or between the Kerygma and the later Church; for it correctly realized that the admission of such a break at any point in the historical line between Jesus and the Church

---

[19] Marlé, *Au cœur*, pp. 84 f. 'This is why', says R. Haight, implicitly disagreeing with Poulat, 'the position vis-à-vis Harnack is so important. What is at stake and to be proved historically is the relation between the gospel and the Church, and not the validity of either.' (R. D. Haight, 'The Unfolding of Modernism in France: Blondel, Laberthonnière, Le Roy', in *Theological Studies*, 35 (1974), p. 649.) Haight thus presents Loisy as bracketing the truth of Christianity while concentrating on the homogeneous relationship between Gospel and Church doctrine. This attitude was precisely what Blondel regarded as irresponsible and indefensible from a Christian standpoint, as we shall see in the next chapter.

would simply invalidate the coherence and unity of the Catholic position as it was then understood and presented. In a word, Lessing's 'ugly, broad ditch' between the accidental truths of history and the necessary truths of reason, occurs, when translated into Roman catholic categories, between history and dogma. Protestantism, by its concentration on the subjective dimension of faith, could cross the ditch either by a Kierkegaardian leap, or by extracting from the Gospel a timeless essence which virtually freed the Christian believer from the contingencies of history. Roman Catholicism, weighed down by its subscription to doctrinal assertions (often interpreted literally and without historical nuance) and by its apologetical preoccupation with credibility, could not begin to contemplate either a Kierkegaardian leap (which it would construe as fideism) or Harnack's essence (which it did construe as Protestant anti-intellectualism). It therefore denied the ditch.

We are concerned here, not directly with Loisy's work as the exegete he proclaimed himself exclusively to be, but with the theologian and philosopher he disclaimed being whenever it seemed tactically desirable for him to do so. When the need for prevarication had passed, he was quite ready to admit freely to being a philosopher of religion, and, indeed, as we have seen from his remark to M. de Boyer de Sainte Suzanne, to evaluating his work as a religious philosopher more highly than his exegetical work. Miss Petre wrote to him in 1917 questioning him on the similarity between his 'religion of humanity' and Comte's. He replied that, to his shame, he had never read Comte. He went on: 'Comte denies any spiritual beyond; I am fully disposed to affirm without defining it; I am perfectly conscious of admitting an implicit metaphysic; what I do not admit is the necessity of a learned metaphysic, of a philosophical theology as the foundation of religion and morality.[20] There is no reason to suppose that the opinions

---

[20] M. D. Petre, *Alfred Loisy: His Religious Significance* (Cambridge, 1944), p. 118. He adds that he finds Comte's theory to be 'as absolute as scholasticism' (p. 119). Nevertheless, two years later he wrote to Raymond de Boyer de Sainte Suzanne: 'Vous ne vous étonnerez pas que j'aime mieux Comte avec sa religion de l'humanité, que Renan avec sa religion de la science . . . *Le scientisme* est une damnable hérésie.' (R. de Boyer de Sainte Suzanne, *Alfred Loisy*, p. 194.)

he expresses here were significantly different from those he held ten years earlier. He affirms an undefined 'spiritual beyond'. The phrase is too elastic for us to take from it any satisfactory theory of transcendence. It is his 'implicit metaphysic' which invites attention. The pure historian, the decipherer of texts, declares himself incompetent to discover the supernatural. What, however, does the implicit metaphysician have to say? We shall examine this question under three heads: (1) the notion of God, (2) the notion of religion, revelation, and dogma, and (in the following chapter) (3) the relationship between history and dogma.

In 1905 Loisy told von Hügel that he was thinking of writing a book 'on God and the essence or basis of religious faith'.[21] In the event, this book was never written and he later came to regard his *La Religion*[22] as taking its place.[23] The reason, as he saw it in 1930, for his failure to get beyond the rough planning stage of his proposed book on God was a sort of impotence, which he regretted but carefully distinguished from scepticism. He found himself unable to employ with any conviction the categories of transcendence and immanence in his effort to resolve the conflict which he felt existed between the traditional theological and metaphysical idea of God and the world-view provided by history.[24]

A letter which he wrote to Semeria in 1906 is probably the best index we have to his theodicy at that time.[25] We are of course not surprised that he finds the traditional metaphysical proofs for the existence of God to be inconclusive. The God arrived at through the classical Thomistic proofs is eternal, immutable, omniscient, and omnipotent. Loisy remarks that he cannot easily conceive of a God so transcendent to the evolving world that he possesses the infinite totality of his being independently of the universe he has created more or less by benevolent caprice.[26] Von Hügel's God, he goes on, is too like Harnack's, available largely to feeling and a mystical cast of mind.

Our idea of God, wrote Loisy to Semeria, is a sort of projection on to God of idealized human personality, a

[21] *Mémoires*, vol. ii, p. 450.   [22] A. Loisy, *La religion* (Paris, 1917).
[23] *Mémoires*, vol. ii, p. 451.   [24] Ibid.   [25] Ibid., pp. 469 f.   [26] Ibid., p. 469.

projection resulting in a mythology which needs to be pro-
gressively purified by theology. God is, as it were, a higher
self overseeing a lesser self and doing so with all the more
right because it is also a transcendent personification of
society, of humanity.[27] 'La grande puissance' from which
everything proceeds must needs be something more marvel-
lous, more august, more benevolent than anything we can
conceive. The Anselmian overtones of this remark are
smothered by a subsequent and laconic 'Nous sommes
quelque chose d'elle. L'invoquer est sans doute une façon
un peu ancienne de communier à son énergie.'[28] The
immanentism expounded in this letter to Semeria in effect
simply dictates Loisy's position on the relative character of
revelation and dogma, as he himself notes. Christianity
cannot be considered as a revelation having absolute value. Its
function in human progress is determinable. Its dogmas were
not revealed in the generally accepted sense. 'Les dogmes ont
leur raison d'être comme symbole encourageant au devoir.'
(This last remark reminds us that Le Roy's article 'Qu'est-ce
qu'un dogme?' had appeared in *La Quinzaine* almost exactly
a year earlier.) To what extent had Loisy's idea of God become more immanentist since the Firmin articles and the first
two 'livres rouges'? His own later assessment was that the
position on revelation, Church, and dogma expounded in his
letter to Semeria was 'clearly implied, indeed explicitated'
in the Neuilly essays and in the Little Red Books, but that as
regards his position on God and religion these articles and
books contain rather the adumbration ('pressentiment') of
the needed critique than the critique itself. If one interprets
'pressentiment' as a vague, perhaps even unconscious, direction of thought, there is no serious reason to question this
judgement. In default of the promised work on God we are
therefore thrown back on sources like the letter to Semeria
as a guide to his theodicy at this time.

An earlier source, an important letter to the Abbé Maubec

---

[27] 'Dieu est comme un moi supérieur, qui surveille un moi inférieur auquel
nous demeurons identifiés; et la conscience individuelle étant aussi une conscience
sociale, ce moi supérieur est également la personnification transcendante de la
société, de l'humanité.' (*Mémoires*, vol. ii, p. 469.)

[28] Ibid., pp. 469 f.

in 1902,[29] suggests a more conservative idea of God, though
it is by no means free of characteristic Loisian ambiguities
such as 'If the idea of God corresponds to reality, if religion
is not a chimera, if humanity is on its way towards an eternal
future, no human being can deny to Jesus the honour of
having revealed God, lived religion, and provided the foundations of hope.' Poulat tells us that this letter was widely
circulated at the time as evidence of Loisy's essential orthodoxy. Félix Klein, professor of French Literature at the
Institut Catholique in Paris, who knew Loisy well at this
period, said of this letter to Maubec that it was 'perhaps the
document which most clearly revealed Loisy's true thought
in the most decisive period of his life', concluding: 'In my
view a document such as this is sufficient to show that at the
end of 1902 and at the beginning of 1904 Loisy had in no
sense lost the Catholic faith.'[30]

There is weighty evidence to suggest that in the spring of
1904 there occurred a watershed in Loisy's life. Five of his
books had been placed on the *Index of Prohibited Books* in
December 1903. His appeal to the Pope had been rebuffed
in February 1904. On 12 March he dispatched a short letter
of submission which was judged unsatisfactory by the authorities and which he almost immediately regretted having
sent, since it compromised him as a scholar without helping
him as a priest.[31] He may well have undergone something
like a nervous breakdown during these weeks.[32] It is not un-
reasonable to suppose that the events of early 1904 had a
considerable effect upon Loisy's idea of God. His disillusionment with the Church was almost total, and this had the

[29] This letter is printed in full by Poulat in *Une œuvre clandestine*, pp. 92 f.

[30] Ibid., p. 90. Three years earlier one of the Firmin articles made an explicit
and unambiguous statement about divine transcendence. In 'La théorie individualiste de la religion' (*R.C.F.* 17 (1899), p. 208). Loisy argues against Sabatier's
individualistic conception of religion. Religion, he writes, everywhere and in every
age has been social and objective; 'elle a mis Dieu près de l'homme, mais au-
dessus; elle est fondée sur la distinction réele de Dieu et de l'homme.' However
contentious this remark may be from the standpoint of the history of religions,
it is strong evidence of Loisy's anti-monism at that time.

[31] See *Simples réflexions*, pp. 207 f., where Loisy defends the sincerity of his
reservations in making the submissions of 1902 and 1904. 'Je suis resté dans
l'Église parce que ma conscience ne me prescrivait pas d'en sortir.' (*S.R.*, p. 208.)

[32] Cf. Poulat, *Alfred Loisy*, p. 126.

effect of leaving his beliefs, including his ideas on transcendence, in disarray. There is no disagreement that his 'dogmatic faith' was in ruins. Whether his 'mystical faith' (or whatever one wants to call what could be salvaged from those ruins) included belief in God as a transcendent and personal being is indeed disputable. What evidence there is suggests a weary and disillusioned scepticism.

In so far as one can speak of philosophical influences on *L'Évangile et l'Église* and *Autour d'un petit livre*, there are, wrote Loisy, only two possible names: Renan and Newman.[33] The admission of such intellectual parentage would probably produce a shrug of despair in the average professional philosopher. Renan might be described as a reluctant positivist with sentimental leanings towards an impossibly vague transcendent, or, more harshly, as a positivist without the courage of his convictions. Coupling him with Newman has all the appearances of intellectual miscegnation. Their role in Loisy's formation seems fortuitous in the extreme. He happened to attend Renan's lectures at the Collège de France and to read Newman at a critical moment in his mental development.[34] Renan, in addition to demonstrating the importance of a historical approach to religious questions, presumably also nourished Loisy's own positivistic leanings; while Newman suggested an evolutionary framework which would facilitate a marriage between historical method and an epistemology based on the relative, because evolutionary, character of truth. Loisy responded enthusiastically to Newman the maverick, the most open theologian in the Church since Origen,[35] the only Catholic theologian that Loisy found it worth his while to study at a time when all his reading was of Protestants,[36] a great teacher, lacking disciples perhaps, but badly needed by contemporary Catholic theology.[37] Loisy appreciated Newman's personalism,

[33] *Mémoires*, vol. ii, pp. 560 f.

[34] 'Durant ces années (1881–1883), mon auteur de prédilection fut Renan, que je ne prenais d'ailleurs pas pour un oracle; mais c'est surtout avec lui et contre lui que je pensais. De 1894 à 1900, c'est avec Newman, passablement élargi, que je pense contre les théologiens protestants.' (Poulat, *Alfred Loisy*, p. 86).

[35] *Mémoires*, vol. i, p. 426.   [36] Ibid., p. 363.

[37] A. Firmin, 'Le Développement chrétien d'après le Cardinal Newman', in *R.C.F.* 17 (1898), p. 20.

his grasp of the need to renew apologetics, and of course, above all, his recognition of the need for 'mouvement dans l'Église'.[38] Harnack's *History of Dogma* might be more erudite than Newman's *Essay on the Development of Christian Doctrine*, Loisy remarks, but how inferior the former was to the latter in its general understanding of Christianity's wider reaches.[39]

The first of the Firmin articles, unusually warm and enthusiastic by Loisy's normal standards, nevertheless recognizes the defects in Newman's biblical scholarship but sees these defects as the inevitable product of the age he lived in. Equally, and consequentially, inevitable was Newman's failure to tackle the problem of *how* revelation enters and maintains its relationship with the evolutionary process. It is the biblical question which poses the problem of revelation for the philosopher and theologian.[40] This last observation may seem trite by later standards; but in the context of Roman Catholic theology at the turn of the nineteenth century it was instinct with revolution. The first Firmin article served another eviction order on traditional Catholic apologetics by making the dogmatic and fundamental theologian accountable to the historian. For a brief moment Loisy, Blondel, and Laberthonnière all appeared to be moving by separate paths towards the same goal. For a brief moment, too, Loisy's position *looked* less threatening to received Catholic orthodoxy than did that of the Blondelians.

The second Firmin article attacked Sabatier's individualistic psychologism and Harnack's pursuit of a pure Christian essence unadulterated by later doctrinal development.[41] Loisy was here defending the legitimacy of dogma against Harnack. Sabatier, however, had made more substantial concessions to the need for dogma than had Harnack, and Loisy had not yet differentiated his views from those of Sabatier on this matter.

By the time we reach the third Firmin article we are made aware of Loisy's skill as a tactician.[42] Quarried in large

---

[38] *Mémoires*, vol. i, p. 468.   [39] Firmin, art. cit., p. 20.   [40] Ibid., p. 13.
[41] A. Firmin, 'La Théorie individualiste de la religion', in *R.C.F.* 17 (1899), pp. 202–15.
[42] A. Firmin, 'La Définition de la religion', in *R.C.F.* 18 (1899), pp. 193–209.

measure from the *Livre inédit*, these articles were clearly planned with care and their material deployed in gentle gradation.[43] The third[44] and fourth[45] Firmin articles constitute the core of Loisy's thought on transcendence and immanence in the period preceding the crisis of 1904. Religion, a universal and social phenomenon, is the area in which man encounters God. Amorphous and intangible in itself, it is given form and tangibility in symbols and rites, the latter being the most tangible and consistent. Religion 'consiste dans une certaine réalisation du divin'. This concretization will always be incomplete, relative, and symbolic, which is not to say that it can be reduced to something purely psychological and individualistic.[46] Man's idea of God is 'un anthropomorphisme grandiose' which is subject to constant change.[47] Intellect, conscience, and will all have a vital part to play in the religious sphere (a much more vital part, Loisy adds, than that allowed them by Sabatier and Harnack); but they are ultimately governed by man's *religious instinct* which is characterized by an innate respect for God and an innate need to trust in him.[48] Under the guidance and inspiration of his religious instinct, man's intellect seeks to grasp the truth of things. It soon becomes apparent, however, that his understanding can make direct contact only with the image of things, the 'impression de la réalité; that 'it does not really know either man or the universe in themselves, and that both at the heart of, and over and above everything, there is the Infinite, absolute reality and absolute truth which escape the grasp of the intellect'.[49] Man's religious instinct is expressed in his conscience which impels him towards a perfection which is inaccessible but none the less partly imitable. Above all, that which throws man before the feet of God and drives his mind and conscience forward is 'le sentiment de l'indigence universelle' which he experiences at every turn in his

---

[43] On this see Loisy's letter to Mignot dated 17 November 1898 in M. Bécamel, 'Lettres de Loisy à Mgr. Mignot à propos de la crise moderniste', in *B.L.E.*, 67 (1966), p. 19.

[44] A. Firmin, 'La Définition de la religion', in *R.C.F.* 18 (1899), pp. 193–209. (The page references to this article are wrongly given in Poulat's bibliography in *Alfred Loisy*, p. 315.)

[45] A. Firmin, 'L'Idée de la révélation', in *R.C.F.* 21 (1900), pp. 250–71.

[46] Firmin, 'La Définition de la religion', pp. 197 f.

[47] Ibid., pp. 203 f.   [48] Ibid., p. 206.   [49] Ibid., p. 206.

life, in the physical no less than in the moral order. This sense
of powerlessness forces man to trust in 'the infinite power
which he senses at the heart of all things'. Religion summons
him away from the despair of self-reliance towards the felt
security of reliance on God.[50] (Although these sentiments
put one immediately in mind of Schleiermacher and Sabatier,
Loisy could easily point to such masters of Catholic
spirituality as de Caussade and François de Sales as having
said much that was similar.) To deny God and religion is to
make of man a living nonsense, an immense desire opening
out on to nothing.

Loisy begins his fourth Firmin article with a salvo fired at
Sabatier in which there is more noise than grapeshot. The
attack follows the usual pattern, with one highly significant
addition. Firmin attributes to Sabatier a doctrine of
immanence which verges on a sort of Hegelian pantheism.
According to Firmin, Sabatier seems to hold that revelation is
the consciousness which God has of himself in man. It is hard
to resist the conclusion that Loisy is quite frankly using
Sabatier, as he was later to use Harnack, and even less fairly.
Revelation, says Loisy, considered objectively as the manifestation of God to man, takes place in man himself.
Although this manifestation is immanent in man, as is God
himself, it is transcendent to man by virtue of its origin, its
content, and its destination.[51] As the argument unfolds we
notice that Loisy's purpose in emphasizing the immanent
aspect of revelation is different from Sabatier's modified
version of Schleiermacher's pietism (not in one's wildest
imaginings would one expect to find Loisy exhorting us to
an enjoyment of religion). It is vital for Loisy to establish
a firm immanent dimension to revelation so that he can
combat scholastic immobilism on the one hand and secure
a hearing for his relativistic epistemology on the other. 'Every
religion must express itself in certain forms of belief, but no
religion can claim absolute immobility for its beliefs, since
such immobility is incapable of realization and is opposed to
the nature of man who makes religion his concern.'[52] Here we
have Loisy's controlling thesis, a leitmotif brought into play

[50] Ibid., p. 207.   [51] Idem, 'L'Idée de la révélation', p. 251.   [52] Ibid.

whenever his adversaries, Protestant or Catholic, put forward the claims of an objective point of reference, whether that point of reference be an essence of Christianity or dogma as a conservative principle of faith.

Reiterating his thesis of the amorphous character of religion, he here claims that the truth of faith subsists as authoritatively in each successive dogmatic assertion as it did in the primitive assertion.[53] The 'native form' of revealed truth is 'a supernatural intuition and an affirmation of faith, not an abstract consideration and systematic definition of their object'.[54] All religions are conceived of as revealed, that is, as received and cherished, not created, by the believer.[55] Sabatier and Harnack, says Firmin, treat religious thought as the human reflection of religious feeling ('sentiment') in the mind. They make it impossible to distinguish between God and the human mind. But this distinction must be safeguarded, and when it is safeguarded, 'revelation, in its most general sense, can, from the standpoint of divine action, be taken as transcendent to, and immanent in, the soul itself; while, from the standpoint of its effect, it can be taken as the religious knowledge, completely penetrated by the divine Spirit, which is the product of this action.'[56] Thus, he continues, if we concede that contact between the religious soul and the divine produces a living light which illuminates the mind, we must concede that revelation is 'la production, divinement effectuée, d'une verité substantiellement divine, quoique toujours humainement perçue et formulée'.[57]

Revelation is proportioned to the human intellectual condition and is so given that the mind can explore its inner possibilities and discover new relationships within it. This activity is carried out under the impulse of the heart, of religious and moral feeling.[58] There follows a celebrated passage

---

[53] Ibid., p. 253n.   [54] Ibid., p. 254.   [55] Ibid., p. 255.
[56] Ibid., p. 257.   [57] Ibid., p. 258.
[58] Ibid., p. 266: 'A la différence des perceptions d'ordre purement rationnel et scientifique, la perception des vérités religieuses n'est pas un fruit de la seule raison; c'est un travail de l'intelligence, exécuté pour ainsi dire sous la pression du cœur, du sentiment religieux et moral.' (Loisy repeats this sentence, omitting only the word 'purement', in *Autour d'un petit livre*, p. 197). There is a marked similarity between this epistemological construction of the revelatory and theological process and Sabatier's three 'moments' in the perception of 'religious phenomena'

which Loisy was to repeat word for word in *Autour d'un petit livre*:

C'est l'homme qui cherche, mais c'est Dieu qui l'excite; c'est l'homme qui voit, mais c'est Dieu qui l'éclaire. La révélation se réalise dans l'homme; mais elle est l'œuvre de Dieu en lui, avec lui et par lui. La cause efficiente de la révélation est surnaturelle comme son objet, parce que cette cause et cet objet sont Dieu-même; mais Dieu agit *dans* l'homme, et il est connu *par* l'homme.[59]

Revelation makes the divine accessible by humanization,[60] while man communicates the original experience by means of metaphors and symbols, 'une sorte de notation algébrique représentant des quantités ineffables'.[61] Loisy takes considerable care to ward off suspicion that he regards revelation as the purely human discovery of religious truths. It consists in 'communications réelles de vérités divines'.[62] He trusts that he has also made quite clear the difference between what he has been saying and the 'intellectualisme sentimental' of M. Sabatier.[63]

But has he in fact done so? Thirty years later he wrote that although his presentation of 'l'économie de la foi' had something in common with the views of Ollé-Laprune and Blondel, his ideas 'on the essentially relative value of religious symbols had a greater affinity with those of Sabatier.[64] This is a considerable concession, even when placed in the context of Loisy's subtle dialectic of affirmation and denial. It is not without significance that he chose Harnack rather than Sabatier as his adversary in *L'Évangile et l'Église*. His debt to Sabatier was too great, and the similarity of his position to Sabatier's too marked, for him to achieve a convincing discrimination between them.[65]

(cf. *Outlines*, p. 235). The only difference between Loisy's 'pression du cœur' and Sabatier's 'subjective piety of man' would appear to be the inclusion of a moral element alongside the religious one. In short, Loisy completes Sabatier's pietistic presentation by including a Ritschlian moral dimension.

[59] Firmin, art. cit., p. 266; *Autour*, p. 197 f.

[60] 'La divine en soi est pour nous l'inaccessible et l'indéfinissable. La révélation n'est et ne peut être que du divin humanisé, on pourrait presque dire humainement personnifié . . .' (ibid., pp. 266 f.).

[61] Ibid., p. 267.　　　　[62] Ibid., p. 268.　　　　[63] Ibid., p. 271.

[64] *Mémoires*, vol. i, pp. 454 f.

[65] There is considerable evidence in Sabatier's writings of Catholic influence upon his thought (he refers explicitly to Pascal and Newman). French Liberal

Neither of the first two Little Red Books adds substantially to what the Firmin articles had said about God, religion, and revelation. The sixth chapter of *Autour d'un petit livre*, on the origin and authority of dogma, contains an important passage on the philosophy of truth preceded by a character-istic disclaimer by its author of any philosophical competence. Truth exists in us as something necessarily conditioned, relative, always perfectible, susceptible also of diminution. Truth is no more immutable than man himself. 'Elle évolue avec lui, en lui, par lui; et cela ne l'empêche pas d'être la vérité pour lui; elle ne l'est même qu'à cette condition.'[66]

Autour d'un petit livre then simply spells out the implica-tions of this epistemology for the theology of revelation. Revelation is the consciousness acquired by man of his rela-tionship with God.[67] Dogmas are symbolic utterances designed to strike answering chords in the human spirit. These utterances not merely can, but must, change with man himself. Revealed truths live pre-conceptually in the Church's dogmas. Only in this restricted sense can dogmas be said to be revealed. The supernatural origin of dogmas is not open to historical investigation, which can take cognizance only of the secondary formulas designed to effect a bridgehead between religious belief and scientific development.[68] Ecclesiastical formulas are not statements of absolute truth, since they cannot embody the full reality of what they rep-resent. The Church is therefore in full control over them and can change them if and when it wishes.[69] *L'Évangile et l'Église* is, he remarks, a very Catholic book, since nothing is less consonant with the true spirit of Catholicism than the cult of the formula.[70] All of this has yet to be realized in Catholic theology, in which biblical criticism is still like tight-rope walking. The time has come to put an end to 'le scandale des intelligences'.[71]

Harnack saw dogma as the destruction of the simple

Protestantism owed more to Schleiermacher, Pascal, and the 'theology of the heart' than to Ritschl, Harnack, and the 'return to Kant' movement within German Liberal Protestantism.

[66] A. Loisy, *Autour d'un petit livre* (Paris, 1903), pp. 191 f.

[67] Ibid., p. 195.   [68] Ibid., pp. 200 f.   [69] Ibid., p. 206.

[70] Ibid., p. 208.   [71] Ibid., pp. 217 f.

message of the Gospel brought about by the infiltration of Hellenistic philosophy. Athens, in Harnack's view, had encompassed the fall of Jerusalem, largely by means of the *Logos* concept. Sabatier took a milder view, insisting merely that the Christian should appreciate the historical limitations of all philosophical attempts to express the primitive revelatory experience. Writing within the Catholic tradition, Loisy had to take the question of dogma with greater seriousness than either Harnack or even Sabatier had done. If he was seeking to end 'intellectual scandal', he was, in 1902, nevertheless committed to doing so within the framework of the Roman Catholic Church and its theology. He further committed himself to doing so as a historian and biblical critic rather than as a philosopher of religion. He was, of course, unable to stay within his self-appointed brief, attempting, as he did, to chart a course between Protestant individualism and Catholic ecclesiasticism. Harnack had argued that the essence of the Gospel could be detached from all historical cultures, whereas the Catholic Church had fused it with medieval culture. Loisy replied that the Catholic Church 'is only bound to the science and political form of the middle ages because it does not choose to detach itself from them'. He appeals therefore from the scholastic conception of orthodoxy to the biblical and historical one of the kingdom as 'a great hope' working itself out in the Church through changing historical forms and formulas. 'Dogma' thus becomes a portmanteau term which designates much more than ecclesiastical formulations of Christian belief. It extends to the whole area of the relationship between faith and history, between the transcendent origin and goal of revelation and its incarnation in space and time.

Having considered Loisy's idea of God and revelation, we shall turn in the next chapter to an examination of his views on the relationship between history and dogma in the context of his debate with Maurice Blondel.

4 History and Dogma: The Debate between Alfred Loisy and Maurice Blondel

Any consideration of Loisy's view of the role of history in the faith-process entails an examination of his abortive debate with Blondel initiated by the latter's reservations about *L'Évangile et l'Église*. In many respects it was scarcely a debate, more a statement and counter-statement of seemingly irreconcilable positions. First of all there was no meeting of minds and no search for common ground. Each of the contestants defended his position with little concern to understand why the other thought as he did. Secondly, neither man seemed to realize that the issue in contention between them had long been the subject of extensive examination and discussion by Protestant theologians like Ritschl, Herrmann, and Troeltsch, whose treatment of the problem (under the rubric of history and faith rather than history and dogma) was rooted in the great questions raised by Strauss, Lessing, Schleiermacher, and Kierkegaard. The ugly, broad ditch which Lessing has pointed to as existing between the accidental truths of history and the necessary truths of reason had not seriously troubled Roman Catholic theology in the nineteenth century, and, with the condemnation of modernism in 1907, would not become a live issue until the Second Vatican Council had freed Catholic theology from the restrictions of mandatory scholasticism and had recognized the importance of a historical dimension in theological thinking. Lack of a genuinely critical interest in the Bible, coupled with a dogmatic theology rooted in substantialist metaphysics, protected Roman Catholic theology from the abrasive questions with which historical consciousness presents any kind of Christian Church dogmatics which is alive to the demands of relevance.

Biblical and systematic theology must of their nature exist in tension, as Protestant religious thought has abundantly shown; but the tension can be creative, as the best

Protestant theology has equally abundantly shown. The contemporary situation in Christian theology, Protestant and Catholic, testifies to the relevance of what Loisy and Blondel began to say to each other before Loisy extinguished the smoking flax of Blondel's attempted dialogue with him. Since then modernist commentators have tended to take sides, with the radicals (usually historians) siding with Loisy in his impatience with Blondel's apparent failure to appreciate the scope and limitations of historiography, and the theologians and philosophers siding with Blondel in his condemnation of Loisy's alleged 'historicism'. Today, the Christian theologian can no longer with impunity allow himself the comfort of a position rendered secure mainly by the evasion of difficulties brought forward by the members of the other camp. It is a fact of theological life that the most obstinate and painful problem in Christian thought centres on the point of contact between transcendent Being on the one hand and historically structured human life and awareness on the other. To historicize — and every Christian theologian is committed to some degree of historicization — is to work on the slippery slope at the bottom of which lies the ravine of total immanentism. To attempt a metaphysical synthesis — and every Christian theologian must to some extent do so if his thought is to have minimal unity and consistency — is to risk creating abstractions which lack negotiability in terms of space and time.

Professor Van A. Harvey states the problem thus:

The problem of faith and history is not merely a problem of two logics or two methodologies. It is a problem . . . of two ethics of judgement. Otherwise, it is impossible to account for the fierce sense of honesty, the suspicion of one's desire to believe, the sense of resentment against obscurantism, which underlie so much unbelief.[1]

This statement of the problem is shaped by developments in Protestant theology from Strauss down to the New Quest. As formulated by Protestant theologians, the problem of the relationship between faith and history is a critical extension of the *sola fide* principle. Belonging as they did to the Catholic tradition, Loisy and Blondel did not evince this

---

[1] Van A. Harvey, *The Historian and the Believer* (London, 1967), p. 104.

Protestant anxiety to ensure that historical research should not be resorted to as a validation of Christian faith. Nor were they greatly concerned with the ethical dimension. (In this respect Laberthonnière comes nearest of all the modernists to the Protestant position.) For Loisy and Blondel the problem is preponderantly one 'of two logics or two methodologies'.

For a brief moment, in the early spring of 1897, it looked as if the leading French Catholic biblical scholar and the leading French Catholic philosopher might join forces. 'We are innovators', wrote Loisy to Blondel after reading the *Letter on Apologetics.* 'Your philosophy can complement my exegesis.'[2] Blondel replied courteously that he was at the moment completely taken up with *L'Action*, and that being a slow worker, he did not feel able to write for Loisy's *Revue d'histoire et de littérature religieuse.*[3]

The publication of *L'Évangile et l'Église* in the winter of 1902 was of course the proto-event of the modernist crisis. Reaction to it was varied. Diehard scholastics condemned it instantly and without reservation. According to Albert Houtin, however, many French Catholics 'were happy to see a Prussian Lutheran put through the hoop and they appeared to be astonished not to be allowed to admire without reserve the vigour with which a French Catholic threw down the gauntlet before him.'[4] The initial reaction of many 'progressistes' was favourable to the point of enthusiasm. They saw in Loisy 'our only scholar worthy of the name in these exegetical questions'.[5] Blondel, having read the book carefully, found himself unable to share in the enthusiasm of his friends.

[2] R. Marlé, *Au cœur de la crise moderniste* (Paris, 1960), p. 35. Marlé quite gratuitously describes this overture as 'un peu suspecte', giving as his reason that the *Revue d'histoire et de littérature religieuse*, to which Loisy invited Blondel to contribute, was a journal which bade fair to promote a ' "historico-philosophical" spirit diametrically opposed' to Blondel's.

[3] H. Bernard-Maitre, 'Un épisode significatif du modernisme: "Histoire et dogme" de Maurice Blondel d'après les papiers inédits d'Alfred Loisy (1897–1905)' in *Recherches de science religieuse*, 57 (1969), p. 56. This article is an important supplement to Marlé's more selective documentation, though it does not reach conclusions notably different from Marlé's.

[4] A. Houtin, *La Question biblique au XXe siècle* (Paris, 1906), p. 89.

[5] Wehrlé to Blondel, cited in Marlé, *Au cœur*, p. 54.

Blondel's objections were soon to be systematically developed in his essay 'Histoire et dogme'. His basic reservations
remained constant from the outset. A fortnight after the publication of *L'Évangile et l'Église* he wrote to Loisy con-
gratulating him on a fine book and expressing admiration for
the subtle artistry with which the latter had exposed the
'fixisme' of Harnack 'who is a scholastic in his own way'.[6]
Loisy had charted an admirable and original course between
'ultramontane caesarism and idealist anarchy'.[7] Then, with
that curious, though characteristic, mixture of diffidence and
firmness, Blondel made his fatal reservation: one senses, he
says, an underlying christology in what you have written.
Blondel's point of departure, and what he made the central
plank of his case against Loisy, is arguably the weakest part
of that case. Christology is not the most suitable theological
terrain for examining the problem of transcendence and
history. Blondel was clearly disturbed by Loisy's limiting of
Christ to local and temporal contingencies with an apparently
consequent limitation in Christ's knowledge. He feared that
the further consequence would be a relativizing of the very
Person of Christ.[8] Some days later (11 January 1903) Blondel
wrote to von Hügel that he appreciated the formidable difficulty of constructing a psychology of the incarnate Word
which would totally avoid the snare of docetism. His own way
out of the difficulty was 'not by admitting two conscious-
nesses in the one Person of Christ, but by incorporating in him
the consciousness of all our unconsciousnesses, by making of
Jesus the Man who includes all men, the explicit [expression]
of all that others possess only implicitly'.[9] By this typically
opaque theory, which he described as 'panchristisme', Blondel
set out to demonstrate that the consciousness of Christ realized
in itself the provisionally inadequate relationship in ordinary
human beings between consciousness and Being.[10]

[6] Bernard-Maitre, art. cit., p. 58.   [7] Ibid.
[8] Blondel to Wehrlé, cited in Bernard-Maitre, art. cit., p. 60.
[9] *Au cœur*, pp. 64 f.
[10] Ibid., p. 61. Although Blondel himself attached great importance to his
'panchristic' theory, one has some sympathy with Loisy's impatient dismissal of
the christological issue as irrelevant to the matter in hand. For further treatment
of 'panchristisme' and of christology in general see Blondel's long and important
letter to Wehrlé in *Au cœur*, pp. 54–63.

By the time he came to write 'Histoire et dogme' Blondel had removed some of the emphasis he had initially placed on the psychology of Christ and was distributing his attention over a wider speculative field. He had initially been diverted into the psychological question by Loisy's consistent eschatology. Jesus, according to Loisy, had died confident in the future of his work and in his own approaching triumph. 'The idea of the divine sonship was linked to that of the kingdom: it had no signification of its own, so far as Jesus was concerned, except in regard to the kingdom about to be established.[11] All Blondel's instincts rose up against what he saw as a casual ambiguity about a central doctrine of the faith; but by the time he came to write 'Histoire et dogme' he had realized that it was not the, or even a, crucial issue in Loisy's thesis. If battle was to be joined, then it must be joined on the methodological question of the role of history in the theological enterprise *as a whole*.

Some of the letters Blondel wrote in early January 1903 show him at work on the ideas which he was shortly to systematize in 'Histoire et dogme'. Loisy, he wrote to Wehrlé, has segregated theology and history into two watertight compartments, and in doing so has gratuitously fabricated an insoluble dilemma: either one limits one's investigations to questions of fact, i.e. to the 'sensible', the 'natural', in short, to the historical; in which case one restricts one's consideration of Christ to the purely human and temporal and thus evades the vital question of his transcendent reference. Or one maintains that, taking one's point of departure from the facts, one can logically proceed to theology; in which case one is up against the obstinate truth that 'facts as facts will never give you the supernatural; that the critical method alone will never connect you with the transcendent; that you are irremediably imprisoned in naturalism'.[12] Already it is clear that Blondel's subscription to his method of immanence is total and pervasive of all his religious thinking. 'The Bible cannot with impunity and legitimately be approached only through the methods of common exegesis . . . Because if the problem of the supernatural is not, from the very beginning, immanent to all your study of the Sacred Books, you will end up in a bottomless abyss.[13] At the close of this long letter Blondel is in a position to formulate the question which will dominate 'Histoire et dogme': 'How and why does one proceed from history to dogma?'[14]

The first instalment of 'Histoire et dogme' appeared in *La Quinzaine* in mid-January 1904.[15] Henri de Lubac has described this essay as 'l'œuvre de philosophie religieuse la plus classique de Blondel'.[16] We have already considered its attack on scholastic extrinsicism. The positive core of the essay is to be found in the third part where Blondel puts forward his theory of tradition as an alternative to the extremes of 'extrinsicism' and 'historicism'. It is his refutation of the latter that concerns us here. *L'Évangile et l'Église* was of course the immediate occasion of Blondel's essay. He was later to remark that he had to be hard on extrinsicism so that he might make his case against 'loisysme' with full effect.[17] His motives were not unmixed. He was anxious to dissociate himself from Loisy's position;[18] at the same time he did not want to make life harder for Loisy, who had just seen five of his books consigned to the *Index*. Loisy's name is nowhere mentioned in 'Histoire et dogme', but the anonymity was purely a gesture, since the readers of *La Quinzaine* knew perfectly well who was meant.[19]

Blondel in his opening section remarks that he has isolated certain abstract theses in order to present them with a rigour which they lack in their normal presentation.[20] In a letter to von Hügel shortly after the publication of the second instalment of 'Histoire et dogme', Blondel claimed that his tactic was to bring each of the opposing camps, i.e. the scholastics

[13] *Au cœur*, p. 57.   [14] Ibid., p. 63.

[15] M. Blondel, 'Histoire et dogme: Les lacunes philosophiques de l'exégèse moderne', in *La Quinzaine*, 56 (1904), pp. 145-67. The following two instalments appear in the same volume, pp. 349-73; 433-58. All three were edited as one long essay in *Les premiers écrits de Maurice Blondel*, vol. ii (Paris, 1956), pp. 149-228 [*H.D.*]. Eng. trans. and edn. by A. Dru and I. Trethowan, *Maurice Blondel: The Letter on Apologetics and History and Dogma* (London, 1964), pp. 221-87.

[16] *B.V.*, vol. i, p. 36.   [17] Ibid., p. 124.

[18] Portalié, among others, had already linked Blondel's philosophy with Loisy's biblical criticism (*Au cœur*, p. 213).

[19] In a letter to von Hügel Laberthonnière claimed that Blondel's thesis against historicism was aimed at least as much at Lagrange and Battifol as at Loisy (Poulat, *Histoire*, p. 563).   [20] *H.D.*, p. 154.

and Loisy, face to face with two caricatures, thus allowing each to repudiate the caricature with the remark that his position had been distorted, 'the final outcome being that both sides would clarify their positions and perhaps come to terms — if only in opposition to me'.[21] Early in his argument against historicism Blondel asks rhetorically 'will the texture of critical history be strong enough to carry the infinite weight of the ancient faith and the whole richness of Catholic dogma?'[22] Both Loisy himself and his friends, together with a fair proportion of modernist commentators, have pounced on this question as irrelevant and incompetent, a paper tiger set up for easy destruction. Loisy flatly denied that he ever claimed this prerogative for historical criticism.

Curiously enough it was the scholastics who were vulnerable to the charge, not alone of extrinsicism, *but of historicism as well.* It was scholastic fundamental theology, not Loisy's biblical criticism, which placed the infinite weight of Catholic dogma on historical fact. Admittedly the history was spectacularly uncritical; but that makes no difference to the historicism involved. One need hardly add that Blondel, Loisy, and the scholastics, all had a positivistic view of history, though Blondel came nearest of them — as his friend Laberthonnière most certainly did — to a theory of interpretation.

Blondel's case may be summarized as follows. Historicism cannot meet the problem posed at the beginning of the essay, namely, how to proceed from 'Christian facts' (history) to Christian beliefs (dogma). History (-as-science) operates under certain limitations. 'While the historian has, so to speak, a word to say in everything concerning man, there is nothing on which he has the last word.'[23] What the historian does not see, and what he must accept as escaping him, is the spiritual reality which is not exhaustively represented by historical phenomena.[24] 'Real history takes place in human lives; and human life is metaphysics in act.'[25] Historicism stands condemned not so much by what it says as by what

---

[21] *Au cœur*, p. 213.　　　　　　　　　[22] *H.D.*, p. 163.

[23] Ibid., p. 167. It is a point which might perhaps be made today about sociology.

[24] Ibid., pp. 167 f.　　　　　　　　　[25] Ibid., p. 168.

it excludes. It depersonalizes by substituting the portrait for
the person. It allows the evolutionary principle to obscure
the teleological principle, i.e. it takes stock of the means but
not of the end.[26] If there is no other way to the 'real Christ'
but through the portrait drawn by his first witnesses, then
the critic, the exegete, and (curious addition) the philosopher,
hold the keys of theology. If, on the other hand, we can
reach the real Christ through generations of believers and
'direct back to their source all the streams of life and thought
which have accrued to the gospel during nineteen centuries',[27]
we can regard as rudimentary the understanding which
Christ's earliest followers had of him.

There are, then, two methods of approach to Christianity.
The first proceeds from Christ's present action in the Church;
the second sees the Church as stemming only from what
Christ 'consigned to the determinism of history'.[28] We have
no right to exclude the first of these alternatives on the
grounds that it is unscientific. To exclude the christological
problem, as historicism does, is to 'immobilize Christ in the
past, sealing him in his tomb beneath the sedimentation of
history and to consider as real and relevant only the natural
aspects of his work'.[29] The historicist sees the facts of
Christian history as the temporal, and therefore relative,
translation of eternal truth. Neither science nor philosophy,
however, can rule out *a priori* the possibility that the truth
of Christianity derives from the facts, and that Christian ideas
and dogmas must gravitate around the facts.[30] The early
Church's rejection of Gnosticism was a striking affair which
demonstrated how important were the facts even to the most
refined speculative thinking.[31] Blondel focuses his case into
a dilemma with which he faces the historicist: '. . . if one
remains in the logic of historicism, there follows either an
untenable claim to seize the supernatural in history and

---

[26] This observation places Blondel in firm opposition to a controlling thesis
of Bergsonian metaphysics.

[27] *H.D.*, p. 177.   [28] Ibid., p. 178.

[29] Ibid., p. 180. 'Have we really the right, in the name of historical science, to
exclude even the possibility of an antecedent finality and of a unity of design in
this historical plan? And, if so, could one still speak of it as a divine work?' (ibid.,
p. 185).

[30] Ibid., p. 182.   [31] Ibid., pp. 187 f.

through history, or a total abdication of criticism in the face of faith.'[32] The outcome of historicism is to expose faith to the 'danger of finding itself suspended between heaven and earth, either evaporating into a mystical symbolism or lapsing back into scientific positivism'.[33]

Blondel's essay was greeted with both applause and protest. The case against it hardly needs restatement. In so far as it was aimed at Loisy's position it was a damp squib. Loisy had every right as a scholar to treat of Christian origins in a purely critical manner; and he lost no opportunity of pointing this out and of holding Blondel up to ridicule. In 1908, commenting on *Pascendi*'s treatment of the modernist as philosopher, he once again stated his resolve to avoid philosophical questions and went on to remark tartly on the irony of the fact that it was the *immanentistes* (he does not mention Blondel or Laberthonnière by name) who allowed him to understand that his exegesis complemented their philosophical system.[34] He seems to have forgotten that the suggestion of complementarity came initially from himself. A quarter of a century later his comments had lost nothing of their acerbity: Blondel, he claimed, was a philosopher not an exegete and he had no business getting himself embroiled in a biblical controversy. The fact that he did so demonstrates that he was merely seeking an excuse to put forward his own philosophy of action.[35] It was Blondel, not he, who invented historicism and, having misapplied it to Loisy, went on to substitute for it his own 'personal method'. The petulance of these remarks should not be allowed to detract from a point which Loisy might have made more effectively if he had made it with greater restraint. Blondel's philosophy of action was basic to all his religious thinking, and quite consistently so, since for Blondel philosophy arises out of, and must be nourished by, lived experience. His real fault lies not in applying his philosophy to the matter under debate — that was, after all, his right — but in his failure to appreciate Loisy's mind and the circumstances under which the exegete had written *L'Évangile et l'Église* and *Autour d'un petit*

---

[32] Ibid., p. 191.   [33] Ibid., p. 194.
[34] Loisy, *Simples réflexions*, pp. 209 f.
[35] *Mémoires*, vol. ii, pp. 392 f.

livre. M. Poulat has observed that Blondel did to Loisy what
Loisy had done to Harnack, i.e. used him as an occasion for
putting forward a thesis.[36]

If Loisy's sympathizers have dealt unsympathetically with
Blondel, Blondel's disciples have tended towards an adulation
verging on the uncritical.[37] Perhaps von Hügel, who admired
and respected both men and was himself both an exegete and
a philosopher of religion, comes nearest to a balanced and by
no means unsympathetic critique of Blondel's thesis. In an
article written for *La Quinzaine*[38] von Hügel took Blondel
gently to task as a philosopher for inconsistency with his own
conviction that the different sciences should not be hermeti-
cally sealed off from one another. Blondel has forgotten, says
the Baron, that while there is objective unity in God and in
the essence of things, this unity is only an ideal for man the
knowing   subject   who   experiences   tension   ('un   certain
conflict') between the various intellectual and moral elements
which go to form his belief. The mystery of Christ is inexhaustible; but M. Blondel, setting out from this indisputable premiss, 'reasons as if the manifestations of this reality
in time and space were not necessarily limited in number and
degree'.[39] Has not this intrepid pioneer, by his depreciation

---

[36] *Histoire*, p. 564. Poulat, who was notably cool towards Blondel in 1962,
has since adjusted the balance slightly towards Blondel's side in an article published
eight years later, 'Critique historique et théologie dans la crise moderniste', in
Recherches de science religieuse 58 (1970), pp. 535-50. In this article Poulat
concedes to Blondel 'une extrême finesse d'analyse dont la valeur stimulante reste
entière' (p. 545), but he goes on to reiterate his view that Blondel was too preoccupied with his own thought and anxieties and insufficiently aware of the need
to share from the inside the experience of the historian. Blondel 'believed that he
had found in Loisy's conception of history a sufficient explanation of the theological disagreement between them: he never envisaged the possibility, put to him
by Loisy, that this explanation might be found in his own theological concepts
which he threw into opposition to history' (art. cit., p. 545).

[37] Even so scholarly a commentator as Jean Lacroix can remark that 'Histoire
et dogme' 'attacked a particular religious problem' with 'extraordinary audacity
and complete success' (J. Lacroix, *Maurice Blondel: An Introduction to the Man
and His Philosophy* (New York, 1968), p. 45; emphasis added). R. Saint-Jean
(*L'Apologétique philosophique, Blondel 1893-1913* (Paris, 1966), pp. 101-35)
believes that '*Histoire et dogme* nous fournit les prolégomènes à toute apologétique du fait externe', p. 135.

[38] F. von Hügel, 'Du Christ éternel et de nos christologies successives', in *La
Quinzaine*, 58 (1904), pp. 285-312. Bremond helped with the translation of this
article.   [39] Ibid., p. 307.

of the role of history in the believer's approach to Christ, achieved 'a premature peace by leaving aside one part [of the whole picture] and by delighting in an illusory harmony, forgetting that one of the essential elements of this harmony is missing from the full score'?[40] Von Hügel concluded by expressing the fervent hope that his two friends, the exegete from Bellevue and the philosopher from Aix, 'would try to respect the respective rights of each other's craft, and so combine harmoniously in the unity of the intellectual life as a whole'.[41] These pious and avuncular sentiments had no noticeable effect either at Bellevue or at Aix.

The case against Blondel, then, is clear and strong. The case in his favour is rather more difficult to state as soon as one steps outside the charmed circle of his disciples, many of whom seem to share his inability to understand what Loisy was trying to say. Blondel believed that philosophy, and, *a fortiori*, theology, was the product of total commitment. A purely phenomenological approach to religion, as Blondel saw it, introduced an invalidating note into the entire process. He deprecated Loisy's lack of commitment to what he, Blondel, regarded as indisputable Catholic truth. He saw through Loisy's disingenuous claim to be only 'un pauvre déchiffreur de textes', and he sensed an underlying and undisclosed philosophy of religion which he totally rejected. Furthermore, he was worried by the destructive effect which he believed Loisy's writings were having on some of the younger French clergy. He therefore translated his instinctive spiritual and moral disapproval into an academic argument. The crux of his case seems to have turned on whether the Christian believer ought to produce a book about his faith based only on historical (i.e. phenomenological) method. Blondel never claimed that it *could* not be done, only that it *ought* not to be done, since such an approach betrayed the Gospel by implication. Academically Loisy was able to argue that he was not attempting to base Christian faith on history alone. This was theoretically true. In practice, however, Loisy appeared to be using historical method as a cover for his lack of subscription to any statement of Christian

---

[40] Ibid., p. 312.   [41] Ibid., p. 312.

faith which would have an objectively valid transcendent reference. Both of the first two Little Red Books, together with the Firmin articles, made plain his radically relativistic theory of truth.

The really surprising feature of Blondel's case against Loisy is that it attacked the exegete at his strongest point, namely, his competence as a historian and biblical critic, while it unaccountably failed to attack him where he actually disclaimed competence, namely, in the philosophical area. This omission is understandable in the publications which of set purpose avoided mentioning Loisy by name. It is much less understandable in the letters which Blondel sent to Wehrlé for forwarding to Loisy. Although Blondel saw through Loisy's disingenuous disclaimer of philosophical intent and competence, he failed to press home his advantage in a matter of crucial importance to the whole debate. In *Autour d'un petit livre* Loisy had written that he had no intention of expounding a theory of truth, since he was 'too ignorant of philosophy'.[42] This ignorance did not, however, deter him from immediately proceeding to write a piece of full-blooded philosophy which committed him to a remarkably decisive theory of truth.

It seems evident to me, from common experience, that truth is in us something necessarily conditioned, relative, always perfectible, susceptible, too, to diminution. It would appear to be the residue of repeated and co-ordinated perceptions which have the real for their object, which are real in themselves and in the notions which remain in them. But our perceptions do not attain to the basis of reality. Still less do notions exhaust themselves. They are faint images of subjective impressions which imply, to be sure, the reality of the subject and object, but which do not adequately represent to the subject either the object or the subject himself . . . The general laws of knowledge are like hereditary customs. Truth does not enter our heads ready-made; it comes about slowly, and one can never say that it is complete. The human mind, at least as possessed by the élite of our species, is always at work . . . Truth is never complete in our mind, and there is always a beyond opening out before our enquiries . . . But truth . . . is no more immutable than man himself. It evolves with him, in him, by him; but that does not prevent its being truth for him . . .[43]

Blondel had all the resources for subjecting this and other epistemological statements in Loisy's writings to a rigorous

⁴² *Autour*, p. 191.   ⁴³ Ibid., pp. 191 f.

critique. Yet he failed to do so. The theory of knowledge outlined here lies at the core of Loisy's theology of revelation and dogma. If these epistemological foundations had been shown to be faulty (and surely Blondel could have criticized its 'common-sense' assumptions and made a case for greater emphasis on the objective and stable elements in knowledge?), Loisy would have been forced to modify his conception of dogma, or at least might have been rendered less peremptory in his removal of dogma from the field of history.[44] Instead, Blondel strayed into territory in which he was self-confessedly inexperienced.

Blondel not unnaturally resented the proprietary attitude — amounting almost to one of hegemony — taken by Loisy in the name of history towards Christian 'facts'. He saw quite correctly that Loisy's thesis entailed an undisclosed philosophy. He did indeed make this point more than once, but he left it strangely undeveloped, whereas we might have expected him to make it the controlling element in his case against the exegete who had an unacknowledged philosophical position. Instead, therefore, of fighting the action on a philosophical front, Blondel chose a difficult theological terrain to deploy his principal thesis, namely, that of Church tradition.

His theory of tradition was an attempt to vindicate the objectivity of certain Christian beliefs which cannot be validated by historical investigation but the truth of which is inseparable from their objective historicity. 'Something in the Church escapes scientific control', he had written towards the end of 'Histoire et dogme', 'and it is she who, without ever departing from or neglecting the contributions of exegesis and history, controls them, because she possesses, in the very Tradition which constitutes her, another means of knowing her author, of sharing in his life, of linking facts to dogmas, and of vindicating both the capital and the interest of Church teaching.'[45] It is not the high ecclesiology of this remark which concerns us here (today many Roman Catholic theologians would be as unwilling as their Protestant colleagues

---

[44] One must constantly remember that 'dogma' here extends to every statement concerning the manifestation, or alleged manifestation, of the transcendent and supernatural in history. [45] *H.D.*, pp. 205 f.

to speak of the Church's 'control' over the contribution of exegesis and history); rather, it is Blondel's postulation of 'another means' of knowing Christ which demands our notice. The Protestant answer to Blondel's problem has normally been a dilation on the nature of faith, often accompanied by reflection on 2 Cor. 5:16. In this way of looking at things Blondel might be credited with the view that Loisy's historicism presented a Christ totally *kata sarka*. If the believer's spiritual approach to Christ were indeed to be limited to the evidence of the New Testament, Loisy's case would be unassailable. Blondel's objection to this limitation, however, is based on its lack of concern for the over-all design, the divine plan, which gives the Gospel its meaning for post-apostolic Christians. Loisy, as Blondel saw it, consigns Jesus to the hands of historians and the Church to the making of mystical reflections which are embodied in symbolic utterances of which the truth is relative to the needs of the age which produced them.

'God is not an historical person', Loisy had written as shorthand for the conviction that transcendent reality is historically unattainable in every respect, even indirect and tangential. Blondel saw this as being in effect gnostic and he represented the *loisystes* as seeking 'to save faith from the assaults of historical science by suppressing sacred History, that is to say, by liberating dogmas from their obligation to incorporate ("représenter") positive facts and to formulate ideas which are rooted in [historical] realities'.[46] The terminology forged by Blondel to deal with the problem thus envisaged centres on the key terms 'fact' and 'idea'. Dogmas, he would say later, are the 'idealization of facts'; but to this idealization there must correspond a 'realization in the facts' of the ideas contained in dogma.

At the beginning of 'Histoire et dogme' he had postulated a 'two-way passage between fact and faith, as it were, a going-out and a coming-back'.[47] He returned to this reciprocal movement in an essay written in 1905 for the *Bulletin de littérature ecclésiastique*, the journal of the Catholic Institute of Toulouse. The *Bulletin* had carried an unsigned article by

---

[46] *H.D.*, p. 198.   [47] Ibid., p. 152.

the young Abbé Louis Venard, editor of the 'Chronique biblique' in the *Revue du clergé français* and already a respected scholar.[48] Venard's aim was eirenic, for he admired both Loisy and Blondel and regretted the acrimony which had entered their debate. Loisy thought highly of the article;[49] but Blondel was rather less pleased and felt that Venard had failed to appreciate his position — a failure evidenced in particular by the absence of any reference to Blondel's theory of tradition. Blondel thereupon wrote a reply which was published in the *Bulletin* in the Spring of 1905.[50] In this reply he restates the problem thus:

. . . if it is true that one would no longer be a Catholic if one denied that the religious value of certain facts is indissolubly bound to their historical reality, though without historical demonstration, an urgent need appears: What, in this case, can act as justificatory evidence for dogmatically historical beliefs ('croyances dogmatiquement historiques') that can neither be based on a purely mystical inspiration nor limited to simple affirmations of a subjective and symbolic character, nor validated ('se contenter') by objective data properly declared inadequate by scholarly judgement ('la critique')?[51]

It was to meet this difficulty, he remarks, that he had put forward his theory of tradition. He has, he claims, been misunderstood by those who have ascribed to him the view that we can have a better idea of the *external* aspects of the Saviour's life than his contemporaries had. It is certainly not a matter of *deducing* historical realities themselves from dogmatic formulas. It is a matter of seeing more clearly what was implied in (1) the 'direct and concrete impression of the first witnesses' which was scarcely capable of being conveyed in language but which was 'the true cause of their initiative';[52] in (2) the Saviour's acts which are open to 'un approfondissement infini de leur sens réel' and of which the documents provide a rudimentary interpretation; and in (3) the collective experience of believers which constitutes a moral verification derived from a light stemming not merely subjectively from

---

[48] 'La valeur historique du dogme. A propos d'une controverse récente' in *B.L.E.* 9–10 (1904), pp. 338–57. This article is summarized in Poulat, *Histoire*, pp. 594–8.   [49] *Mémoires*, vol. ii, p. 427.

[50] M. Blondel, 'De la valeur historique du dogme', in *B.L.E.* 10–11 (1905), pp. 61–77; reprinted in *Les Premiers écrits de Maurice Blondel*, vol. ii (Paris, 1956), pp. 229–45; references here are to this latter edition.

[51] Ibid., p. 232.   [52] Ibid., p. 233.

their action but also from the 'objective theme put before thought by history itself as matter subjected to the laboratory of life'.[53] If it were merely a question of scientific methodology, a provisional reserve would indeed be in order. Not so if we are dealing with religious truth. 'To speak accurately, the journey from facts to dogmas is inescapably bound up with the return journey from dogmas to facts: separable for purposes of scientific analysis, these two moments are emphatically inseparable in concrete reality and in the living exercise of the faith.'[54] To limit historical inquiry to the first journey [sc. from facts to dogmas] and not to regard the return journey [sc. from dogmas to facts] as in any way historical is, in Blondel's view, to fall into fideism.

What I have described as *historicism* does not therefore consist, as I have been credited with thinking, in 'justifying by history alone the connection between facts and beliefs'; it consists rather, and especially, in believing that there are not *many modes of access to, and regress from*, faith to facts, modes which must be taken into scientific consideration as much to explain the dogmatic interpretation of the documents as to validate the historical truth of dogmas.[55]

As long as Christian beliefs appeared to coincide with Christian facts, there was no obvious need to seek a ground for dogma outside history. But the tutored mind, aware today both of critical research and of the progressive analysis of religious psychology, can no longer rest in this primitive simplicity. Therefore if one believes that Catholicism is bound up not merely with human states of consciousness but with divinely incarnated realities, one needs a theory of tradition, analogous to the philosophy of action, which will account for Christian knowledge ('la science chrétienne').

In short, Blondel's theory of tradition is consistent with his desire to find an immanent dimension which would avoid the snare of immanentism. He will not allow the *fait intérieur* to do duty for the *fait extérieur*. But the *fait extérieur* may be of a type that escapes historical verification. It has its objective reality in the life and reflections of the Church.

[53] Ibid., p. 233. As Venard suggested in a letter, Blondel's position here is curiously close to Tyrrell's conception of revelation as experience and dogma as reflection upon that experience (see *B. V.*, vol. i, p. 216).
[54] Ibid., p. 233.   [55] Ibid., p. 235, original italics.

For Blondel openness to historical verification is not the only test of objective givenness and presence; hence his remark that something in the Church escapes scientific control, namely, Tradition. More specifically, the Church believes some conditions and events in the life of Christ to have been historical (by which Blondel means having objective existence and reference in time and place), but these conditions and events cannot be historically substantiated. That Jesus was virginally conceived, that he was not in error about the Parousia, and that he rose from the dead are truths which cannot be demonstrated historically, but the Catholic must believe them as being, not simply true, but *historically* true. This was precisely the sort of remark which left him wide open to Loisy's criticisms. Blondel's views on Jesus' attitude to the Parousia were based on current Catholic *theological* convictions about error and not on an impartial inspection of the Gospel evidence. Blondel believed that dogmatic faith made it *a priori* impossible to attribute to Jesus any historically false expectations about the Parousia.

Having read Blondel's article in the *Bulletin*, Venard wrote him a friendly and perceptive letter[56] in which he remarked that Loisy had told him that Blondel was absolutely correct in his refusal to *separate* the religious value of facts from their historical value. One may not separate them, said Loisy, but one must *distinguish* them. Venard went on:

Nevertheless — and here we return to the difficulty and profound divergence [between you] — he refuses to apply this distinction to the case where, in his view, there are no *facts* (that is, phenomena which are historically verifiable and verified), where there are only spiritual realities which escape historical experience, as is in his view the case with the virginal conception and the resurrection. Whence, if I understand his thought, we have the precise point of difference [between you] : While for you the supplementary means you have appealed to allow of certitude, a certitude which is extra-historical, but nonetheless a real certitude, concerning historical phenomena which cannot be verified, or at least not sufficiently verified, in establishing realities which presuppose the existence of these phenomena; for M. Loisy, on the contrary, these extra-historical means serve only to interpret the phenomena established by historical methods and [to enable one] to arrive at the spiritual realities behind these phenomena,

[56] Published in full in *B. V.*, vol. i, pp. 213–16.

[namely] the metaphysical being which they presuppose and of which they are but the imperfect translation and revelation.[57]

The point is well made; but it also highlights the ambiguity which rendered the terms 'history' and 'fact' so unstable as agreed intellectual currency.

Although Blondel realized the fundamental ambiguity of the term 'history', he failed to explore the implications of the distinction between history as objective event and history as interpretative record. One can tackle this problem under the rubric of *Geschichte* and *Historie*, discuss it as a problem in existential analysis, or simply treat it as one of the many variants of the critical question concerning the subjectivity and objectivity of human thought. However one chooses to approach it, it remains the basic problem in any philosophical analysis of the concept of history. Loisy was not constrained by the exigencies of his argument to tackle it. Blondel, aware as he was of the consequences of the Kantian critique, had much less excuse for evasion or neglect. Moreover, the sort of argument he was seeking to advance demanded such attention. The 'algebraic' distinctions (between the different senses of the word 'fact') which he makes in the second part of his article in the *Bulletin*[58] quite simply bypass, if indeed they do not beg, the question of the relationship between event and interpretation as the crucial issue in any theological reflection on the meaning of transcendent reference in historical religion.

The 'positivist thaw', which Alan Richardson has indicated as characterizing historiographical thinking during the course of the twentieth century,[59] has made it easier to appreciate 'that "sources", like "facts" themselves, are only judgements of evidence, and that earlier sources are inevitably partial and lacking in historical perspective'.[60] In this respect Blondel, with his insistence on the reciprocal relationship between 'faith' and 'fact', was anticipating the move away from a positivist conception of history and of the task of the historian.

---

[57] *B.V.*, vol. i, p. 214.

[58] Ibid., pp. 236–44. Blondel describes his scheme as an 'algèbre de distinctions': A, a, a', a'', a 1, a'' 2, a'' 3, Bb, C 1, C 2, C 3, Z.

[59] A. Richardson, *History Sacred and Profane* (London, 1964), p. 237.

[60] Ibid., p. 239.

But his approach was oblique. A Protestant commentator might reasonably feel compelled to observe that Blondel was tackling the right problem for the wrong reasons and with the wrong weapons. His conception of 'faith' can be seen as being too closely bound up with the notion of dogma prevailing in the Roman Catholic Church of the period for it to serve as an acceptable currency among Christian theologians of all traditions and schools. His conception of 'fact' is too undifferentiated to be of much use in an age which has grown increasingly aware that the hermeneutical problem can no longer be left to immensely learned Germans writing for each other in splendid isolation from the rest of reflective Christianity. If, however, the two termini of Blondel's journey are open to criticism, as they certainly are, he can at least be credited with the appreciation that a journey has to be made between faith and fact (however one may choose to define each) and that it is a two-way journey. In this he saw further and deeper than Loisy (though not von Hügel) had done. He was however prevented from working out the implications of his position by all the limitations of a scholastic christology which accepted no break whatever in the line connecting the Jesus of history with the Christ of faith. Anxiety about preserving the continuity of the Christ-line forced Blondel into an attitude of distrust and hostility towards any claim to autonomy made by historians in matters of religion on behalf of their craft. It also put him in a position of some inconsistency with his own stated conviction that the different sciences should not be sealed off from one another.

Friedrich von Hügel was the one who gently pointed out this inconsistency.[61] Von Hügel's article was greatly resented by some of the Blondelians (especially by Wehrlé, whose response, expressed in an article and several letters, was intemperate and maladroit). They were unwilling to accept any distinction between the 'Eternal Christ' and the Jesus presented by the Synoptists. Blondel referred to the Baron's 'bi-ontologisme' and went on to deliver himself of an aphorism which has more sound than sense: 'The heavenly Christ cannot be what you say he is if the earthly Christ is

[61] F. von Hügel, 'Du Christ éternel', pp. 306 f.

not more than you say he is.'[62] This remark is evidence of
that total failure of comprehension on Blondel's part which
made Loisy and von Hügel wonder how such an intelligent
man could be so wilfully obtuse.

Von Hügel had argued for a clear distinction between
phenomena and their interpretation and had taken Blondel to
task for failing to 'distinguish adequately between historical
phenomena and their spiritual significance' and for seeming
to believe that Loisy had claimed for critical history the
power to discern and demonstrate the existence of spiritual
realities.[63] For von Hügel the deeper realities must lie behind,
or rather within, the phenomena available to historical
inspection. Blondel chose to describe this as 'mystico-
positivisme'.[64] Laberthonnière, who had seen facts as having
'un dedans', was initially more disposed than the other
Blondelians to appreciate what von Hügel was saying,[65] and
Blondel told Wehrlé that Laberthonnière was 'un peu trop
sous le charme, quoiqu'il repousse la christologie nestorienne
du Baron'.[66] The outer, historically available, phenomenon is
seen by von Hügel as being in inevitable but fruitful tension
with its inner eternal meaning, in that the phenomenon
cannot of itself show forth the Infinite. This was a controlling thesis of all von Hügel's thought. The paradox of religion
— *all* religion and not merely Christianity — consists in the
manner in which the Infinite reaches the soul by means of
the contingent and finite.[67] The Infinite in fact *needs* the
contingent in order to awaken the soul to the presence of
spiritual realities. All religion must, he believed, evince some
factor of this kind. 'Plus une religion sera complète et profonde, plus elle devra présenter ce paradoxe du permanent
saisi à travers les choses qui passent, de l'éternel manifesté
dans le temps.'[68] Such a relationship entails a tension, which
may not be resolved as Blondel has sought to resolve it, by a
specious and premature harmony.[69] This deepest and most

---

[62] *Au cœur*, p. 222.   [63] 'Du Christ éternel', p. 305.
[64] *Au cœur*, p. 225.   [65] *B.L.*, pp. 175 f.
[66] *Au cœur*, p. 231. This was clearly a matter in which Blondel expected the
team to remain solid.
[67] 'Du Christ éternel', p. 290.   [68] Ibid.
[69] Art. cit., p. 287. 'Entre ces deux séries, entre le *phénomène* saisi et le
noumène deviné, il y a forcément conflit, frottement, et dans notre désir d'arriver

enduring of von Hügel's insights was, under pressure from Blondel, interpreted by Laberthonnière as a species of occasionalism in which the Jesus of history becomes an occasion for the exercise of faith.[70] This diagnosis comes strangely from a proponent of the method of immanence, of the philosophy of action, and of moral dogmatism. Laberthonnière would have done better to have trusted his first reactions, expressed less than a month before,[71] instead of capitulating in the face of Blondel's relentless and rather feverish communications.[72]

Perhaps the last word may most fittingly be left to the man who had tried to make peace between the philosopher from Aix and the exegete from Bellevue. The problems raised by Loisy and Blondel clearly continued to exercise von Hügel's mind over the next year, and he sought to give them a wider frame of reference. In May 1905 he read a paper before the London Society for the Study of Religion entitled 'The Place and Function of the Historical Element in Religion'.[73] The second section of the paper carries the heading: 'The Mind's Movement from the Apprehension of Historical Events at their Phenomenal Level to the Conviction as to their Spiritual Depth and Significance; and the Mind's Movement back from this Conviction to that Apprehension'.[74] Von Hügel's exquisite academic tact would not allow him to refer explicitly in such a setting to an internationally obscure French Catholic philosopher; but it

---

plus vite à l'unité, à la paix, nous sommes tentés de simplifier ce qui est complexe, d'identifier les dehors et le dedans et d'établir en nous une unité prématurée.' (Ibid.)

[70] In view of *Pascendi*'s thesis of 'transfiguration' as attributed to the modernists, one ought to note Laberthonnière's precise words: Von Hügel, he says, appears to share our view that the phenomena must be interpreted. 'Mais on s'aperçoit ensuite que par interprétation il entend une *transfiguration*, une *idéalisation* par la foi. Le Christ historique est *l'occasion* − et ce mot revient plusieurs fois − pour la foi de s'exercer. Il apparaît comme révélateur . . . sans le vouloir.' (*B.L.*, p. 178.) Von Hügel had written 'C'est la foi qui, en les [sc. phenomena] accueillant, les transfigure.' ('Du Christ éternel', p. 293.)

[71] *B.L.*, p. 175 f.   [72] Ibid., pp. 176–8.

[73] F. von Hügel, *Essays and Addresses on the Philosophy of Religion*, 2nd series (London, 1926), pp. 27–55. This paper must surely be among the most dense and opaque of all von Hügel's writings, and one can only marvel at the sheer stamina of the Society which listened to it.

[74] Ibid., p. 35.

is impossible to read this section of the paper without recognizing that the Baron was here deploying on a wider and less confessional canvas the conviction of his obstinate and touchy friend that 'le passage des faits aux dogmes est inévitablement solidaire du retour des dogmes aux faits.'

5 Lucien Laberthonnière's 'Critical Mysticism'

Lucien Laberthonnière is one of those luckless figures who are dislodged by events into the interstices of history. Encyclopedias and general histories tend to represent him as the largest planet circling Blondel's sun but going into more or less permanent eclipse after being forbidden to publish in 1913. The scholastic hegemony which followed upon the condemnation of modernism ensured that Laberthonnière would not be read by the majority of Roman Catholics; while those modernist commentators who have focused their attention on the radicals have treated him with much the same lack of fundamental interest and sympathy as they have Blondel. Yet his place in the modernist movement was central and his contribution to the theology and philosophy of immanence notable and in many respects original. It has more than once been observed that Laberthonnière frequently anticipates future preoccupations in theology, here and there throwing out a suggestion or insight which others would later develop at length.[1]

Some remarks on his character and preoccupations may help towards an appreciation of his position. First and foremost he needs to be read in his own right and not merely as Blondel's principal champion. This is not to underestimate his debt to Blondel, which he constantly acknowledged. It is simply to recognize that however much his interests and sympathies chimed with those of Blondel, they were nevertheless his own and had begun to take shape before he read and met Blondel.[2] In 1925 he wrote to his friend Enrico Castelli:

---

[1] Thus J. Lacroix remarks, 'ce qui est devenu banal il [sc. Laberthonnière] est souvent le premier à l'avoir dit', cited in P. Beillevert, *Laberthonnière: l'homme et l'œuvre* (Paris, 1972), p. 238.

[2] Blondel, having read 'Le dogmatisme moral', wrote to Laberthonnière to advise him not to emphasize 'notre solidarité'; '. . . vous êtes votre propre initiateur, comme le prouve ce premier article . . .' (*B.L.*, p. 120). Loisy's *mot* that Laberthonnière's system was 'Maurice Blondel translated into French' (*Choses*

From my earliest youth I experienced the most lively disquiet within myself. And before long I felt the need of giving the religious problem a philosophical expression, that is to say, of not separating religion from philosophy, as, since the middle ages, there was a tendency, indeed a compulsion, to do. Pascal and Maine de Biran confirmed me in this way of seeing things; and thus I linked up with the Augustinian tradition.[3]

The disquiet of which he speaks was for him a driving force throughout his life. But the word 'rejoignais' is carefully chosen. It was his profound conviction that Aristotle's philosophy, christianized by St. Thomas Aquinas, had paralysed the dynamic relationship existing in Augustinian thought between intellect and will, or rather — to avoid terminology which has an Aristotelian ring to it — between man's cognitive and conative sides. Laberthonnière was a sworn enemy of speculation divorced from life, and he claimed that such a divorce occurs in Thomism. His Thomistic critics have in their turn claimed that he had no first-hand knowledge of Aquinas and that he misrepresented the views of his Thomistic contemporaries. It can immediately be admitted that he exaggerated their 'intellectualism'. Exaggeration, however, is not necessarily misrepresentation, especially when it is employed in a polemical situation where everybody knows the rules of the game and where exaggerations occur at the opposite pole. Thus Aubert's judgement is itself a legitimate exaggeration when he says of Laberthonnière: 'Essentiellement polémiste, il ne pouvait penser que contre quelqu'un et, pour mieux mettre en relief son point de vue, poussait à leur extrêmes consequences les points faibles des systèmes qu'il critiquait.'[4] Bremond described Laberthonnière playfully as 'le violent de la rue Las-Cases'.[5] Tyrrell met him for the first time in 1906 and was captivated by the delightful amalgam in his character of sweetness and humility on the one hand and verve and courage on the other.[6]

passées, pp. 307 f.) probably helped to support the idea that Laberthonnière was nothing more than a Blondelian commentator.

[3] E. Castelli, *Laberthonnière*. Traduit de l'Italien par Louis Canet (Paris, 1931), p. 6.   [4] Aubert, *Le Problème de l'acte de foi*, p. 298.

[5] A. Blanchet (ed.), *Henri Bremond et Maurice Blondel: Correspondance*, vol. ii (Paris, 1971), p. 66. The house to which Laberthonnière moved in 1903, after the French government's refusal to authorize the Oratorian school at Juilly, was situated in the Rue Las-Cases in Paris.

[6] M. D. Petre, *Autobiography and Life of George Tyrrell*, vol. ii, p. 264.

Laberthonnière in fact resembles Tyrrell in his integration of thought with life, in his courage and integrity, and in his tendency to exaggerate the perversity of the case to be attacked. Although he shared Tyrrell's indignation at the manner in which authority was conceived and used in the Church of his time, he was less astringent than Tyrrell in his personal comments. His political and social sympathies lay, one need hardly remark, with Marc Sagnier and the Sillonists, while his dislike of Thomism was intensified by the support given by so many French Thomists to *Action Française*. According to Marc Boegner,[7] a Protestant friend, Laberthonnière's condemnation was brought about largely by the influence of members of *Action Française* who were smarting under his attack on them in his book *Positivisme et catholicisme*.[8]

When Laberthonnière took over the editorship of the *Annales de philosophie chrétienne* in 1905, he placed on its title page the celebrated text from St Augustine's *De Trinitate* (ix, 1): 'Cherchons donc comme cherchent ceux qui doivent trouver, et trouvons comme trouvent ceux qui doivent chercher encore; car il dit "l'homme qui est arrivé au terme ne fait que commencer" (Eccles. xviii, 6).' It was a reminder of precisely that strand in Augustinian thought which he believed to be lacking in Thomism. In his inaugural article he exhorted his readers to abandon the effort to think in two compartments, one philosophical, the other religious. There must be a thoroughgoing integration of the two, reaching into the very depths of the believer's being. 'If there are two orders, the natural and the supernatural, which are distinct, they [nevertheless] interpenetrate each other and do not constitute two realities in life.'[9] These words summarized the position he had taken since his intervention in support of Blondel nearly ten years earlier. It was a position in open conflict with Loisy's historical positivism and with the doctrinal positivism of contemporary scholastic orthodoxy.

[7] M. Boegner, *The Long Road to Unity: Memories and Anticipations* (London, 1970), p. 46; Eng. Trans. of *L'Exigence oecuménique* (Paris, 1968).
[8] L. Laberthonnière, *Positivisme et catholicisme* (Paris, 1911).
[9] *A.P.C.* 1 (1905–6), p. 23. Cf. his remark to Blondel many years later, 'J'entends être chrétien philosophiquement et être philosophe chrétiennement' (*B.L.*, p. 330).

Many of the guidelines to his thought can be found in his first major article, 'Le problème religieux à propos de la question apologétique'.[10] With Schwalm and Gayraud in mind he sets out to give theological support to Blondel's thesis by approaching the question 'from above'. Blondel had found himself driven by philosophical inquiry to postulate 'from below' the supernatural and had in consequence been accused of 'naturalism', of denying, that is, the otherness and gratuitousness of supernature. Laberthonnière proposes to take his point of departure from Christian faith, accepted and established as true, and to work backwards by asking about the competence of philosophy in the matter.[11] This involves him in a statement of 'the religious problem', which is quite simply that since there are 'deux ordres de vérités', the primordial human drive towards unity demands that we define the relationship between these two orders.[12] 'Two orders of truths, is not a happy phrase, making, as it does, too great a concession to the position he was attacking. By 1900 not merely had he replaced 'vérités' by 'vérité', but he had moved further and with complete consistency to speaking of 'affirmation de l'être' in place of 'affirmation de la vérité'.[13]

As one works one's way through this phase of the modernist controversy, one becomes increasingly convinced that the issue of the gratuitousness of the supernatural order was a diversion from the real task in hand. Nevertheless it had become, and was to remain for the next sixty years, a major issue in Roman Catholic theology. Catholic theologians after the Second World War were to discover that all attempts to relate the natural and supernatural orders more homogeneously were met by the same arguments supporting the 'gratuitousness' of supernature. 'Naturalism' and 'concordism' were stock terms of disapprobation levelled against such

---

[10] Laberthonnière, *Essais de philosophie religieuse* (Paris, 1903). The edn. referred to here is C. Tresmontant (ed.), Lucien Laberthonnière, *Le Réalisme chrétien: précédé de: Essais de philosophie religieuse* (Paris, 1966) [*E.P.R.*], pp. 135-67. This edn., the only modern one available, is unsatisfactory in many respects. It provides no editorial information about the individual essays. It incorporates a jejune preface and lacks an index. More seriously, it omits three important appendices: 'Réponse à M. l'Abbé Gayraud'; 'Réponse à M. le Chanoine Gombault'; and 'Le Kantisme et M. Blondel'. These appendices can be found in the 1903 edn., pp. 313-25.

[11] *E.P.R.*, p. 137.　　　　[12] Ibid., p. 138.　　　　[13] Ibid., p. 115.

initiatives. Yet, as Laberthonnière had ceaselessly claimed, this was quite simply beside the point. The point at issue was not the relationship between nature and supernature, but the mode of contact between transcendent being and human experience and action. As we have seen, Blondel had tentatively indicated that the disjunction 'supernature/ nature' was not co-extensive with the disjunction 'transcendence/immanence'.[14] What Laberthonnière was trying to say did not lend itself to discussion in terms of nature and supernature, with the result that a great deal of time, energy, and goodwill was lost in the attempt to debate a question in language which quite simply did not fit it. To some extent Laberthonnière allowed his scholastic adversaries to choose both the weapons and the terrain for the contest. In theory he could have taken either or both of two courses: he could have shown that the contemporary scholastic understanding of nature and supernature derived not from St. Thomas but from sixteenth-century commentators; and/or he could have shown that the problem he was tackling demanded a different sort of language from that employed by the scholastics. As it happened, he was not suitably equipped for, or temperamentally inclined towards, the first course; the second he did indeed partially undertake by his inchoate theory of interpretation.[15]

The cooling of his friendship with Blondel (many years after the modernist crisis) has a certain relevance to this question. In general he came to feel that Blondel was making too many concessions to the neo-Thomists, more especially in respect of the theory of nature and supernature. It was a matter on which Laberthonnière was utterly committed and utterly consistent. 'I cannot concede that there is something

[14] See above, pp. 77 f.

[15] In the event, it was Henri de Lubac, aided by the atmosphere generated by the Second Vatican Council, who delivered the *coup de grâce* to the sort of Roman Catholic theology which insisted on the concept of 'pure nature' as indispensable to orthodoxy. See his *Le Mystère du surnaturel* (Paris, 1965) (Eng. Trans., *The Mystery of the Supernatural* (London, 1967)), in which, with patient scholarship he shows that the concept of 'pure nature', in spite of being a late arrival in Catholic theology, nevertheless achieved an astonishing degree of unquestioned authority. Referring to W. Lossky's *Essai sur la théologie mystique de l'Église d'Orient* (Paris, 1949), de Lubac points out that the theory never penetrated the theology of the East.

called "nature" constituted by an *ought* and something called
supernature constituted by gift . . . Everything is gift in the
work of God', he wrote to Blondel in 1925,[16] and his reason
is based on his conception of morality: we have to be reborn
so that we can actively co-operate with God in the work of
creation and sanctification. Our 'natural' life is 'une sorte
d'égocentrisme natif' from which we need to be freed by our
co-operation with God's creative as well as redemptive
action.[17] 'Qu'on appelle ce que nous sommes "nature" et
"surnature" ce que nous devons être, j'y consens volon-
tiers.'[18] He will not allow that 'supernatural elevation' (to use
the neo-scholastic term) is a process before which man is in
any way morally or ontologically passive. In fairness to the
neo-scholastics it should be said that their view of faith and
justification was not as exclusively intellectualist as Laberthonnière customarily assumes. Nevertheless one can hardly
deny today that their emphasis on faith as intellectual assent
based on an extrinsic motive extrinsically manifested
amounted to a serious neglect of the moral and metaphysical
unity existing between the creative and salvific process.
Laberthonnière reacted against this dualistic tendency by
exaggerating it in order to combat it. Nature is graced not by
a serene possession of the truth, but by a constant striving to
reach truth, each level of which, once attained, reveals a
further level to be conquered.[19] This is why in 1896 he
applauded Blondel for transposing the religious problem from
the object to the subject[20] and attacked neo-scholastic apologetics as 'Socratic determinism'.[21] Faith must be shown to be
reasonable, but not by geometry-type arguments. Faith is
the meeting of two loves, not the coupling of two ideas.[22]

He now comes to what he later singled out as the most
original part of the essay.[23] 'We must', he writes, 'set out
from the living reality that we are.'[24] Something in us must
correspond with extrinsic revelation, otherwise the revelatory
process amounts to no more than a crude juxtapositioning
of grace and nature — a process devoid of moral content.

[16] *B.L.*, p. 328.   [17] Ibid., pp. 329 f.   [18] Ibid., p. 330.
[19] Ibid., p. 90.   [20] *E.P.R.*, p. 142.   [21] Ibid., p. 144.
[22] Ibid., p. 147.
[23] R. P. Lecanuet, *La Vie de l'Église sous Léon XIII* (Paris, 1930), p. 528.
[24] *E.P.R.*, p. 151.

At this point he explicitly invokes his fellow Oratorian, John Henry Newman,[25] in support of his observation that the meaning we give to revelation is conditioned by the sort of persons we are. As if forestalling the accusing cry of 'Kantian immanentism', he goes on to remark that what he has said in no way implies that each man makes his own truth.[26]

He concludes his essay with a challenge to those who wish to be both 'intellectualist' and Christian. They must show (1) how nature and supernature heteronomously construed can be brought together to form a rational system subject to scientific observation (Schwalm had written: 'Nous ne recevons la foi, comme la science, que par l'instrument de nos sensations');[27] and (2) how the freedom of faith together with its personal and individual character can be reconciled with science, the conclusions of which are necessary, impersonal, and universal. He himself will maintain that only the method of immanence can resolve 'these antinomies'; abstract speculation most certainly can not.[28] Thus the very manner in which Laberthonnière laid out 'the religious problem' made clear his conviction that contemporary scholasticism was incapable of meeting it.

In espousing the method of immanence against such critics as Schwalm, Gayraud, and Fontaine, he drew some of the fire away from Blondel. This was, as he fully realized, 'a delicate and dangerous task',[29] for he was a priest and a member of a religious congregation and therefore far more vulnerable to disciplinary action than a layman would be. Under Leo XIII, however, he was relatively safe. The atmosphere of the late 1890s in France was conducive to creative thinking and to hope for the future. In 1899 Bremond was speaking cheerfully of 'un vrai *Oxford Movement*'. Blondel and von Hügel

---

[25] The absence of Laberthonnière's name from the list of French thinkers influenced by Newman which B. D. Dupuy discusses in his essay, 'Newman's Influence in France' (J. Coulson and A. M. Allchin (eds), *The Rediscovery of Newman: An Oxford Symposium* (London, 1967), pp. 147–73) is surprising. No French thinker during the modernist period was more faithful to the *spirit* of Newman than was Laberthonnière.

[26] 'Le sens que chacun de nous en son for intérieur attache à la doctrine révélée est relatif à ce qu'il est. Mais ceci ne veut pas dire que la vérité dépend de nous, et que chacun peut se faire à son gré sa vérité.' (*E.P.R.*, p. 161).

[27] Cited by Laberthonnière in *E.P.R.*, p. 153.

[28] *E.P.R.*, p. 164 n.   [29] Lecanuet, op. cit., p. 525.

were to be its Newman, while Laberthonnière would be its Dean Church.[30]

In 1899 Laberthonnière published a three-part article in the *Annales de philosophie chrétienne* under the title 'Le dogmatisme moral'. This was in fact to be the phrase by which his position would be commonly known by friend and foe alike.[31] 'Dogmatisme' for Laberthonnière means the affirmation of a position. It is the opposite of scepticism, in which one refrains from affirmation for fear of illusion.[32] He devotes a section of his essay to the refutation of scepticism. Significantly and typically his condemnation is less of scepticism from an epistemological standpoint than of sceptics from a moral one. Sceptics abandon the search for truth. There is a strong element of Augustinianism in his view that the stance of sceptics is immoral because, having declared the phenomenon empty of reality, they continue to live selfishly in it.[33] One must take up a position; one must affirm *Being*, even at the risk of illusion. What is Christian life but the constant breaking of idols? It is a Christian duty to attack illusions even though one be accused of impiety.[34]

If the sceptic reduces all to himself, the illusioned dogmatist reduces himself to his beliefs; he substitutes thought for action and, like the sceptic, he is content to live in the phenomena he has created by his formulas.[35] It is at this point in his argument that Laberthonnière comes nearest by implication to Tyrrell's position on doctrine as instrument and representation of experience. 'In any case, our ideas, even when they come from our own depths, can never

---

[30] Bremond to Von Hügel, 21 October 1899, printed in E. Goichot, 'En marge de la crise moderniste: la correspondance Bremond–von Hügel', in *Revue de sciences religieuses*, 48 (1974), pp. 209–34. Goichot interprets Laberthonnière's role thus: '[Dean] Church incarne une adaptation plus pratique, moralisante, des directives doctrinales d'un Newman' (p. 230). Interestingly, Bremond cast himself in the role of Mark Pattison, the eventual sceptic of the group.

[31] The phrase 'moral dogmatism' is used here because it is the one normally used to describe Laberthonnière's most characteristic theory. The English word 'dogmatism' is not an accurate translation of Laberthonnière's word 'dogmatisme'. An approximate English word might be 'affirmation' or, perhaps, 'commitment', though both words are a trifle too active.

[32] *E.P.R.*, p. 49.   [33] Ibid., pp. 57 f.   [34] Ibid., p. 49.

[35] 'Ce qui caractérise le dogmatisme illusoire c'est donc d'attribuer, soit aux sensations, soit aux idées comme telles, une existence en soi ou de les considérer comme représentant adéquatement des existences en soi.' (*E.P.R.*, p. 60.)

be anything but a simplified substitute for our internal experience.'[36] In words which recall Loisy and Tyrrell, Laberthonnière remarks that 'truth is not something ready-made which falls from on high into the human mind',[37] but he refuses to discuss doctrine in terms of symbolic utterance, precisely because, to his way of thinking, the symbol merely becomes a substitute for an abstraction.[38]

Biblical criticism caused Laberthonnière no anxiety in spite of his being in no sense a biblical scholar. Of course the Bible is full of symbols, he remarks, but they are never symbols of the abstract and the logical, always of the concrete and the living.[39] The very mention of symbolism conjures up in his mind visions of Platonic and Spinozan idealism.[40] Ideas, and therefore doctrines, do not fall from heaven into the mind. They are fashioned as a response to facts and it is with facts that the Bible has to do. The material accuracy of biblical narratives is not essential to their basic meaning. Laberthonnière refused, however, to adopt the stratagem of distinguishing between 'essential' and 'accidental' content in the Bible. It is not the facts as such, whether historically true or not, which matter; it is the *meaning* of the facts which conveys their metaphysical and moral teaching. This, he says, is what distinguishes the Bible from other historical narratives.[41] The facts themselves, we might say, become doctrinal.'[42] It is a mistake to consider facts as purely empirical: 'Les faits ont aussi un dedans'.[43] Here we find Laberthonnière breaking away from the historical positivism of his age in anticipation of a much later conception of hermeneutics. One may justly regard it as perhaps the most original aspect of his work, of particular interest today because he reaches his conclusions by a different route from that taken by later exponents of biblical hermeneutics. His theory is virtually an *a priori* one, arrived at not by historical analysis of biblical texts but as the logical consequence of his 'moral dogmatism'. If the Bible is the word of God, then it *must* conform to the ontologically analysed pattern of all God's

---

[36] *E.P.R.*, p. 60.   [37] Ibid., p. 105.
[38] *Le réalisme chrétien et l'idéalisme grec* [*R.C.I.G.*], pp. 262 f.
[39] Ibid., pp. 262 f.   [40] Ibid., p. 262.   [41] Ibid., p. 261.
[42] Ibid., p. 263.   [43] Ibid., p. 263.

dealings with man. It *cannot* be a purely extrinsic record of divine intervention in man's life and history. Laberthonnière would have been as severe on Protestant biblicism, had he encountered it, as he was upon scholastic intellectualism, since such biblicism would be for him just another species of 'illusioned dogmatism'.

His hermeneutical theory can be found partly in his 1899 essay and more fully in his 1904 book. It stems from his understanding of Being and of the ontologico-moral relationship existing between God, others, and the self. Laberthonnière is explicit that for him *Being is always a subject.*[44] He refuses to extend the term Being to objects. Being cannot be affirmed on the basis of either empirical sensation or intellectual abstraction.[45] Laberthonnière thus appears to understand by 'Being' what the existentialists were to understand by 'existence'. In this way he breaks with Wolffian essentialism and quite palpably anticipates the change in perspective brought about in Roman Catholic theology during and after the Second Vatican Council.[46]

[44] *E.P.R.*, p. 58, where he also makes it clear that he is using Kantian language.

[45] It is instructive to note Blondel's reaction to Laberthonnière's thesis (*B.L.*, pp. 122–7). In general he is delighted. With extreme delicacy, however, he expresses some reservations about Laberthonnière's conception of *Being*. He finds it somewhat equivocal (ibid., p. 124). In defining Being in such exclusively personal and moral a manner, is Laberthonnière not restricting its application too much? Instead of rejecting realism, idealism, and intellectualism, would it not be better to subsume them as inferior but necessary elements into his theory of moral dogmatism? Blondel feels that his friend, in defining Being so rigorously in terms of the subject, has left himself open to criticism from adversaries like Schwalm. In effect, Blondel, in his characteristically roundabout and apologetic way, is reminding Laberthonnière of the scandalous particularity of Christian faith. One recalls Cullmann's criticism of Bultmann's position as 'gnostic'. (Blondel actually mentions the word 'bouddhisme'.) 'D'un mot, il ne faut pas exclure l'empirisme ou intellectualisme, être contre eux, mais les intégrer dans une philosophie qui les comprenne et les convertisse en elle.' (*B.L.*, p. 127.)

[46] Cf. M. D. Chenu, 'Vérité évangélique et métaphysique Wolffienne à Vatican II', in *Revue des sciences philosophiques et théologiques*, 57 (1973), pp. 632–40. In this short but important article Chenu claims that the essentialism of Leibniz and Wolff was imported into Roman Catholic scholastic theology in the eighteenth century and remained firmly entrenched there up to and including the preparatory drafts submitted to the Second Vatican Council. Chenu makes theologically explicit an implication contained in E. Gilson, *Being and Some Philosophers* (2nd edn. Toronto, 1952), pp. 112–21, where it is argued that Wolff had derived his ontology from Suarez, who was one of the prime distorters of classical Thomism. According to Gilson, Wolff's contention, 'Ens dicitur quod existere potest, consequenter cui existentia non repugnat', gave philosophy a direction

Significantly, and with commendable imprudence, Laberthonnière praises Kant's incessant quest for Being, his adoption of a moral affirmation in place of an empirical or idealist
one, and his role in initiating a philosophy of will and freedom.[47] In this, says Laberthonnière, Kant was not inventing,
he was simply reflecting systematically on something which
Christian mystics have always known. It is understandable
that the intellectualists have called Kant a sceptic, for that
is how he looks from the perspective of Socratic determinism.
Instead of salvation by intellect and science Kant proposes
salvation by the good will. 'He understood that certitude,
which has Being for its object, instead of being imposed from
outside as a modification to be undergone, is an action.[48]
But there is a debit side too. Laberthonnière finds Kant's
distinction between the phenomenon and the noumenon to
be artificial and scholastic. In fact it is the very negation of
the method of immanence, a major ontological assumption of
which is precisely that Being is immanent in the phenomenon
but has to be discovered and affirmed by a free and interior
act.[49] The task of the method of immanence is not to throw a
bridge across the Kantian abyss between transcendence and
immanence; on the contrary it is to discover transcendence
within experience. 'Here we have what may be called the
philosophical meaning of the word belief ('croire')'.[50] Faith
is thus an interior and free response of the good will stimulated by grace. It is not the same as belief on the authority of
another: it is an interior affirmation of the being of oneself,
the being of God, and the being of others.

Laberthonnière seems here to leave himself open to the
charge of espousing the stratagem of the double truth.
He is, as he constantly claims, a Christian philosopher and a

which was to prove fateful. 'When Kant wrote that Hume had "aroused him from
his dogmatic slumber", what he really meant to say was that Hume had aroused
him from his Wolffian sleep' (ibid., p. 121). Although Gilson is severe in his judgement on Laberthonnière's alleged ignorance of (classical) scholasticism (*La Vie
intellectuelle*, 34 (1935), pp. 303 f.), he expresses marked approval of the sound
Augustinianism of *Le Réalisme chrétien et l'idéalisme grec*, which, in spite of
what Gilson regards as its lack of nuances, he nevertheless describes as a 'livre
classique' (E. Gilson, *Introduction à l'étude de Saint Augustin* (3rd edn., Paris,
1949, p. 8 n).

[47] *E.P.R.*, pp. 88 f.   [48] Ibid., p. 89.
[49] Ibid., pp. 89 f.   [50] Ibid., p. 90.

philosophically minded Christian. He finds all his authentic convictions in his philosophical analysis of lived Christian experience. But he remains an avowed Roman Catholic and is therefore in some way bound to take cognizance of the traditional understanding of faith as formulated by the Council of Trent and the Vatican Council. Unfortunately his hermeneutic of Being did not include the interpretation of ecclesiastical documents. This neglect made it possible for his adversaries to hurl conciliar texts at his head and thereby put him in a position of some apparent inconsistency.

Although Laberthonnière did not engage in the scientific interpretation of texts, his theory of the interpretation of facts is original, especially when we remember that hermeneutical theory from Schleiermacher onwards was the almost exclusive preserve of Protestant philosophical theology, and Laberthonnière shows no sign of having been even indirectly influenced by it. There are moments in 'Le dogmatisme moral' and *Le Réalisme chrétien et l'idéalisme grec* when one is irresistibly put in mind of Heidegger and even more recent exponents of hermeneutical theory.[51] What gives Laberthonnière's conception of interpretation its own peculiarity is the emphasis he lays upon its moral character. Interpretation of facts is an affirmation of the subjectivity of others and it calls for conversion,[52] because one will not find in others what does not resonate in some way, however faintly, within oneself. To interpret is to take something into oneself *and also* to project something of oneself into what one interprets. The discovery of God, of others, and of oneself constitutes one inextricably interrelated series of actions. Because of its moral character the interpretative process breaks down the opposition between subjectivity and objectivity: the subject is no more sacrificed to the object than the object to the subject.[53] If it is true that the Christian has

[51] Thus, for example, R. E. Palmer in his book, *Hermeneutics: Interpretation Theory in Schleiermacher, Dilthey, Heidegger, and Gadamer* (Evanston, 1969), p. 242, writes that both understanding and language are ontological but 'they do not disclose being as an object over against subjectivity; rather they light up the being in which we are already standing. Nor is the being that is disclosed merely the being of an object but our own being, that is, "what it means to *be*".' This remark might have come straight from Laberthonnière.

[52] 'une transformation intérieure' (*E.P.R.*, p. 93).   [53] *R.C.I.G.*, p. 283.

nothing that he has not received, it is equally true that he has nothing that he has not acquired. We begin life in morally neutral ignorance in respect of ourselves, God, and others. The logic of action then faces us with two alternatives: either rest in sceptical or illusioned inactivity, and thus convert ignorance into error; or diagnose the gradual and inevitable transformation of ignorance into error, and seek to pass from it into truth. 'The passage from error to truth, together with the passage from doubt to certainty, is brought about by a change of heart',[54] and it is expressed in the comprehensive act whereby the believer affirms Being.

Laberthonnière is greatly concerned with the ontological and moral conditions under which it is possible for man to affirm Being. He propounds the thesis that it is impossible to affirm Being without (whether or no one realizes that one is doing so) affirming God.[55] The core of his position is that the affirmation of Being involves the affirmation of self, of God, and of others as subjects. This position he expounds in sections iv to vi of 'Le Dogmatisme moral'. It is no accident that his theodicy is to be found as much in his section on the affirmation of self as it is in that on the affirmation of God. The argument is profoundly Augustinian in its consciousness of the tension which the believer experiences between the transitory and the permanent.

Moral and ontological self-affirmation is an act performed in full consciousness and freedom; it is at once an act of faith and an act of knowledge. It is preserved from egotism by its indissoluble link with the affirmation of God and of the selfhood of others.[56] I need more than intuition, he says, in order to be able to affirm that I am. The affirmation takes its value from what I mean by 'am'.[57] If I mean nothing more than presence in space and time, what I affirm is simply an illusion, not in the sense that it is empirically false but in the deeper sense that it is ontologically empty. It is a description

---

[54] *E.P.R.*, p. 107. [55] Ibid., p. 73.

[56] Cf. D. M. Eastwood, *The Revival of Pascal: A Study of His Relation to Modern French Thought* (Oxford, 1936), p. 123. Miss Eastwood observes that Laberthonnière is here at one with Pascal in the dynamism and universality of his notion of the affirmation of Being. 'Both . . . would replace a static and narrow self-sufficiency by a sense of dependence with its corollary of expansive, open-minded effort.' [57] *E.P.R.*, p. 71.

of existence in the flux of phenomena.[58] 'Ce n'est pas être que d'être en passant.'[59] Descartes, says Laberthonnière, was right when he said that there is no certitude apart from God. He was wrong in imagining that the affirmation of God and self was a mathematical procedure. 'Mais pour se trouver soi-même et pour trouver Dieu il ne suffit pas d'analyser, il faut se constituer en Dieu et aussi constituer Dieu en soi: il faut agir, il faut vouloir Dieu et se vouloir en lui.'[60] To him who experiences only emptiness in existence, the affirmation 'je pense, donc je suis' is no more than a vanishing shadow.[61] Certitude about Being is a very different thing from logical or mathematical certitude.[62] Being is characterized by unity and permanence, but existence in space and time is multiple and ephemeral. Thus in order to affirm Being, i.e. oneself, God, and others as subjects, one must transcend by intention the conditions of space and time.[63] To do this is to live no longer 'par le dehors' but 'par le dedans'.[64]

The argument now moves into territory which gives colour to Enrico Castelli's description of Laberthonnière's thought as 'mysticisme critique'.[65] All Being is an act of, and affirmation by, God; but if *we* are to affirm Being, it must become ours without ceasing to be God's. 'Dieu agit en nous pour que nous agissions en Lui.'[66] The Kantian critique fails most seriously 'in supposing that we are totally extrinsic to the absolute and that in order to reach it one must, as an act of desperation, make a leap into the unknown'.[67] As if charting a dangerous course (and indeed foreseeing the charges that would inevitably be brought against him), he is anxious to clear his theory from suspicion of ontologism. He is not, he says, postulating a suprasensible vision of God in

---

[58] *E.P.R.*, p. 70.   [59] Ibid., p. 71.   [60] Ibid., p. 74 and note.
[61] Ibid., p. 78.   [62] Ibid., p. 80.

[63] *E.P.R.*, p. 80. If one were to take such statements as this in isolation from Laberthonnière's commitment to the historical particularity of Christianity (expressed most clearly in *Le Réalisme chrétien*) one might be inclined to represent him as mildly gnostic. Taken as a whole, however, his position is neither gnostic nor even Platonist. The beyond is always in the midst for Laberthonnière. When he speaks of transcending space and time he is merely affirming the inherently transcendent intentionality of time- and space-bound man.

[64] *E.P.R.*, pp. 68, 81.   [65] Castelli, *Laberthonnière*, p. 6.
[66] *E.P.R.*, p. 81.   [67] Ibid.

order that we may affirm Being.[68] His main purpose is to exclude the idea that one can reach God through abstract meaning. In saying this, he avers, he is in no way excluding reason from the process. His protest is against reason appealed to, and employed, in isolation from the moral dynamism of lived reality, and he hopes he will not be accused of fideism for speaking in this way.[69]

Laberthonnière's brief but trenchant comments on the traditional proofs for the existence of God cut right across the apologetic of his age. The proofs do not, he observes, operate like theorems in geometry. To people of good will they are useful signposts of a knowledge already reached, but they always point beyond themselves. Of their very nature they are incomplete; to regard them as complete in themselves is to pull God down to our level rather than to seek to rise to his.[70] 'Consequently, to imagine that of themselves the proofs, by virtue of their demonstrative form, can give us God or enable us to know him, is a supposition so constantly belied by the facts that it is astonishing to see it still put forward.'[71] Here he puts his finger on what was perhaps the most serious weakness in scholastic apologetic. Having stated that the proofs (not merely for God's existence but, implicitly, for every stage of the case for Roman Catholic Christianity) are apodictic, it simply cannot account for the failure of these proofs to produce an inevitable result. Bad faith, darkened intellect, and weakened will are the normal and extremely lame reasons offered. Just as neo-scholasticism could never give a satisfactory analysis of what it was forced to call 'implicit faith', meaning by this term a faith which accepted truths without conscious awareness of their meaning or even of their existence, neither could it account for the failure of men and women of good will to be convinced by the arguments offered them. Billot's analysis of the act of faith, with its distinctions between 'credibilitas', 'credenditas', 'fides', and 'cognitio', leaves us

---

[68] *E.P.R.*, p. 82. Doubtless this is true; but he is resonating sympathetically with some elements in classical French Traditionalism and Ontologism. Tyrrell and Bremond, for example, recognized this when in writing to one another they refer playfully to Laberthonnière as 'Malebranche'.

[69] *E.P.R.*, p. 83.　　　[70] Ibid., p. 82.　　　[71] Ibid., pp. 82 f.

with a beautifully dissected corpse, a masterpiece of logical surgery. All it needed was the breath of life and a heart of flesh. As Laberthonnière saw it, death had occurred with the creation of the first and most fundamental dichotomy, namely, that between knowledge and faith. Years later when making an assessment of his own contribution to the debate, he chose a statement from 'Le Dogmatisme moral': 'We do not set out from knowledge so that faith may follow. We believe as we know and we know as we believe. The outcome is a complete transformation of the soul.'[72] Only thus, he comments from the wilderness, can one bring dialectical speculation into fruitful union with 'la méthode ascétique et vivante des mystiques'.[73]

The stock charge brought against Laberthonnière by his Catholic critics is that he simply did not understand the scholasticism he attacked. This charge, made by such judicious commentators as Étienne Gilson and Roger Aubert, cannot be shrugged off. Aubert writes of Laberthonnière:

Anxious to react against the exaggerated extrinsicism (which he exaggerated still more) of some of his adversaries, he came eventually to give the impression of criticizing the very idea of a faith which would have for its sole motive the authority of a revealing God instead of a kind of direct intuition of truth.[74]

That Laberthonnière exaggerated the rationalism of his neo-scholastic opponents is probably true. That he exaggerated their extrinsicism must remain a matter of opinion. The point at issue is one not of degree but of kind. It is a question of one's basic conception of how divine revelation takes place and is certified as divine in origin. Aubert's implied antithesis between 'the authority of a revealing God' and 'direct intuition of truth' repeats in gentler language the case brought against Laberthonnière by Lebreton.[75] It seems to assume that divine authority as a motive for faith must be *empirically* certifiable. In reply to Lebreton, Laberthonnière made it abundantly clear that his employment of the method of immanence implied no neglect, still less denial, of the authority of God as a motive for faith. He merely located the

[72] *E.P.R.*, p. 84. Lecanuet, op. cit., p. 530.   [73] Ibid.
[74] R. Aubert, *Problème*, p. 310.   [75] See below, pp. 113–15.

manifestation of that authority within, rather than outside, the believer. In his opinion scholasticism failed completely to appreciate that divine authority as a motive for faith, not merely can, but must, have an interior reference which takes precedence over any external manifestation which may be present.

Laberthonnière shared Blondel's view that scholastic apologetic was ineffective because of its refusal to see that contemporary philosophical critique advanced a case to which any worthwhile apologetic had to respond, if it were to be taken seriously as apologetic and not simply as ideological reiteration. He went further than this: he held that such an apologetic was not only intellectually deficient; it lacked a moral dimension. He described the method it employed as 'empirical' and to this he contrasted the method of immanence.[76] Empirical apologetics in his view simply juxtaposed supernatural revelation alongside natural man as an appendage ('superfétation').

> Religion would thus be nothing more than a *superstition* (in the etymological sense of the word) foreign to moral life; and the God of religion would have for us no other character than that of a *power* commanding us from on high, arbitrarily, as slaves are commanded. It would therefore become truly something *heteronomous*, that is to say, a slavery, to use the language of contemporary philosophers.[77]

Empirical apologetics thus creates for itself the problem of reconciling two orders of truths. This false dualism, he remarks, is a pseudo-problem.

The method of immanence, however, avoids this false and harmful dichotomy. With Pascal it accepts a dualism, not the abstract dualism of two orders, but the concrete dualism of man divided within himself.[78] Supernature heals this division not by juxtaposition or superimposition, but by penetrating and impregnating nature from within.[79]

> Being Christian does not mean adding supernatural thoughts and acts to natural thoughts and acts; it means imparting a supernatural character to all our thoughts and acts. It is, as it were, a raising of our entire being to a new power.[80]

[76] L. Laberthonnière, 'L'Apologétique et la méthode de Pascal', in *E.P.R.*, p. 171.

[77] *E.P.R.*, pp. 173 f.   [78] Ibid., p. 178.

[79] Ibid., p. 181.   [80] Ibid., p. 182.

The effect of supernatural grace is unification of the whole man, not his stratification into two levels of existence, one natural, the other supernatural.

Thanks to this conception (which in the last analysis is the Augustinian and Thomist conception, of a supernature which, for all that it is transcendent, is not any the less immanent in nature, since it penetrates and informs nature) there no longer exists for Pascal philosophy on the one hand and Christianity on the other.[81]

Aubert's claim that Laberthonnière had forced an opposition between the fact of divine revelation as a motive for faith, on the one hand, and a direct intuition of the truth, on the other, seems to overlook the implications of the scholastic distinction between the preamble to faith and the act of faith itself. It was this distinction which Laberthonnière wished to repudiate, for it construed divine revelation and the motives for accepting it as externally imposed. Remove the distinction and the objection falls away. God's authority is resplendently present in the *fait intérieur*. Laberthonnière's 'ontologism' is not an intuition of the divine essence; it is an apprehension from the inside ('du dedans', as he never tired of saying) through which the believer recognizes the presence *and authority* of God operating within the being of the believer. Laberthonnière's conception of immanence is designed to avoid 'heteronomy', that is, the acceptance of a divinely authenticated package in advance of knowing its contents. For him the divine authority is manifested in the content, which unifies human experience so that faith and knowledge are fused into a graced dynamic. Thus there is no more reason for seeking to reconcile natural knowledge with supernatural faith than there would be for seeking to reconcile mathematics with morality.

Since Laberthonnière did not lack for enemies we might expect that he would have been grateful for as many academically reputable allies as he could find. Edouard Le Roy could not understand Laberthonnière's rejection of a common intellectual bond between them.[82] In point of fact,

---

[81] *E.P.R.*, p. 183.

[82] 'Vous me dites une fois de plus que vous sentez une divergence entre nous. Je serais content de la voir se préciser, car je n'arrive pas à l'apercevoir. Il me semble qu'il y a seulement un malentendu verbal.' (M.-T. Perrin (ed.), *Laberthonnière et ses amis* (Paris, 1975), pp. 128 f.)

however, both Laberthonnière and Blondel were frankly embarrassed by Le Roy's intervention, initiated in 1905 by an article written for *La Quinzaine* and entitled 'Qu'est-ce qu'un dogme?'.[83]

Le Roy was a disciple of Henri Bergson, but his case against the scholastic understanding of revelation, faith, and dogma had much in common with that of Blondel and, especially, of Laberthonnière. There was a certain brashness about Le Roy which Blondel and Laberthonnière found distasteful. They seem to have regarded him as a well-intentioned bull in an already damaged china shop. There is a directness and clarity about Le Roy's style which is refreshing when placed alongside the tortuous prose of Blondel. He was perhaps too similar to Laberthonniére for the latter's comfort. Le Roy relished academic conflict and entered into it with the sort of panache which seemed to Blondel to lack philosophical gravity and balance.[84] Le Roy simply cut the knot which Blondel and Laberthonnière were trying laboriously to untie. Like them he attacked the 'intellectualism' of traditional Catholic theology and apologetic. Like them too he made his criticisms as a philosopher who wished to commend Catholicism to the scholars of his age but found himself unable to do so as long as Catholic orthodoxy insisted on presenting dogma as revealed truth directed towards the intellect considered as a faculty separated from the will. He described this separation as 'morcelage' and regarded it as the most damaging feature of the intellectualist conception of dogma. For him, intellect and will are immanent to each other, and this mutual interpenetration is made perfectly evident by psychological observation and the data of religious experience. The intellectual conception of

[83] E. Le Roy, 'Qu'est-ce qu'un dogme?', *La Quinzaine*, 63 (1905), pp. 495–526. In 1907 Le Roy incorporated an amended version of this article in a book entitled *Dogme et critique* (Paris, 1907), pp. 1–34, together with responses to it published in a variety of journals, and his own reply to these responses. *Dogme et critique* was placed on the Index of Prohibited Books two months after its publication. Le Roy submitted but changed nothing of his views.

[84] Blondel accused Le Roy of wielding an over-facile pen 'which achieves clarity at the expense of accuracy and balance' (*B.V.*, vol. 1, p. 225). Le Roy's ideas on miracle, together with criticisms of them by Blondel, Laberthonnière, and others, are discussed in F. Rodé, *Le Miracle dans la controverse moderniste* (Paris, 1965), pp. 183–242.

dogma is based, as he sees it, on a denial of the freedom and autonomy of the human person. This is why he treats dogma as the test-case for an understanding of the relationship between transcendent reality and the believer.

Le Roy is careful to define what he means by dogma. It is the 'dogmatic proposition', the 'dogmatic formula', that he is referring to, not the truth which underlies the formula.[85] He then poses the problem. As a Catholic he accepts the authority of dogma. As a philosopher, however, he finds himself faced with a universal rejection by his fellow-philosophers, not of this or that dogma, but of the very notion of dogma.[86] Modern thought will not accept a generalized system of unproved and unprovable propositions of allegedly transcendent origin.[87] If the proffered proof is an extrinsic one bearing no relation to the autonomy of the human mind, it does violence to that mind.[88] Even if dogmas, thus extrinsically understood, possessed the authority attributed to them by scholastic theologians, they would need to be perfectly intelligible and utterly unambiguous if they were to be accorded a firm assent. Expressed as they are, however, in concepts and language which constantly become outmoded, the problem they occasion becomes one, not of acceptance or rejection, but of meaning.[89] Finally, and most fatally of all, dogmas, by the claim of immutability made on their behalf, purport to use language in a manner totally different from that of other branches of learning.[90] As a philosopher he accepts these objections as valid. Therefore as a Catholic he must search for a manner of interpreting dogma which will not be vulnerable to them. An intellectualist interpretation is fatal from the start. God is not a learned professor who, by the sheer weight of his authority, imposes on his audience notions they are incapable of understanding for themselves.[91] Such extrinsicist pedagogy would lead only to anthropomorphism. Le Roy then gives as instances the dogmas of divine personality, the resurrection of Christ, and the real eucharistic presence. Literal understanding of these

[85] Le Roy, *Dogme et critique* [*D.C.*], p. 3 n.   [86] Ibid., p. 6.
[87] Ibid., pp. 6 f.   [88] Ibid., pp. 7–10.
[89] Ibid., pp. 10–12.   [90] Ibid., pp. 12–13.
[91] Ibid., p. 16.

dogmas is, he remarks, philosophically impossible. A closer examination shows that dogmas are essentially negative: they seek to exclude erroneous beliefs.[92] The correct way to approach them critically is through the historical method. He then states his basic thesis: 'A dogma has principally a *practical* meaning. It states first and foremost a prescription of the practical order.'[93] He here quotes Laberthonnière: '[Dogmas] have a moral and practical meaning; they have a living meaning ("un sens vital") more or less accessible to us in a manner commensurate with the intensity of our spirituality.'[94] 'Why not, therefore', asks Le Roy, 'bring theory into harmony with practice?' He emphasizes that his understanding of 'practice' is very wide and is broadly synonymous with the terms 'action' and 'experience'.[95] He does not intend to contrast it with thought, and therefore he coins the phrase 'pensée-action' to describe his theory. 'Pensée-action' becomes for him a mode of interpretation of dogma. A dogma must be lived in before it can be understood. This moral pragmatism ensures that the scholar has no advantage over the charcoal-burner. Cleverness is of no avail in understanding dogma.[96] Le Roy closes his essay by summarizing his case in two propositions. (1) 'The intellectualist conception in vogue today makes it impossible to answer the majority of objections arising out of the nature of dogma.' (2) 'On the other hand, a doctrine of the primacy of action allows the problem to be resolved without any denial of the rights of thought or the demands of dogma.'[97]

Le Roy's position becomes still clearer in his replies to his critics. In answer to Wehrlé he develops his thought in a few masterly pages. 'Those who have manufactured the barbarous term *Immanentism* and are guilty of the crude mistake of transforming a *method* into a *doctrine* are themselves creating the enemy they are fighting and are fabricating the absurdity over which they then triumph effortlessly.'[98] The principle of immanence and the scholastic notion of 'nature' are totally incompatible. The concept of nature is static.[99]

---

[92] *D.C.*, pp. 21 f. [93] Ibid., p. 25. [94] Ibid., p. 25.
[95] Ibid., pp. 25–30. [96] Ibid., p. 32. [97] Ibid., p. 34.
[98] Ibid., p. 60.
[99] Le Roy takes his definition of nature from H. Hurter, one of the principal manualists of the age: 'quidquid rei definitione continetur' (*D.C.*, p. 61).

Nature thus understood is a thing, an abstraction, incapable of change or movement. It is curious, he shrewdly remarks, that both the scholastics and Kant are guilty of 'the same abuse of spatial metaphors' and both display 'the same attitude of a logician imprisoned in the timeless and immobile world of abstractions'.[100] Under these conditions of thought there is a total and irrefragable incompatibility between the principle of immanence and the affirmation of the supernatural.[101] Le Roy shows a greater courage and logic than the Blondelians. In bold terms he states the basic problem as that of reconciling the principle of immanence with an affirmation of the supernatural. His solution is, as one would expect, a thoroughly Bergsonian one. 'Human nature is more a *progression*, a *becoming*, than a *thing*'.[102] The principle of immanence respects this conception of nature by its recognition that what matters is not so much 'truth in itself as our manner of entering into a relationship with it'.[103] Supernatural truth therefore does not come to us as a thing, extrinsic and heterogeneous to our mind. 'A heavenly body ('aérolithe') of this kind, falling from above, can reach you only by clouting you on the head.'[104] Any life-giving truth must have its roots within us; if it did not, 'it would be like discussing philosophy with an animal'.[105]

In the same year as *Dogme et critique* Le Roy published an article in the *Revue de métaphysique et de morale* on the problem of God.[106] In it he examined the classical proofs for the existence of God[107] and concluded that the arguments were insufficient but not without value. In the second part of the article he turned to the problem of our knowledge of God. His Bergsonian vitalism results in something like Process theology. We know God, he says, by God's very life within us making for our deification. 'In this sense we can go so far as to say that, for us, God does not exist but becomes. His becoming is our very progress, and like all progress, can be

---

[100] *D.C.*, p. 61.   [101] Ibid., p. 62.   [102] Ibid.

[103] Ibid., p. 63.   [104] Ibid., p. 63.   [105] Ibid.

[106] Le Roy republished this article ('aujourd'hui introuvable') as the first part of his book, *Le Problème de Dieu* (Paris, 1930), pp. 13-133. References here are to the book.

[107] Le Roy, *Le Problème de Dieu*, pp. 13-75.

known only by lived intuition, not by conceptual analysis.'[108]
Le Roy does not deny that concepts have a role to play, but
he specifies the role carefully: they are signposts on the road
marking experience already acquired, indicating direction and
reminding us of the 'énergie motrice' impelling us along the
road. In the last analysis it is religious experience which
matters.[109] Religious experience, however, 'is essentially a
traditional and social experience' resulting from our solidarity with each other, both living and dead. 'Faith in God
manifests itself as the envelope of all moral experience:
acquiring it, increasing it, and verifying it is not the task of
a moment or of an individual, but of all life.'[110]

In September 1907, Laberthonnière began a series of long
articles in the *Annales* under the title 'Dogme et théologie'.[111]
Over-long, repetitive, and argumentative, these articles do not
show him at his best and tend to bear out the truth of
Aubert's remark that he needed 'to think against someone'.
In them he sought to situate himself somewhere between
Le Roy's pragmatism and the scholastic intellectualism of
Jules Lebreton who took Laberthonnière to task in an article
published in 1908.[112] Lebreton's case against Laberthonnière
was a firm restatement of the Vatican Council's teaching that
faith is a supernatural virtue by which the believer accepts as
true what God has revealed, not because of the intrinsic
truth of what has been revealed, but because of the authority
of God who makes the revelation. 'From the start', wrote
Lebreton, 'one point is beyond doubt: certain objects of
faith are such that no natural intuition can attain to them,
and that revelation alone can bring them to our knowledge.'[113]

Laberthonnière, comparing Le Roy's pragmatism with
Lebreton's scholasticism, finds that in spite of the radical

---

[108] *Le problème de Dieu*, p. 131.
[109] Ibid., p. 132.   [110] Ibid., pp. 132 f.
[111] L. Laberthonnière, 'Dogme et théologie', I, in *A.P.C.*, 4 (1907), pp. 561–
601; II, 5 (1907), pp. 10–65; III, 5 (1908), pp. 479–521; IV, 7 (1908), pp. 5–79;
V, 9 (1909), pp. 279–313. Incidental to 'Dogme et théologie' see also 'Réponse
à M. Lebreton', in *A.P.C.* 5 (1908), pp. 624–33; 'Discussion – Réponse à M.
Rousselot', in *A.P.C.* 9 (1910), pp. 397–420, 527–35.
[112] J. Lebreton, 'La Connaissance de foi', in *Études*, 117 (1908), pp. 731–57.
It is worth recalling Tyrrell's remark that Lebreton was a fair-minded opponent
(G. Tyrrell, *Through Scylla and Charybdis* (London, 1907), p. 310).
[113] Lebreton, art. cit., p. 733.

differences between the two positions, they share a common extrinsicism. Pushing paradox as far as it would go, he declared that both positions were not merely extrinsicist but agnostic.[114] 'If the pragmatism of one is a self-confessed agnosticism, the intellectualism of the other is an unacknowledged agnosticism. There you have the difference between them.[115] Extrinsicism leads to agnosticism; and it is the extrinsicist conception of revelation which forces both Le Roy and Lebreton into fighting an essentially pointless battle, trying to settle the false problem posed by the urge to reconcile intellectual autonomy with an externally imposed truth.[116] The piquancy of this challenge lay less in describing Le Roy as an extrinsicist than in the labelling of Lebreton as an agnostic. By implication Laberthonnière was stigmatizing as agnostic the view of revelation implied in Pius X's encyclical *Pascendi*. Le Roy, says Laberthonnière, interprets dogma as an extrinsic communication about conduct, while Lebreton interprets it as an extrinsic communication about truth.

The truth thus communicated is as extrinsic to the mind, as inaccessible, as impenetrable, as unknowable for him [Lebreton] as it is for M. Le Roy. He wants dogma to be a notion, but a notion extrinsically transcendent, one might even say spatially transcendent, through a noumenal transcendence implying radical disjunction, since the reality expressed by this notion can in no way enter into our experience and be the subject of mental intuition. In his eyes, as in those of M. Le Roy, the supernatural character of dogma can be preserved only under these conditions. That is why I say that at the roots of both positions you find the same agnosticism.[117]

This is the sort of polemic which makes Laberthonnière so stimulating — or infuriating — to read. The point is implicit in Blondel's case against scholasticism, but Blondel lacked the intrepidity to make it explicitly. Lebreton, arguing the scholastic case with greater cogency than most of his contemporaries, had nevertheless to construe divine revelation as extrinsic to the believer, precisely because his conception of supernature demanded this radical disjunction between the believer's personal dispositions and the truths put forward

[114] Laberthonnière, 'Dogme et théologie', in *A.P.C.* 7 (1908), p. 6.
[115] Ibid., pp. 7 f.   [116] Ibid., p. 8.   [117] Ibid., p. 10.

for his belief.[118] 'And when M. Lebreton speaks directly of transcendence and supernature, he always allows it to be understood, if he does not say so explicitly, that this transcendence and this supernature demand this radical disjunction.[119] Faith is thus robbed of its moral and personal dimension. 'With the liberal protestants it was faith without belief: here it is belief without faith.'[120]

Laberthonnière's insistence on the 'moral and practical' meaning of dogma forced him to discriminate between his position and that of Le Roy who had cited him approvingly in this connection. He made the discrimination by rejecting what he described as Le Roy's radical dichotomy between pure speculation and pure practice.[121] If he repudiated the sort of segregation ('separatisme') which made pure speculation sufficient to itself, it was, he observed, certainly not in order to reaffirm it in favour of a doctrine of pure practice. The concept of action demands a dynamic reciprocation between thought and practice.[122] Laberthonnière concludes the last part of his extremely long article with the claim that what he was trying to say about the harmony between faith and knowledge is no more and no less than fidelity to one of St. Augustine's most characteristic insights.

Perhaps it is Laberthonnière's Augustinianism which most sets him apart from his scholastic contemporaries. He was able to read Augustine without scholastic spectacles and to find in Augustine that concern for the 'heart', the 'affections', and the conative side of life, which was so conspicuously lacking in the scholastic tradition. As a philosopher by profession Laberthonnière was in no danger of underestimating the importance of the mind in the things of the spirit. He would, however, have applauded Blake's conviction that 'thought alone can make monsters, the affections cannot.' He had therefore to face the problem of harmonizing thought with total human experience. As a Blondelian he redefined truth as the alignment of the intellect, not with a

---

[118] *A.P.C.* 5 (1908), p. 503.　　　　[119] Ibid., p. 495.
[120] 'Avec les protestants libéraux c'était la foi sans croyance: maintenant c'est la croyance sans foi', ibid., p. 511.　　　　[121] Ibid. (1907), pp. 30–31 n.
[122] This attempt to discriminate his position from that of Le Roy is unconvincing and rests in part on a misrepresentation of Le Roy, who was careful to rule out just the sort of disjunction impugned by Laberthonnière.

given object, but with life. The result was 'la métaphysique de la charité'.[123] The intellectual programme entailed by this kind of metaphysic could not be deployed in terms acceptable to the schools. It presupposed that unfocused use of the mind which is sometimes loosely described as intuition. Coleridge would have described it as imagination and seen in it a corrective to literalism. Laberthonnière postulated it as the only mode of understanding capable of full and authentic resonance with the Word of God addressed to man. He therefore rejected with impatience the blander securities of scholastic intellectualism and embraced the rigours of a never-ending search. Augustine had linked hunger of the heart with the quest for truth, virtually sacramentalizing both the hunger and the quest. The role which Laberthonnière gave to disquiet ('l'inquiétude') in his own life and thought was exactly similar. Towards the end of his life he wrote to a friend:

Far from shaking off and seeking to escape the disquiet which possessed me from about my twentieth year and which arose out of the problems that life forced me to put to myself, I have entertained it to the best of my ability and I continue to entertain it in spite of my near seventy years. And I have the very strong feeling that it has directed me into the way that leads to light. I could say that . . . I am 'at peace' ('apaisé') . . . but it is the peace of one who is not afraid to look problems in the face.[124]

---

[123] M.-M. d'Hendecourt (ed.), *Les Fruits de l'esprit: Instructions pour une retraite*, par Lucien Laberthonnière (Paris, 1961), p. 24.
[124] Ibid., p. 10.

6 Friedrich von Hügel: Experience and Transcendence

Every instinct of Friedrich von Hügel, the whole cast of his mind, ensured his participation in the modernist movement. In the event he did more than participate in it; he became its communications and documentation centre. His command of the languages and theological literature of Protestant and Catholic Europe, his indefatigable letter-writing, his massive, though autodidact, learning, all equipped him to act as clearing office for the truncated renaissance which became the modernist crisis. His competence in both biblical scholarship and religious philosophy greatly enhanced the unifying influence he exerted upon a movement which never possessed the cohesion that its enemies bestowed on it. A radical in biblical and historical criticism, von Hügel was fundamentally conservative in philosophical theology and devotional life. After 'those terrible years' before the First World War, his highly idiosyncratic conservatism won out, and he finished his life in an Olympian isolation produced partly by his deafness and partly by the fact that he was never able to contract his conception of Catholic orthodoxy completely within the limits prescribed by a reaffirmed and mandatory neo-scholasticism. Some English Roman Catholic intellectuals, together with many Anglicans, honoured him to the end of his life and kept his memory alive in the years which followed. His thought was broad and unfinished enough to allow it to influence different people in different ways.[1] There were, for example, English Roman Catholics who drew

---

[1] John Coulson remarks that von Hügel has had a considerable influence upon Anglican theologians, 'who have been tempted to regard [him] as unrepresentative of his Church and unorthodox in his descriptions of its nature' (*Newman and the Common Tradition: A Study in the Language of Church and Society* (Oxford, 1970), p. 175). Coulson's book is a fine study of the alternative view of the Church to be found in Newman, F. D. Maurice, Blondel, Möhler, and von Hügel. As found in Newman, and through Newman in von Hügel, it derives, as Dr Coulson shows, from Coleridge.

sustenance from his spiritual teaching while discreetly, or unconsciously, ignoring the theological and philosophical thought which underlay it. Such a dichotomy was facilitated by that divorce between theology and spirituality which the triumph of neo-scholasticism had reinforced. If von Hügel appeared unorthodox, it was only from the standpoint of scholastic integralism.[2]

Opposites met quite frequently, though not always comfortably, in von Hügel. His capacious mind found room for ideas and attitudes which were not merely diverse but, in the experience of other thinkers, irreconcilable. A lesser, or at least a tidier, mind would have blown a fuse if asked to accept the input of which von Hügel's was capable. It was not the material load of information which constituted the phenomenon. Other scholars have read as widely as he; but most of them have been equipped with a filter-system which allowed for intellectual selectivity. Von Hügel was an eclectic in the non-pejorative sense of the word. He not merely considered ideas, he entertained them. Some he then excluded courteously by the back door; others he relegated to the attic to be occasionally visited; most he kept in vigorous and at times disjointed conversation in the several large living-rooms of his mind. One idea alone was banished at the front door: the doctrine or philosophy of pure immanence. Any suspicion of its presence in the attitudes, conversation, or writings of others put an immediate strain on his old-world courtesy and on the ample sympathies of his mind. Thus when the London Society for the Study of Religion, of which he was a founder, seemed to be attracting more pure immanentists to its membership than he thought desirable, he began a campaign to limit their number and even to ration their contributions (one out of every six immanentist papers was as much as he was prepared to stomach).[3]

---

[2] This contention is strongly argued by Lawrence F. Barmann in his *Baron Friedrich von Hügel and the Modernist Crisis in England* (Cambridge, 1972). See, however, Thomas M. Loome, 'The Enigma of Baron Friedrich von Hügel — as Modernist' (*Downside Review*, 91 (1973), pp. 13-34, 123-40, 204-30) where Barmann is taken severely to task on several issues, including this one. On this issue it appears to me that Barmann carries his point.

[3] M. de la Bedoyère, *The Life of Baron von Hügel* (London, 1951) [Bedoyère], pp. 256-7.

Reading von Hügel is an exercise in intellectual asceticism; the rewards are as great as the process is exhausting. His style is altogether *sui generis*. Where some writers achieve clarity by exclusion, he achieves it by accumulation. All his adjectives and adverbs, and — more dauntingly — his adjectival and adverbial phrases and clauses, are important, even where they conspire to ruin his style. To come to grips with von Hügel one must simply abandon literary aesthetics while reading him.

Von Hügel's life falls naturally into three periods: the premodernist (1852-94), modernist (1895-1910), and postmodernist (1911-25). Since his writings were the product of long maturation, I shall here extend by a few years the limit of his second period.

Von Hügel regarded the question of divine transcendence as the most crucial issue in the religious thought of his age. Some of his fellow modernists thought him obsessive about it.[4] Maurice Nédoncelle, writing in 1962, probably comes nearest to a balanced judgement when he writes: 'From 1910 on, between his two great works, *The Mystical Element* and *Eternal Life*, he was especially preoccupied with establishing the existence of a transcendent reality, and he became hypersensitive to any contrary opinion.'[5] Radical biblical criticism and considerable disillusionment with Church government barely ruffled the surface of his mind and had no perceptible effect on the deeper reaches of his faith. He had a curious facility for keeping these problems in isolation from his spiritual and devotional life. It was quite otherwise in the matter of God's transcendence. Any move away from the otherness of God, ontologically considered, threatened the very fabric of his belief and indeed of his concept of religion. (The phrase 'religionless Christianity', however one chose to interpret it, would not merely have appalled him, it would have struck him as a contradiction in terms.) Maude Petre claimed that he was 'to a great extent, reacting against his

---

[4] See, for example, Loisy, *Mémoires*, vol. iii, p. 24 where the Baron's concern for the transcendence of God is described as 'un cauchemar angoissant'; see also M. D. Petre, *Alfred Loisy: His Religious Significance* (Cambridge, 1944), p. 36.

[5] M. Nédoncelle, 'A Recently Discovered Study of von Hügel on God', in *International Philosophical Quarterly*, 2 (1962) [*I.P.Q.*], p. 6.

own previous convictions and attitude. He had dipped on the side of Immanentism further than he judged right in his later developments . . .'[6] His biographer, Michael de la Bedoyère, varied the diagnosis without reaching any greater plausibility when he suggested that

just as Loisy played a critical part in guiding von Hügel towards excessive historico–critical positions so hard to reconcile with his own great Catholic faith, so Loisy himself, in revealing the spiritual consequences in his outlook and character of the implicit denial of the basis of religion, became the occasion of von Hügel's increasing mistrust of the whole immanentist trend in Modernism . . .[7]

Bedoyère goes on to wonder why the Baron failed to extend that mistrust to an examination and revision, point by point, of his earlier beliefs. This suggestion simply misses the point that von Hügel never viewed historico–critical positions in the same light as he did ontological ones.[8]

Bedoyère made his comment in the context of a long and important letter which the Baron wrote to Professor C. C. J. Webb and which makes it perfectly clear that his only concern is with Loisy's immanentism and not at all with historico–critical matters. The letter to Webb, written in August 1910, refers to 'symptoms big and small' which

point to the *increasing prevalence of but two forces*, which certainly each is *the* very stimulant and producer of the other — *a tyrannous Transcendentalism and a sceptical Immanentism*. Is it not right, a duty, to point out that the Ontological element of Religion does not necessarily involve those abuses and hence the escape into a pure Immanentism; and to show how tyrannous, and hence again productive of the

[6] M. D. Petre, *Alfred Loisy*, p. 36. Miss Petre does not specify when and where these dips had occurred. Possibly she was thinking of some such expression as he had used in a letter to her in 1900, in which he speaks of God who '*made us in order that in a sense we might* make Him, — in and for our minds and wills' (B. Holland (ed.), *Baron Friedrich von Hügel: Selected Letters, 1896–1924* (London, 1928) [*S.L.*], p. 90, original italics). The letter, however, makes it perfectly plain that God's transcendence is not in question; but von Hügel was then far less anxious about the dangers of immanentism than he was to be later.

[7] Bedoyère, p. 247.

[8] Von Hügel sometimes failed to realize how disturbing his radical criticism could be to others, including his daughter, Gertrude. Tyrrell, who was much wiser in this respect, took him to task over the effect he was having on Gertrude (see M. D. Petre, *Von Hügel and Tyrrell: The Story of a Friendship* (London, 1937), pp. 14–26). The Baron felt remorse whenever he became aware that he had unwittingly disturbed the faith of others (see F. von Hügel, *Letters from Baron Friedrich von Hügel to a Niece* (London, 1928) [*L.N.*], p. xxxix).

counter-tyranny, can be or become such Immanentism, which, besides, kills religion and with it all Religion's special benefits?[9]

It was not the only occasion when von Hügel sought to occupy and defend middle ground,[10] but it is one of the most significant. The 'tyrannous Transcendentalism' to which he refers was, at the moment of his writing, in the process of being ruthlessly re-established by decree in Roman Catholic theology where it was to hold general sway until the 1960s. Von Hügel saw its re-establishment as unquestionably the lesser of two evils, but he justly diagnosed its counter-productive relationship with sceptical immanentism. His call for an ontological basis to religious belief implied no blanket approval for neo-scholastic metaphysics. As we shall see, he recognized, implicitly and explicitly, that all religious thinking which genuinely seeks a hearing in the post-Kantian world has to be done on the slippery slope of immanental attraction. The most one can reasonably reproach him with is the manner in which he expressed that recognition and the extreme steps he took to avoid the hazard.

In his article 'Experience and Transcendence', written in 1906, von Hügel posed the question which remained for him the most fundamental of all religious questions: '. . . how can man, the Finite and Contingent, solidly experience the Abiding and Infinite?'[11] The question, together with the answer suggested in his article, shows precisely where his theological priorities lay. Lessing's broad, ugly ditch between fact and faith was for von Hügel an interesting feature on the theological landscape, not the dominating hazard it was for other religious thinkers, including Blondel. Von Hügel's ditch lay not between fact and faith but between the contingent and the absolute; and it is noteworthy that he depicts the problematic link which connects them as not merely

---

[9] Bedoyère, p. 247, original italics.

[10] See, for example, his letter to Wilfrid Ward in which he adopts a position in the centre between 'un-catholic Liberalism' and the late nineteenth-century brand of ultramontanism (M. Ward, *The Wilfrid Wards and the Transition* (London, 1934), p. 301).

[11] F. von Hügel, 'Experience and Transcendence', in *Dublin Review*, 138 (1906) [*E.T.*], p. 357. This article is a reworking of an earlier paper with the same title read in 1903 to the Synthetic Society; see J. W. Beatie, 'Von Hügel's "Sense of the Infinite" ', in *Heythrop Journal*, 16 (1975), pp. 160 f.

cognitional but experiential. It is, however, important to register accurately what he meant by experience. The article of 1906 is our best guide towards this.

He opens his essay with the remark that whereas contemporary scientific methods have become largely inductive, Catholic theology 'remains predominantly deductive', Greco-Roman in its preoccupation with 'discursive and abstractive' method, and in consequence neglectful of the 'intuitive method' which has always had a place in Christian and Catholic thought.[12] It is this neglect which has tended to divorce theology from spirituality. Having posed his question about the contingent and the absolute, he proposes 'to show how modern is the clear conception and empirical demonstration of our actual Experience, as ever distinct from and exceeding our concurrent Attention or even our subsequent reflex Knowledge . . .' This distinction between experience, attention, and reflex knowledge is crucial to an understanding of von Hügel's epistemology. He credited Leibniz with something like a philosophical breakthrough in being the first to make the distinction between 'dim Experience' and 'reflex Knowledge'.[13] He returned to the point again two years later in his book *The Mystical Element of Religion*:

As we have already found, it is only since Leibniz that we know, systematically, how great is the range of every man's Obscure Presentations, his dim Experience as against his Clear or distinct Presentations, his explicit Knowledge; and how the Clear depends even more upon the Dim, than the Dim upon the Clear.[14]

Von Hügel's epistemic link between the contingent and the absolute is to be found expressly in 'dim Experience' which offers a middle ground between reflex knowledge and no knowledge at all.[15] He adopts towards Kant something like the approach that Kant adopted towards Hume. As von Hügel saw it, Kant's efforts to prevent Hume's ship

---

[12] *E.T.*, p. 357.　　　　　　　　[13] Ibid., p. 358.

[14] F. von Hügel, *The Mystical Element of Religion: As Studied in Saint Catherine of Genoa and Her Friends* (2nd edn., London, 1923) [*M.E.*], vol. ii, p. 338. References here are to this 2nd edn. (in the reprint of 1927) which, as von Hügel observes (p. xviii), is a 're-issue of the work of 1908' with some slight modifications and the correction of misprints.

[15] *E.T.*, p. 360. On von Hügel's epistemology see A. H. Dakin, *Von Hügel and the Supernatural* (London, 1934), pp. 3–42.

from being driven aground resulted in driving his own ship aground. Von Hügel therefore takes the wheel out of Kant's hands and points the ship towards 'dim Experience', where he claims it will find sufficient metaphysical water to keep it afloat and capable of arriving at the transcendent. It was here in the soft cognitional focus of experience that von Hügel located the primary meeting of God and man. It is hence that man is driven by the 'stinging sense of the relative and finite'.[16] The very clarities of relative and finite existence produce a longing for the absolute and infinite which is necessarily apprehended as dim. The infinite and absolute otherness to which we are thus drawn must not be separated from the contrasting relativity, lest the very medium which makes it present should disappear. A developed sense of contingency is the indispensable vehicle by which man is put in touch with the absolute: '. . . what seems the sheerest, the most fleeting of contingencies is strictly necessary for the awakening of even the simplest idea and assurance of something profoundly different, of persistent being, of space and time, of Eternity, of God Himself.'[17] We snap the delicate link between the absolute and the contingent whenever we 'treat our at first vivid experience and apprehension of it [sc. 'the contrasting Other'] as an articulated "distinct" comprehension and as a starting-point and object of strict ordinary science of the mathematico–deductive type'.[18]

It is against this epistemological background that one should examine von Hügel's tempered criticism of neo-

[16] *E.T.*, p. 362. Von Hügel had already, in 1899, postulated a 'theory of spiritual dynamics' to diagnose the presence of the transcendent in human experience. 'Stop the machinery to look, and you must not expect to see it moving; there is no such thing as a science of statics for the living forces of the soul . . .' (J. J. Kelly (ed.), 'Von Hügel on Authority', in *The Tablet*, 6 May 1978, p. 446).

[17] F. von Hügel, *Essays and Addresses on the Philosophy of Religion* [*E.A.*], vol. ii (London, 1926), pp. 106 f. See also F. von Hügel, 'Du Christ éternel et de nos christologies successives', in *La Quinzaine*, 58 (1904), p. 296: 'Suppress all contact with these lesser realities and you weaken in proportion the spiritual life.'

[18] *E.T.*, pp. 362 f. In his earlier paper on 'Experience and Transcendence' von Hügel compared our awareness of the Infinite to the awareness we might have of a 'broad-stretching, mist covered lake, only on occasion of the leaping of some fish upon its surface, and of the momentary splash accompanying the momentary glimpse of the shining silver' (cited in J. W. Beatie, 'Von Hügel's "Sense of the Infinite" ', in *H.J.* 16 (1975), p. 169).

scholasticism.[19] The 'tyrannous Transcendentalism' of contemporary Roman Catholic theology was the very seed-bed of the 'sceptical Immanentism' he so greatly dreaded. Thus he refused to bypass Kant and Feuerbach, as theologians like Billot, Pesch, and Hurter were doing. Kant's Copernican Revolution must be faced honestly and such concessions made to it as were seen to be necessary.

Kant was for von Hügel an adversary to be opposed with respect. Kant's 'greatness undoubtedly lies, not in Religion, but in Epistemology and Ethics; and, even in these, more in his acute detection of the precise nature and whereabouts of certain crucial problems and complications, than in the consistency and satisfactory character of the solutions proposed'.[20] Kant the epistemological diagnostician must be carefully heeded if Kant the theological agnostic was to be refuted. Nevertheless, even on the epistemological plane Kant's position was open to an objection which von Hügel regarded as cogent, since he makes it at several places in his writings. Its briefest expression occurs in *The Mystical Element of Religion*. Kant, says von Hügel, never admits 'the possibility that our subjective conceptions of Objective Reality may have some true relation to that Reality'.[21] He gives this observation its most forceful expression in an essay of 1909, 'Religion and Illusion',[22] in which he writes

Kant's interestingly unconscious self-contradiction here — that we can know nothing whatever about trans-subjective reality, yet that we know for certain it is in no sense like what even our deepest and most closely criticised experiences indicate it to be — can doubtless not be maintained as reasonable by any mind once vividly aware of the inconsistency.[23]

Kant's position, then, disastrous as it is for religious thought, is open to serious epistemological and logical

[19] Though he agreed with most of what Tyrrell had to say about scholasticism, he always felt that the violence of Tyrrell's language detracted from the effectiveness of his case.

[20] F. von Hügel, *Eternal Life: A Study of Its Implications and Applications* (Edinburgh, 1912) [*E L.*], p. 136.

[21] *M.E.*, vol. ii, p. 278, cf. *S.L.*, p. 356.

[22] Published in an Italian translation by Angelo Crespi in *Coenobium*, 5 (1911), pp. 5–59; republished in an expanded English version in *The Quest*, 9 (1918), pp. 353–82; and finally published in *E.A.*, vol. i (London, 1921), pp. 20–66. References here are to this latter edition.   [23] *E.A.*, vol. i, p. 51.

objection. Von Hügel, however, does not rest his case on this objection. He proceeds to an openly *a posteriori* argument: 'Can I thus experience and know God?' he asks; and he replies: 'The question is, in the first instance, *not whether I can, but whether I do*';[24] and there is no hesitation in his affirmative. His impatience with Kantian subjectivism is paralleled by an equal impatience with classical and medieval 'naif Realism',[25] and he claims support from the 'newer' sciences of Biology, Sociology, and History which 'are now fast bringing us to a third stage where truth and life will more and more evidently be found to consist in the fullest and most manifold interaction between Subject and Object . . .'[26] One is reminded in all this of Laberthonnière's description of Pascal as 'a sort of positivist, but a positivist for whom interior reality, living reality, is the essential and primordial fact'.[27] The description would fit von Hügel perfectly. Interior reality is for him something *given*, not something reached by argument. It is nothing less than the self-manifestation of God's Spirit which, together with the human spirit's response to it, 'renders superfluous all attempts, always more or less hopeless, to construct God *a priori*, or even to demonstrate Him, from the facts of nature and of human life, by any single, deductive argument of a strictly constraining force'.[28]

Our experience of God is for von Hügel (1) a fact (2) objectively given, (3) dimly apprehended, (4) together with the painful experience of contingency. Can this experience be described as revelation in the sense normally employed by Christian theology? Von Hügel is cautious in his answer. He was well aware of the hornets' nest stirred up by Blondel and Laberthonnière in their appeal to the 'method of immanence', but, like them, he had no time for scholastic extrinsicism.[29] God is experienced, and therefore self-disclosed,

---

[24] *E.A.*, vol. i, p. 52.   [25] Ibid., p. 56.

[26] Ibid. On von Hügel's critical realism see M. Nédoncelle, *Baron Friedrich von Hügel: A Study of his Life and Thought* (London, 1937), pp. 71-9.

[27] L. Laberthonnière, *Le réalisme chrétien: précédé de: Essais de philosophie religieuse*, ed. C. Tresmontant (Paris, 1966), p. 195 n.

[28] *E.A.*, vol. i, p. 57.

[29] In 'Experience and Transcendence' von Hügel shows solidarity with the Frenchmen by citing from Cardinal Dechamps, who had written that there never

in the 'natural' sense of finite and contingent insufficiency. Supernatural revelation is an intensification of the experience 'which, to become characteristically religious, requires to meet and accept fuller, more articulate manifestations of the presence and grace of God in other human lives'. The argument remains impressionistic, suggesting rather than developing lines of further investigation. Revelation is experienced as a twofold operation of the Spirit: (1) 'the general and inevitable'; (2) 'the characteristic and free'. Each requires the other 'as the ear and sense of music, stimulated only by the sounds of nature, require the organized tones of music to actually reveal the full soul of music to them . . .'[30] The distinction between general and special revelation was of course a commonplace of scholastic theology, but von Hügel employed it in a non-scholastic manner, allowing for an ebb and flow between the general and special which was quite foreign to run-of-the-mill scholasticism. He was also, it need hardly be said, much more receptive to the truth in other people's religious positions.[31]

In a letter to Wilfrid Ward, von Hügel wrote:

Is it not this, that minds belong, roughly speaking, to two classes which may be called the mystical and positive, and the scholastic and theoretical? The first of these would see all truth as a centre of intense light losing itself gradually in utter darkness; this centre would gradually extend, but the borders would ever remain fringes, they could never become clear-cut lines. Such a mihd, when weary of border-work, would sink back upon its centre, its home of peace and light, and

had been 'pure nature' in man, since human nature had been 'positively destined by its Author to a supernatural end, and consequently *interiorly prepared and disposed for such an end*'. (*Œuvres complètes de S. E. le Cardinal Dechamps*, vol. ii, pp. 373–5, as translated and cited by von Hügel in *E.T.*, p. 369; the emphasis is Dechamps's.) Dechamps's position is, he says, 'largely Platonic': there is no logical place for it in Aristotelianism, where the correlatives are intellect/truth.

[30] The concert-hall has interesting possibilities as a model for special revelation, but the Baron does not, to my knowledge, develop the analogy elsewhere in his writings. He may have borrowed it from Tyrrell's Oxford sermon, 'Insufficiency of Internal Religion', G. Tyrrell, *External Religion: Its Use and Abuse* (2nd edn., London, 1900), pp. 41–3. Neither of them appears to have been particularly musical, so perhaps the analogy lacked for them an immanent resonance.

[31] Loisy (*Mémoires*, vol. ii, p. 577), maintained that von Hügel was envisaged in *Pascendi*: 'In the conflict between different religions, the most that Modernists can maintain is that the Catholic has more truth because it is more vivid, and that it deserves with more reason the name of Christian because it corresponds more fully with the origins of Christianity.'

thence it would gain fresh conviction and courage to again face the twilight and the dark. Force it to commit itself absolutely to any border distinction, or force it to shift its home or to restrain its roamings, and you have done your best to endanger its faith and to ruin its happiness.[32]

This extremely revealing insight into von Hügel's psychology and intellectual method goes far to explain why he remained fundamentally untroubled by radical positions, including his own, on biblical and doctrinal criticism,[33] but became profoundly disturbed by any apparent attenuation of the notion of divine transcendence. The former was 'border work'; the latter bore on the 'centre' to which one withdrew for prayer, refreshment, and ultimate religious security. At that centre one encountered God, immanently present and dimly experienced, yet present and experienced as *transcendent reality*. It is this God, not the God of theological and philosophical speculation, whom one adores and before whom one enters into 'such states of recollection which, though the soul, on coming from them, cannot discover definite ideas or picturings to have been contained in them, leave the soul braced to love, work, and suffer for God and man, beyond its previous level'.[34]

This, then, is von Hügel's conception of what he called the mystical element of religion. Few words appear in modernist writing with greater frequency than 'mysticism', 'mystic', 'mystical'. Few words are as difficult to define. Throughout

---

[32] Cited, without date, in M. Ward, *The Wilfrid Wards and the Transition*, p. 301.

[33] See Bedoyère, pp. 214 f., for Tyrrell's amusing comment on the Baron's ability to separate critical thought from devotional life. A. R. Vidler (*A Variety of Catholic Modernists* (Cambridge, 1970), p. 117) quotes Tyrrell's remark in a letter to A. L. Lilley; 'The Baron has just gone, Wonderful man! Nothing is true; but the sum total of nothings is sublime!' Dr Vidler seems to me to make rather heavy weather of Tyrrell's flippancy.

[34] *M.E* , vol. ii, p. 266. He spelt out the spiritual consequences of this doctrine to his niece: 'Religion is dim − in the religious temper there should be a great simplicity, and a certain contentment in dimness. It is a great gift of God to have this temper' (*L.N.*, p. xvi). In literary terms some aspects of von Hügel's understanding of mysticism might be described as romanticism. Thus the 'contentment in dimness' bears a curious resemblance to Keats's notion of 'Negative Capability', i.e. a state of mind and heart in which 'a man is capable of being in uncertainties, mysteries, doubts, without any irritable reaching after fact and reason', cited and commented on by Raymond Williams in his *Culture and Society, 1780–1950* (Harmondsworth, Penguin Books, 1961), p. 62.

the modernist period we find the term 'mystical' most generally employed as á serviceable antonym for scholastic rationalism.[35] Von Hügel often used the term 'mystical' in a broad non-technical sense. He was, however, never as overtly anti-scholastic as Loisy, Laberthonnière, or Tyrrell, all of whom were priests reacting against their former training in theology and philosophy. As laymen, von Hügel and Blondel had not experienced the full rigours of the intellectual and spiritual hegemony of the scholastic system and hence were able to take a more detached view of it. They did not have to exorcize a daimon within themselves.[36]

Nevertheless von Hügel's generalized use of the term 'mystical' evinced a conscious antithesis to 'that mania for deceptive and very superficial clarities' which he found in Hébert. Contemporary Roman Catholic theology suffered, in his view, from the pursuit of a clarity in excess of the facts and in contradiction to the true condition of faith, a clarity which impoverished both the aesthetic sense — he always found lack of interiority to be philistine — and the mystical sense. In the deepest matters of life clarity is not possible, and to insist upon it is to pursue a chimera, thus paralysing faith and prayer.[37] To clarity von Hügel opposed vividness.

[35] Thus for example Tyrrell writes to von Hügel: '[My] . . . language is scholastic though my thought is mystic', British Library Add. MS. 44, 927.

[36] Von Hügel frequently adverts to the tendency in clerical modernists to carry over into their reactive positions the very rigidities of the system against which they were reacting. This point is important enough to illustrate. In 1906 von Hügel wrote to Tyrrell in reference to Houtin's *La Question biblique au XXe siècle* (Paris, 1906): 'That tendency to take the middle distance, — the mathematico-physical clear but artificial construction of a part of Reality, for the whole of our experience, or at least as its adequate and final type and measure: this drift which tends to make our Clerics, as soon as ever they cease to be orthodox Scholastics, into merely heterodox ones, cheerfully "clear" Philistines of the older Unitarian, Deistic kind: I find much of it here.' (*S.L.*, pp. 135–136.) A year earlier he had remarked, also to Tyrrell, '*how* easy it is for a scholastically trained mind to remain in close bondage to precisely the weakest side of its method; and this entirely unbeknown to the mind thus remaining, — through that mind developing a (conscious or unconscious) antithesis, full and relentless against its former task-master. The later dependence is one of angry and bitter, or too deep down to be be conscious, contradiction: the dependence is none the less as complete, or perhaps more mischievous in some ways, as ever it was.' (*S.L.*, p. 131.) In 1902 the Baron had written to Blondel about Marcel Hébert: '. . . je l'ai cru . . . dans l'erreur . . . difficile à expliquer, si là encore l'on ne pouvait bien facilement retrouver l'influence de la scholastique et cette manie des clartés décevantes et très superficielles' (Marlé, *Au cœur*, pp. 325 f.)   [37] *E.A.* vol. i, p. 100.

Thus we find, through actual experience and through the similar experiences of our fellow-men, that the right and proper test for the adequacy of abstractions and of spatial, numerical, mechanical relations is, indeed, clearness and ready transferableness; but that the appropriate test for the truth concerning existences and realities is vividness (richness) and fruitfulness.[38]

The fact that von Hügel employs the epithets 'vivid', 'rich', and 'dim' as being closely related with each other and with the 'mystical' in its generalized sense tells us something about his epistemology of self-transcendence. It is in this pre-analytical ambience that Religion (the word demands a Hügelian capital) takes place. Religion is the response to a conviction about the ontological presence of God, a presence which precedes all subjectivity, is simply 'given' and to which the appropriate response is adoration.[39] Religion is thus mystical by definition. It precedes theology and is even, as we have seen, a sort of refuge from theology.[40]

Having firmly established the ontological priority of the pre-conceptual, pre-analytical character of religion and mysticism, von Hügel then subjects both to careful analysis, synthesis, and even systematization. The mysticism (in its more precise sense) which he wishes to commend and promote

---

[38] *E.A.*, vol. i, pp. 104 f. This letter, in effect a fine essay on the mystery of evil and suffering, raises the question of Newman's influence on von Hügel. The sentence quoted above is a straight gloss, without attribution, on *The Grammar of Assent* and in particular on Newman's distinction between the notional and the real. Discussing Hellenism in *The Mystical Element*, vol. i, pp. 10 f., von Hügel poses the problem in characteristically Newmanian terms: 'We revert then to the apparent interior antinomy from which we started, — the particular concrete experience which alone moves us and helps to determine our will, but which, seemingly, is untransferable, indeed unrepeatable; and the general, abstract reasoning which *is* repeatable, indeed transferable, but which does not move us or help directly to determine the will.' It has been suggested, by R. K. Browne ('Newman and von Hügel: A Record of an Early Meeting', *The Month*, 26 (1961), p. 33) that von Hügel had assimilated Newman's thought so thoroughly that he was no longer conscious of his debt to the latter. John Coulson (*Newman and the Common Tradition*, pp. 174–8) discusses the relationship between the two, concluding that where von Hügel was interested in religion generally, Newman was interested specifically in the Christian Church. 'What Newman gave von Hügel was a logical model for the analysis of religion into its elements.' (Ibid., p. 177.)

[39] He wrote to his niece: 'I want you to hold very clearly the *otherness* of God, and the littleness of men. If you don't get that you can't have adoration, and you cannot have religion without adoration.' (*L.N.*, p. xvii.)

[40] Von Hügel was greatly influenced by Tyrrell's seminal essay, 'The Relation of Theology to Devotion' (*The Month*, 94 (1899), pp. 461–73).

is achieved only by a careful process of checks and balances. Thus rather than define the term in advance of discussing it, he allows its meaning to emerge inductively from his multi-layered impressionistic study of it in *The Mystical Element*.[41] Having established to his satisfaction the existence (rather than the mere possibility) of a direct, experiential, though dim, contact between God and man, von Hügel is anxious to limit that contact by careful qualifications. Above all, he wishes to exclude all forms of gnosticism: his mysticism is rooted firmly in time and place. He will not have transcendence at the price of escaping from the scandalous particularity of Christian faith. He makes this point with great force while treating of Hellenism. From the mystical standpoint the Hellenistic process culminates in Plotinus and Proclus whom von Hügel applauds for their concern with transcendence but whom he finds finally and fatally lacking because of their anti-incarnationalism. Hellenistic realism is one of 'all-devouring Abstraction'[42] 'The system . . . is . . . profoundly anti-Immanental, anti-Incarnational: a succession of increasingly exalted and increasingly empty Transcendences, each of which is, as it were, open upwards but closed downwards . . .'[43] Von Hügel had no time for a purely ascending transcendentalism: God has first descended the ladder which man must ascend. Von Hügel frequently rejects 'pure' or 'exclusive' mysticism and propounds the need for 'mixed', i.e. incarnational mysticism. He will not allow 'a specifically distinct, self-sufficing, purely Mystical mode of apprehending Reality'.[44]

[41] Joseph P. Whelan (*The Spirituality of Friedrich von Hügel* (London, 1971), p. 82) has extracted a definition from the Baron's article on the Gospel of St. John in the 11th edn. of *The Encyclopedia Britannica*, xv, p. 455: Mysticism is 'the intuitive and emotional apprehension of the most specifically religious of all truths, viz., the already full operative existence of eternal beauty, truth, goodness, of infinite Personality and Spirit, independently of our action'. This definition, it will be noticed, while specifying intuition and emotion as the apprehending faculties of mystical response, is characteristically careful to safeguard the transcendence and givenness of the Being to whom the response is made.

[42] *M.E.*, vol. i, p. 24. It is instructive to note that part of his case against Hébert rests on the same conviction: '. . . I am sad only at seeing how entirely the reaction against Scholasticism can remain under the fascination of the Fragestellung of the latter, boiling all things down to the most abstract of abstractions . . .' (*S.L.*, p. 109). Preoccupation with abstraction always signified for the Baron a failure in spiritual maturity.   [43] *M.E.*, vol. i, p. 25.   [44] Ibid., ii, p. 283.

His celebrated analysis of religion into its three elements, viz., the institutional, the intellectual, and the intuitional, experimental, and mystical, is closely relevant to his understanding of man's approach to the transcendent.[45] He sees each of these elements as corresponding to human development from childhood, through adolescence, into mature adulthood. The child's first contacts with religion are on the external, imaginative, plane. He is relatively passive and unquestioning in the face of what is offered to him by those around him. As a youth he needs to question and even oppose what he has previously accepted. His ability to create abstractions provides him with the means of posing his questions. Religion at this stage becomes 'Thought, System, a Philosophy'. The mature adult, however, feels the need to complement the first two stages by the exercise of will and action.

Man's emotional and volitional, his ethical and spiritual powers, are now in ever fuller motion, and they are met and fed by the third side of religion, the Experimental and Mystical. Here religion is rather felt than seen or reasoned about, is loved and lived rather than analysed, is action and power, rather than either external fact or intellectual verification.[46]

Von Hügel is deploying his argument here on two levels. The first level is descriptive, a piece of straightforward educational psychology. By today's criteria it may seem somewhat over-simple. But it is the second level which matters to his main argument. On this level the three educative stages, successive on the first level, became a model for understanding the concomitant and *abiding* elements of religion. The three stages must be seen not as successive but as cumulative. In the language of a later age, they are synchronically rather than diachronically related. Just as, at the first descriptive level of the argument, the passage from childhood to adolescence and from adolescence to adulthood is marked by a crisis, so the synchronic relationship of the three elements is one of fruitful tension.[47] The temptation is to cling to one

[45] For the following see *M.E.*, vol. i, pp. 50-5.   [46] Ibid., p. 53.
[47] Ibid., pp. 53 f. It is worth noting that this is one of the places where von Hügel expresses in a footnote his debt to Newman, citing the Preface to *The Via Media* (1877), vol. i, pp. xv-xciv.

of the three elements while evading the just claims of one or both of the other two. To cultivate the institutional alone is to assimilate religion to economics and politics, thus causing religion to shrivel up into one thing alongside others in life. To cultivate the intellectual at the expense of the institutional and the mystical is to assimilate religion to science and philosophy, causing it to grow hard and shallow. To cultivate the mystical at the expense of the first two elements is to fall into 'shifting subjectivity', and thus exposure to the 'tyranny of mood and fancy', and finally into 'fanaticism'.

By his insistence on the need for an abiding correlation of the three elements of religion in the life of the Christian, von Hügel in effect defined what he meant by genuine mysticism. In analysing the dialectical relationship between mysticism on the one hand and the institutional and rational on the other he showed that his understanding of the term mystical embraced a carefully worked out system of risks, checks, and balances. Something of what he meant by 'mystical' would today perhaps be categorized as existential. His comments on Kierkegaard are illuminating in this respect. He clearly warms to Kierkegaard's existential commitment to the ontological reality of God. He compares 'the deep, melancholy, strenuous, utterly uncompromising' Dane to Pascal and Hurrell Froude.[48] He recognizes that Kierkegaard cannot be classified as mystical in the full Hügelian sense, precisely because Kierkegaard's view of divine transcendence is so radical that it breaks the slender cognitive link between God and man by its denial of any similarity between them. 'Thus it is Kierkegaard's profound apprehension of the Ontology and the Difference [sc. between God and man] which renders him religiously deep and powerful, beyond all the Subjectivists and Identity-thinkers put together; and it is his lack of insight as to the Likeness which leaves his life strained to the verge of insanity.'[49] Paradoxically, Kierkegaard, recognized by von Hügel as profoundly religious, is nevertheless disqualified for inclusion under any of the latter's three categories. Kierkegaard's rejection of the Danish Church, his extreme reaction against Hegel, and his denial of any

---

[48] *E.L.*, p. 260.   [49] Ibid., p. 262.

similarity between God and man involve respectively a rejection of the institutional, the rational, and the mystical
elements of religion. One has the impression that von Hügel
did not quite know what to do with Kierkegaard and was,
indeed, over-hasty in describing him as 'tragically non-
mystical',[50] merely on the grounds of his emphasis on the
otherness of God and the fact that 'continuous volitional
strain and conflict left him no time for mystical contempla-
tion'.[51]

Dim and indistinct as the cognitive link between man and
God might be, it was for von Hügel none the less absolutely
indispensable. This is why he would not allow the mystical
element to be divorced from the rational. He quotes and
flatly rejects Wilhelm Herrmann's claim that 'There exists no
Theory of Knowledge for such things as we hold to be real
in the strength of faith. In such religious affirmations, the
believer demolishes every bridge between his conviction and
that which Science can recognize as real.' Von Hügel
interprets this Ritschlian position as an extreme reaction
from 'the contrary metaphysical excesses of the Hegelian
school'.[52]

Von Hügel's rejection of agnostic transcendentalism,
though firm, is always measured and sympathetic. His rejection of pantheistic immanentism is uncompromising and even
a trifle hectic. Maude Petre's suggestion that his hypersensitivity on the subject derived from his having 'dipped on
the side of Immanentism' misconstrues the situation by
implying that he was, as it were, doing penance for *past*
misdeeds. If there is a personal dimension to his reaction,
apart, that is, from his conviction that several modernists had
gone unacceptably far in an immanentist direction, it was the
realization that he needed to keep a continuing and sharp
watch over his own instincts in the matter. Nor would he
have been unduly embarrassed to be confronted with this
observation.

The orthodox mystic, he remarks, shares three special
attraits with the pantheist: first, a thirst for unity, a distaste
for multiplicity, and a consequent attraction to monistic

[50]*M.E.*, vol. ii, p. 287.   [51]*E.T.*, p. 373.   [52]*M.E.*, vol. ii, p. 269.

immanence; second, a call away from individualistic self-centredness; third, a tendency to escape from the 'Successive and Temporal' to the 'Simultaneity and Eternity of God'.[53] The attraction to pantheism is a good thing and can give depth and interiority to life, provided that it is kept under strict control — a sort of platonic flirtation conducted under the stern glance of a metaphysical policeman.[54] Von Hügel approaches pantheism as something one has to experience in a mild form in order to build up a resistance to its virulent strain. Science can provide the necessary inoculation.

> . . . the principles, ideals, and picturings of Mathematics and Physics (with their insistence upon ruthless law, utter interchangeableness of all individual instances, and flawless determinism) have a very special place and function in the full spiritual life of the soul. For they provide that *preliminary* Pantheism, that transition through fate and utter dehumanization, which will allow the soul to affirm, ultimately and as ultimate, a Libertarianism and Personalism free from all sentimentality or slovenliness, and immune against the attacks of *ultimate* Pantheism, which can *now* be vanquished as only the caricature of the poorer half of a far richer whole.[55]

In this suggestive passage he is more concerned with the deterministic and impersonal aspect of pantheism than with its excessive subjectivism. Christianity has been historically sandwiched between the abstract determinism of both Hellenism and Science, and it must continually relate itself to both, even as it must finally transcend both.[56] The clarity, 'iron Necessity', and monism promoted by Science are 'purgatorial' for the believer,[57] who must be ready to pass through the scientific experience, allowing to Science its proper autonomy and not introducing religion into its processes.[58] Coming from 'such rigorous, disinterested phenomenal analysis', man turns to God 'more happily and humbly'.[59] Von Hügel was a strong proponent of the

---

[53] *M.E.*, vol. ii, pp. 328 f.

[54] Loisy uses the phrase 'gendarme métaphysique' to describe von Hügel's God (*Mémoires*, vol. iii, p. 107).

[55] *E.L.*, p. 388; see also F. von Hügel, 'Petite consultation sur les difficultés concernant Dieu', in P. Scoppola, *Crisi modernista e rinnovamento cattolico in Italia* (Bologna, 1961) [*P.C.*], p. 382.

[56] *M.E.*, vol. i, pp. 48 f.   [57] Ibid., p. 41.

[58] Ibid., p. 44.   [59] Ibid., p. 45.

'costingness' of religious affirmation. He opposes fideism not simply because it seeks to eliminate the rational element of religion, but also because it makes religious affirmation *intellectually* a cheap grace. The affirmation of divine transcendence and personality has real meaning and value only for him who has experienced the attraction of immanent, impersonal monism. It is only after one has passed through this 'preliminary pantheism' and has gone on to affirm the reality and otherness of God that one is ready to formulate the true doctrine of immanence.

This doctrine is called by von Hügel 'panentheism': 'an intense consciousness of the prevenient, all-pervasive presence of God'.[60] Von Hügel's concept of panentheism was a deliberate *via media* between pantheism proper ('affirming the simple Divinity of the innermost centre of the soul') and the 'tyrannous Transcendentalism' of neo-scholasticism which declared 'that the soul ever experiences only by the Grace of God, *i.e.* certain created effects, sent by Him from the far-away seat of His own full presence'. Panentheism, 'whilst ever holding the definite creatureliness of the soul, in all its reaches, puts God Himself into the soul and the soul into God . . .'[61]

Having pondered Tyrrell's article 'Da Dio o dagli uomini?', von Hügel wrote to its author that he regarded the reformulation of the idea of God in immanental terms as 'most tempting' but an 'impoverishing simplification'. Instead, we must learn to interpret spatial imagery in terms of a spiritualized experience which is 'as truly of God transcendent as of God immanent'. Recourse to total immanence would bring to nothing the 'religious experience of tip-toe expectation, of unfulfilled aspiration'.[62] The 'unfulfilled aspirations' argument is one of the central Hügelian convictions. The 'tip-toe expectations' is a pointer to his eventual position on eschatology.[63] Eschatological expectation was, for von Hügel, one of the

---

[60] *E.T.*, pp. 374 f.
[61] *M.E.* vol. ii, p. 336. Dakin remarks (*Von Hügel and the Supernatural*, p. 158) that 'a term like "panentheism" formulates rather than resolves the difficulty.'   [62] *S.L.*, p. 139.
[63] Which he worked out later in an address he gave in 1919 to a meeting of (Anglican) clergy of Birmingham, 'The Apocalyptic Element in the Teaching of Jesus', *E.A.* vol. i, pp. 119–43.

correctives to over-emphasis on the mystical element of
religion. He found it 'profoundly impressive to note how
intractable the Synoptic Jesus remains to all purely mystical
interpretation: Evelyn Underhill's recent attempt is as able
as it is unconvincing.'[64] The 'not yet' is a constant reminder
of the inescapably incarnational, historical, dimension of
Christian life. It supplies a point of friction; and von Hügel
believed in the spiritual benefits of friction.[65]

In the last analysis, however, it is not to eschatology but
to history that von Hügel goes for his understanding of divine
immanence. It is only in history that revelation takes place at
all fully, and only in Jesus Christ that it takes place 'in a
supreme and normative manner'.[66] The answer to pure mysticism is a sound christology, and a sound christology depends
on a correct apprehension of the historicity of Christ. A
superficial reading of von Hügel's emphasis on the mystical
element of religion might lead one to expect at this point an
exposition of 'Christ-mysticism'. On the contrary, he takes
Schleiermacher to task for his insistence on 'the Johannine
picture as so entirely historical and an eye-witness's testimony, and, generally, upon so intense a Christocentrism, as
to prepare acute collisions with Biblical Criticism and with
the patent presence of various lights and graces in the Old
Testament and in the different ethnic religions and spiritual
philosophies'.[67] Furthermore he rejects the panchristism of
both Herrmann[68] and Blondel.[69] Christ is a model not simply
of what we must *be* but also of *how* we must become it:
holiness is born of contact with concrete things.[70] This aspect
of von Hügel's christology derives directly from his conception of the role of the contingent in making the transcendent
reality of God available, and also from his conviction that
'man's spirit is, at first, potential rather than actual, and has
to be conquered . . . by the slow transformation of the

---

[64] *E.A.*, vol. i, p. 132.
[65] See John J. Heaney, *The Modernist Crisis: von Hügel* (London, 1969), pp.
76–82, for a brief discussion of von Hügel's theory of friction.
[66] *M.E.*, vol. ii, p. 266.   [67] *E.L.*, p. 198.   [68] *M.E.*, vol. ii, p. 266.
[69] See his letter of 1903 to Blondel, in Whelan, op. cit., pp. 247–8. 'Du Christ
éternel' is a powerful criticism of Blondel's failure to see that the denial of contingent, humanly perfectible knowledge in Jesus was an implicit denial of his full
humanity.   [70] Whelan, op. cit., pp. 41, 247–8.

animal and selfish nature.'[71] In a long and important letter
to Maude Petre, written in 1900, he spoke of the 'slow, indefinite acquisition of spiritual substances, of a gradual
change, through successive will-acts, in the quality and value
of the spiritual entity in man'.[72] Christianity is defined by its
paradoxical conviction that the Infinite lays hold of the soul
through the contingent and finite.[73]

Von Hügel's position on the relationship between God and
man is deliberately struck in the indeterminate terrain
between the naïve transcendentalism of neo-scholastic thought
and the monistic immanentism to which the more radical
modernists were, in varying degrees, apparently drawn. This
middle position was not chosen as a mere dialectical tactic
(it is, after all, nearly always possible to site any theological
or philosophical position somewhere between two extremes).
Von Hügel makes it abundantly clear that he experienced a
strong dialectical tension in maintaining his position on transcendence and immanence. Whatever may be said about his
later development away from an apologetic based on the
conative towards a more pronounced critico–realist epistemology, he was, during the modernist period at least, in fundamental sympathy with Blondel and Laberthonnière. The
influence exercised over him by Eucken and Troeltsch,
however, stiffened Gallic heart-logic with Germany metaphysics. Maurice Nédoncelle[74] maintains that von Hügel's
theodicy was fundamentally Greek and medieval, since the
philosophical principles he invokes in favour of a transcendent
God are based on causality, necessity, and finality. 'If he
were to be taken to task, it would be for having accepted
them without seeking to perfect them. In this respect his
weapons of thought are pre-Kantian.'[75] Nédoncelle goes on to
remark that von Hügel's theodicy differs from that of St
Thomas only in being brought to bear upon 'objective
interiority' rather than upon 'the physical exteriority of the

---

[71] *M.E.* vol. ii, p. 301.   [72] *S.L.*, p. 92.

[73] 'Du Christ éternel', p. 290: 'Plus une religion sera complète et profonde,
plus elle devra présenter ce paradoxe du permanent saisi à travers les choses qui
passent, de l'éternel manifesté dans le temps. Cf. *E.L.*, p. 281: 'Religion, above
all Christianity, awakens and develops its strength in contact with the visible,
especially the organic . . .'.

[74] *I.P.Q.* p. 20.   [75] Ibid.

cosmos'.[76] Nédoncelle thus seems to imply that the difference is really a rather minor one. This is an area in which Nédoncelle is particularly competent, and one dissents from his judgement with some diffidence. Surely, however, the difference between objective interiority and cosmic exteriority is a fairly radical one? Von Hügel, as Nédoncelle himself points out earlier in his article,[77] was concerned to attack only theories of *pure* immanence. Once divine transcendence had been safeguarded to his satisfaction, von Hügel was as ardent a supporter of the method of immanence as Blondel ever was. We have already seen that von Hügel's main criticism of Kant is that the latter assumes *a priori* that the noumenal *cannot* correspond to the phenomenal. Von Hügel's appeal to 'dim experience' is made in full awareness of the Kantian critique. His rejection of essentialism frees him completely from the sort of Wolffian metaphysics against which Kant was reacting.

I do not wish to enter here into the question of how far the neo-scholastics were unfaithful to Aquinas. What is beyond question is that the neo-scholasticism which triumphed with *Pascendi* set its face resolutely against all theological appeals to any kind of immanence, 'objective' or not. In his *Petite consultation* von Hügel states clearly his conviction that we can have no knowledge of God apart from our immanent experience of him.[78] This conviction is as full a recognition of the Kantian critique as Blondel's, and, as thus expressed, is in flat contradiction if not of Aquinas himself, certainly of the neo-Thomists of the period. It is the word experience which makes all the difference. One can call it 'ontological instinct' and distinguish it from 'idealist hunger' as Nédoncelle does,[79] but it still remains something very different from the scholastic notion of cognition. That fact alone is sufficient to put von Hügel outside the ambit

---

[76] *I.P.Q.*, p. 20. Nédoncelle notes, however, that von Hügel's treatment of contingency has much in common with the Third Way of St. Thomas.

[77] *I.P.Q.*, p. 9.

[78] 'Nous ne pouvons donc point, il est vrai, connaître Dieu en dehors de toute expérience de Lui au dedans de nous-mêmes, mais nous pouvons Le connaître, au moins indirectement au delà de ce que nous sommes nous-mêmes; si nous le connaissons du tout, nous sommes même forcés de le connaître ainsi.' (*P.C.* p. 390.)   [79] *I.P.Q.* p. 7.

of orthodoxy as *Pascendi* defined orthodoxy. While von Hügel's ontology of transcendence was beyond challenge even by the narrow standards of neo-scholastic orthodoxy, his religious epistemology was in open conflict with that same orthodoxy.[80] Nevertheless his epistemology was always realist in the sense that he believed that in knowledge the object known was given in advance of the act of knowing. In the *Petite consultation* he speaks of the 'mysterious trinity' which comprises the subject, the object, and the knowledge which results from bringing them together.[81] It was on the manner of that knowing that he differed from both the idealists on the one hand and the naïve realists on the other.

Von Hügel's God was as radically transcendent as Barth's; but whereas Barth's religious epistemology refused to allow for a cognitional approach to God which was not totally faith-derived, von Hügel accepted, indeed dwelt upon, the cognitional implications of the doctrine that man is created in the image of God.

---

[80] In the important letter to Professor René Guisan (not Guiran, as printed), written in 1921, von Hügel remarked that he was then less influenced by Blondel and Laberthonnière and had turned to authors, mainly German, English, and Italian, who addressed themselves to establishing a '*critico-realist epistemology*' (*S.L.*, p. 334). To claim on the basis of this letter, as Robert Aufieri does in his article 'Baron Friedrich von Hügel: A Doctrine of God' (*Dunwoodie Review*, 14 (1974), p. 7) that von Hügel 'firmly rejects the "*méthode d'immanence*" of Blondel and others' is to go far beyond the evidence for any stage of von Hügel's life. In respect of his modernist period it is demonstrably untrue.

[81] *P.C.*, pp. 376 f.

7   George Tyrrell: Revelation as Experience

In the autumn of 1897 Friedrich von Hügel began a friendship with a thirty-six-year-old Jesuit priest, George Tyrrell, which was to last until the latter's early death in 1909. There can be no doubt about the fact that von Hügel exercised a far-reaching influence upon Tyrrell's theological development.[1] Estimates vary, however, as to how far von Hügel is to be credited with responsibility for what happened to Tyrrell during the last decade of his life. Miss Maude Petre, Tyrrell's friend, apologist, and biographer, blamed the Baron for not seeing the inevitable effect of exposing his friend to the latest conclusions of German critical scholarship. She almost certainly exaggerated. Tyrrell's restless mind and his increasing disillusionment with scholastic thought had already put him on a course which led directly to the roughest theological waters of the age. Von Hügel merely added some sail while counselling caution — which to someone of his own temperament was not the contradiction it sounds. Von Hügel always had his still centre to withdraw to when the going got rough. Tyrrell, an intellectual buccaneer, did not believe in ports for storms.[2] Not for Tyrrell the easy compartmentalizing that von Hügel was able to impose on his spiritual and academic lives. For Tyrrell

[1] In a very carefully considered obituary article written just after Tyrrell's death, von Hügel said: 'I am nine years my friend's senior, and to me he owed his initiation into German, Biblical criticism, and a good deal of the psychology and philosophy of religion.' (F. von Hügel, 'Father Tyrrell: Some Memorials of the Last Twelve Years of His Life', in *Hibbert Journal*, 8 (1910) p. 234.) Shortly before his death, Tyrrell in a letter to the Baron asking him to meet a new acquaintance, the Revd. Albert Cock, remarked: 'I told him [sc. Cock] the simple truth that if I knew anything worth knowing I got it all from you; that at most I was your Aaron with a more facile tongue and pen than his master . . . (Letter published by T. M. Loome in an introduction to his edition of Tyrrell's lecture, 'Revelation as Experience', in *H.J.* 12 (1971), p. 121.)

[2] Tyrrell's character has considerable relevance to his theological positions. I have discussed this point in my article, 'Some Reflections on the Character of George Tyrrell', in *H.J.* 10 (1969), pp. 256–74.

theology was life and life was theology; and this is why he was so passionately hard on what he regarded as bad theology. Fearless to the point of folly he scorned the cult of caution which characterized so much contemporary Roman Catholic theology and spirituality. He had a compulsive urge to face the whole truth, whatever the consequences.[3] As he told von Hügel, he could not bear the thought that he owed his stability 'to any sort of ignorance or half-view'.[4]

Ronald Chapman in his stimulating essay 'The Thought of George Tyrrell'[5] has remarked that 'Tyrrell, in fact, belonged to no party and this is hardly to be forgiven where party and denomination is almost religion itself.'[6] There is, writes Chapman, 'an elusive Cain-like quality about Tyrrell'.[7] Chapman's thesis is that if as a theologian Tyrrell must be judged at best a partial failure, 'as a religious thinker it is another matter'.[8] 'His contribution is to be found in the attempt he made to reconcile transcendentalism with immanentism.'[9] I believe that this judgement is correct; and the present chapter will attempt to explore it further.

The careless (and occasionally malicious) stereotype of Tyrrell one so often encounters is of a proud rebel against ecclesiastical authority driven ever further into modernist excesses until, at the time of his death, his views were so immanentist that he could no longer be described as in any sense a believing Christian, much less a Catholic. The fact is that by the end of his life Tyrrell had become a convinced subscriber to the consistent eschatology propounded by Johannes Weiss and adopted by Albert Schweitzer and Alfred Loisy. But whereas Schweitzer had taken to missionary medicine and Loisy to raising chickens, Tyrrell was still in theological harness when he died, struggling as vigorously against Liberal Protestantism as against Roman scholasticism and trying to formulate a theology of revelation which would accommodate without nullifying the apocalyptic perspective

---

[3] M. D. Petre (ed.), *George Tyrrell's Letters* (London, 1920) [*G.T.L.*], p. 158.

[4] M. D. Petre (ed.), *Autobiography and Life of George Tyrrell* vol. ii (London, 1912) [*Life*], p. 96.

[5] R Chapman, 'The Thought of George Tyrrell' in W. W. Robson (ed.), *Essays and Poems Presented to Lord David Cecil* (London, 1970), pp. 140-68.

[6] Ibid., p. 165.   [7] Ibid.

[8] Ibid., p. 166.   [9] Ibid., pp. 166 f.

of the New Testament as he saw it. The reconciliation of transcendence with immanence was indeed for Tyrrell the major religious problem and he had become convinced that the correct approach to it lay in a proper understanding of revelation.

In 1899 Tyrrell published an article entitled 'The Relation of Theology to Devotion'.[10] He later described this article as 'a brief compendium or analytic index' to his thought on revelation.[11] If we compare this essay with one he wrote a year earlier on Sabatier,[12] we discover a remarkable change of perspective and preoccupation. The 1898 review–article employs standard Catholic procedures for dealing with the Protestant view of faith and reiterates (with some characteristic Tyrrellian shadings) the scholastic understanding of revelation as instruction of the mind[13] and faith as intellectual assent. The intellect is 'our highest faculty'.[14] The 1899 essay, though couched in careful and non-combative terms, points to the future. In his short introduction to its last reprinting Tyrrell wrote: 'it marks a turning-point in my own theological experience.'[15]

It is always important to examine what Tyrrell means by 'theology' in any given context. 'Here we employ the term to signify what is known as scholastic theology, that is, the essay to translate the teachings of Catholic revelation into the terms and forms of Aristotelian philosophy; and thereby to give them a scientific unity.'[16] In this article Tyrrell does not yet make explicit his crucial distinction between revelation and theology; but he prepares the ground for it. He emphasizes the difference between the original deposit of faith, 'this concrete, coloured, imaginative expression of divine mysteries, as it lay in the mind of the first recipients',[17]

---

[10] *The Month*, 94 (1899), pp. 461–73; reprinted in *The Faith of the Millions: A Selection of Past Essays* [*F.M.*] vol. i, pp. 228–52; repr. finally under the title 'Lex Orandi, Lex Credendi', in *Through Scylla and Charybdis: Or, the Old Theology and the New* (London, 1907) [*S.C.*], pp. 85–105.   [11] *S.C.* p. 85.

[12] 'Sabatier on the Vitality of Dogmas', in *The Month* 91 (1898) pp. 592–602; repr. in *F.M.*, vol. i, pp. 115–35.

[13] *F.M.* vol. i, p. 130.   [14] Ibid., p. 134.

[15] *S.C.* p. 85. F. M. O'Connor ('George Tyrrell and Dogma', in *Downside Review*, 85 (1967), pp. 22 f.) ignores both the internal evidence and Tyrrell's own estimate of this article and treats it as belonging to Tyrrell's scholastic period.

[16] *S.C.*, p. 86.   [17] Ibid., p. 95.

and its later systematization through the use of philosophical language and categories. Philosophical theology refines the crudity of the original vulgar statement, but it does so at the peril of forgetting its own deficiencies — a forgetfulness which results in a far more obnoxious crudity. Devotion feeds on a revelation expressed in the language of peasants and fishermen and tends towards anthropomorphism and superstition. Philosophical theology tends towards 'excessive abstraction and vague unreality'.[18] Both, says Tyrrell, 'must be brought to the test of primitive revelation as interpreted by the Church'.[19] That primitive revelation is 'a concrete religion left by Christ to his Church, it is perhaps in some sense more directly a *lex orandi* than a *lex credendi*'.[20] The credal formularies which express it 'are ever to be tested and explained by the concrete religion which they formulate'.[21] 'Devotion and religion existed before theology, in the way that art existed before art-criticism; reasoning, before logic; speech before grammar.'[22] In these seemingly innocuous phrases we have the roots of Tyrrell's future theological growth. He has excavated the ground around 'primitive revelation', detaching it from all later intellectual development. Blondel found a ditch between faith and fact; von Hügel found one between the absolute and the contingent; Tyrrell dug one between revelation and theology. Over the next few years he was to widen it relentlessly. The notion of a revealed theology (and this included dogma) became the enemy which had to be fought to the death.

Our concern here is with the implications of all this for Tyrrell's understanding of transcendence and immanence. His primary interest is not in the transcendent as such, i.e. as the Other, the ontologically absolute — he had a profound respect for the apophatic in theology — but in the manner of contact between the transcendent God and man the believer. Most of Tyrrell's theology of transcendence and immanence flows from his understanding of revelation. Before we examine this relationship, however, we shall consider his

[18] *S.C.*, p. 95. Cf. G. Tyrrell, 'Revelation as Experience: A Reply to Hakluyt Egerton' [*R.E.*] in *H.J.*, 12 (1971), pp. 145 f.
[19] *S.C.* p. 96.   [20] Ibid., p. 104.
[21] Ibid., p. 104.   [22] Ibid., p. 105.

understanding and usage of the terms 'transcendent' and 'immanent'.[23]

'The transcendent is not the spiritual as opposed to the phenomenal; but the whole as opposed to an infinitesimal fraction of possible spiritual experience.'[24] That whole is inaccessible to man except in so far as it is mediated immanently to man through experience, conscience, and the symbolic language of those who have experienced it. 'As such, religion has to do with the transcendent — with the other world, not with this.'[25] The transcendent is knowable, but only through the medium of symbolism and anthropomorphism. 'Man's highest God will be man writ large.'[26] Expressions like this look like a capitulation to Feuerbach, if they are detached from their context. Tyrrell, however, makes it contextually plain that he is speaking of man's *image* of a truly transcendent God. Nearly a decade earlier, preaching to the Roman Catholic undergraduates at Oxford, he had said:

God is not directly reached by our *mind*, or our *imagination*, but only an idea or picture of God which we ourselves have constructed out of the fragments of our experience — a crude, childish representation at the best. It is not God, but only this rude image of God we set before our mind's eye when we pray to Him or think of Him, and try to love Him and find it so hard to succeed. No wonder, then, that He seems so far away, so uncertain, so intangible.[27]

Tyrrell's point is that religious man must recognize that he meets God in his 'own dim spiritual experience and its imaginative symbols'[28] and must school himself 'to submit to the limitation *consciously*; to realize that our best God is but an idol . . .'.[29] The ontological reality of God's transcendence is never questioned in Tyrrell's last book, as von Hügel, for all his hypersensitivity on the issue, recognized in

---

[23] One need hardly point out that Tyrrell's thought on this, as on other matters, evolved between 1900 and 1909. His last book, *Christianity at the Cross-Roads*, published posthumously, is our principal guide to the state of his thought at the time of his death.

[24] *C.C.*, p. 207 f.   [25] Ibid., p. 99.   [26] Ibid., p. 100.

[27] G. Tyrrell, *External Religion; Its Use and Abuse* (2nd edn., London, 1900), pp. 158 f., 204 f. Cf. G. Tyrrell, *Oil and Wine* (London, pub. 1907 but written 1900).   [28] *C.C.*, p. 196.

[29] *Life*, vol. ii, p. 416. Cf. his letter of 1908: 'What saves our "theologia" from being an "eidolopoea" is the sense of its infinite inadequacy to compass the transcendental.' (*G.T.L.*, p. 32.)

a letter to Maude Petre.[30] By the criteria of contemporary Roman theology Tyrrell's position was 'agnostic', but hardly more so than von Hügel's. Tyrrell set more store by, and laid heavier emphasis upon, symbolic representation and contact than did von Hügel, for all the latter's incarnationalism. Tyrrell's conception of symbol was remarkably strong: there is no 'as if' about its representational capacity. The transcendent makes contact with man in symbolic but also inexhaustible ways.

The truth of all these ways is the same if they yield the same control over experience. To say they are but symbolic of the transcendent is not agnosticism; since symbols may be representative. Nor is it pure pragmatism, since the degree of their practical utility is just that of their correspondence to reality.[31]

It is precisely the ability to form, live in, and accept the limitations of, symbols that prevents us from falling into agnosticism in respect of the transcendent, or worse, into literalism and the identification of revelation with theological formulation. Tyrrell's criticism of scholastic theodicy is similar to, and usually more strongly expressed than, that of his fellow modernists. The main burden of his criticism was that scholastic rationalism with its rigidities and clarities stifled the sense of search for God.[32] In the last of his books to receive an imprimatur from Bishop Bourne of Southwark he had written:

It is neither what we seem to understand about God that feeds our love; nor the fact that he is infinitely beyond our understanding; but the fact that we can ever progress in knowledge and love, and always with a sense of an infinite 'beyond'. It is at the margin where the conquering light meets the receding darkness that love finds its inspirations.[33]

[30] '. . . I was so utterly sure of his position . . . that any serious and deliberate attempt to present him as, at bottom or eventually, a pure Immanentist would . . . be met by his "X Roads"; so poignantly emphatic on this point . . .' (cited in M. de la Bedoyère, *The Life of Baron von Hügel*, pp. 238 f.   [31] *C.C.*, p. 104.

[32] His letters were considerably more unbuttoned than his publications. In one of them he wrote: 'Religion dies with the sense of mystery, and worship becomes mere servility. That is why our theologians are so irreligious. Their treatise *De Deo* is as definite as their treatise *De Romano Pontifice*, and they worship God merely as an arch-pope . . . They speak as though the inadequacy of our God-idea were merely quantitative; as though he were comprehensible up to a certain point.' (*G.T.L.*, p. 32.)

[33] G. Tyrrell, *Lex Orandi; or, Prayer and Creed* (London, 1903), p. 49. In his spiritual theology Tyrrell frequently comes close to that of Laberthonnière. Both

In attacking the scholastic conception of transcendence and defending the claims of a properly conceived theology of immanence, Tyrrell appreciated, perhaps more clearly than any other modernist, the inescapable correlativity of the terms 'transcendence' and 'immanence'. He recognized that, taken in isolation from one another, the terms are largely stripped of their meaning. Pure transcendence is pure spirit and 'pure spirit is pure abstraction.' Pure immanence is for Tyrrell the destruction of religion: '. . . if there be no transcendent life . . . we are then but dreams ourselves.'[34]

Tyrrell's theology of immanence is intimately connected with his ambivalent attitude towards Liberal Protestantism. *Christianity at the Cross-Roads* might be fairly described as a sustained offensive against Liberal Protestantism, yet in reading it, we sense, as Tyrrell himself seems to have done, that he was attracted strongly to several facets of the position he was attacking. A few months before his death he wrote to von Hügel that he felt that his past work had been 'dominated by the Liberal-Protestant Christ'.[35] Tyrrell's position here is a faithful reflection of general modernist attitudes to Liberal Protestantism It seems never to have occurred to either Loisy or Tyrrell that it might be a worthwhile exercise to delineate those aspects of Liberal Protestant thought with which they were in substantial agreement before they engaged in refutation. Loisy's 'Firmin' articles are something more than an attack on Sabatier and Harnack: they implicitly show how extensively Loisy had been influenced by the position he was attacking. Tyrrell's remark to von Hügel does, however, suggest that he was at least dimly aware of his own debt to his antagonists' standpoint.

---

of them, in rejecting the primacy of the intellect, found themselves turning to the Augustinian–Franciscan tradition which accorded an importance to the affective and conative that overrode, or at least corrected the excesses of, a purely cognitive dimension in man's quest for God.   [34] *C.C.*, p. 158.

[35] *Life*, vol. ii, p. 398. Maude Petre adds a puzzled footnote to this remark, since it seemed to her to contradict all that he had ever written on the subject. She ought perhaps to have recalled something she wrote in her journal in 1901: 'I cannot get at any unity in him — it seems as though he might fall into pieces that could walk off different ways, and I should not know which to follow.' (M. D. Petre, *My Way of Faith* (London, 1937), p. 281.) What she had written of the man was equally applicable to the theologian.

In the same letter we find further evidence in support of
this contention. 'If we cannot save huge chunks of transcendentalism, Christianity must go.' The sentence which follows
this inelegant apostrophe is interesting: 'Civilisation can do
(and has done) all that the purely immanental Christ of
Matthew Arnold is credited with.' Henri Bremond told Loisy
that a third of Tyrrell could be found in Arnòld's *Literature
and Dogma*.[36] This estimate is an exaggeration (and is difficult to verify or falsify, since Tyrrell rarely quotes sources
or explicitly acknowledges intellectual parentage) but there is
more than a grain of truth in it. In the letter of 1908, already
quoted, Tyrrell describes his own personal experience of
revelation as 'the image of a sort of indwelling Christ-God-my
conscience, my judge, my other and better self . . . with
whom I am often at variance, never at peace. This being, I
know, is a construction of my understanding and imagination
inspired by and explanatory of the Power within me that
makes for righteousness and of whose real nature I have no
idea . . .'[37]

The ambivalence of Tyrrell's attitude to Liberal Protestantism is largely a matter of his conflicting convictions about the
role of morality in religion. Much of his doctrine of immanence is closely connected with the ethical dimension of
religion. So fiercely moral is his attitude to religion that he
is constantly at pains to remove the impression that he is
identifying religion with ethics. Hence his insistence on the
mystical dimension, an insistence that brings him close to
Arnold's idea of religion as 'morality touched by emotion'.[38]
For 'emotion' Tyrrell would substitute 'mysticism', and he
would extend the notion of morality to cover thought and
experience as well as conduct.[39] Morality 'is not our highest
life, but only a particular manifestation of it under certain
contingencies'.[40] It needs 'a religious and transcendent interpretation' before it can effect a conscious union with God.
'The moral life, therefore, is potentially, and may become
actually, religious; it may help to satisfy man's mystical

---

[36] *Mémoires*, vol. iii, p. 268.   [37] *G.L.T.*, p. 35.
[38] M. Arnold, *Literature and Dogma: An Essay towards a Better Apprehension
of the Bible* (Popular Edn., London, 1884), p. 16.
[39] *C.C.*, p. 115.   [40] Ibid., p. 114.

need of conscious union with the transcendent; but it can never be the whole of religion, and need not be religious at all.'[41] No ethic can be truly Christian which is not rooted in mystery, he had claimed in 1902, since without mystery there will not be 'that love which is the substance of the inward immanent life of the Christian soul', but only 'a vague amiability whose roots are nowhere and its branches anywhere'.[42]

Tyrrell held that Liberal Protestantism, by its rejection of the eschatological (or, as he preferred to put it, the apocalyptic) dimension of the Gospels, had removed the transcendent element from Christian revelation. It filled the resulting vacuum with an immanentist humanism that lacked the angularities, the tensions, and the heart-hunger of a drive towards transcendence expressed in apocalyptic imagery. 'The whole tendency of Liberal Protestantism is to minimise the transcendence by establishing a sort of identity of form between this life and the other.' 'Heaven and the Kingdom of Heaven are in our midst; they are the spiritual or moral side of life.'[43] This comfortable accommodation of the Gospel message to the blander securities of nineteenth-century optimism enabled Harnack to give Christ a Liberal Protestant face and rob the Christian message of all friction with the present age. Against this attitude, which he construed as religious by intention rather than in content, Tyrrell affirmed his pessimism,[44] his protest against the removal of eschatological tension, and his rejection of a purely moral conception of immanence.

His campaign against Liberal Protestantism was a relatively detached affair, for all the conviction that went into it. Quite otherwise was the warfare he waged against Roman scholasticism. The battles of this war were fought over a wide front and almost every shot was fired in anger, frustration, and sustained disillusionment. It was a frame of mind which did not make for academic detachment, but it gave his prose a biting intensity which contributes

---

[41] *C.C.*, p. 115.   [42] *S.C.*, p. 190   [43] *C.C*, p. 65.

[44] 'If optimism is usually associated with the youth and pessimism with the age of persons or peoples, it is because pessimism is the verdict of experience.' (*C.C.*, pp. 117 f.)

greatly to the enduring readability of Tyrrell's works.

If Liberal Protestantism, by disposing painlessly of the apocalyptic inspiration of the Gospel, had evaded the claims of transcendence, Roman scholasticism had, as Tyrrell saw it, set up a system of mediated transcendence which exalted the function of ecclesiastical authority in that mediation by removing all traces of immanence in the link between God and man. From the Roman standpoint any appeal to the claims of immanence could be construed as a challenge to lawful authority whose officers found no difficulty in describing 'Modernism' as 'simply a protestantising and rationalising movement'.[45] This was written after the publication of *Pascendi*. A few months before the appearance of the encyclical, Tyrrell published an article in the newly established Milanese journal, *Il Rinnovamento* under the title 'Da Dio o dagli uomini?'.[46] Though basically a study in ecclesiology the essay has some important observations to make on the claims of a properly understood notion of immanence.

Given that the priest is an official with power and authority to teach and govern the religious community, the question arises, 'From whence has he received this power, from Heaven or of men?'[47] Ostensibly on priesthood, defined here by Tyrrell to mean 'all ecclesiastical authority',[48] the essay is in effect a condemnation of 'sacerdotalism' and a plea for democracy in the Roman Catholic Church. Milanese 'modernism' was strongly political in character. *Il Rinnovamento*, its short-lived organ, aimed at providing a lay and democratic alternative to Italian clericalism. Its philosophical programme was to promote 'all aspects of modern, subjectivist, postkantian philosophy in so far as these could be accommodated to faith in the transcendence of a personal God and in revelation'.[49] *Rinnovamento* was thus a near-perfect vehicle for Tyrrell's message. The Milanese in their turn, conscious of their debt to Newman, read avidly what Newman's fellow-Briton had to say.

[45] *C.C.*, pp. 44 f.
[46] *Il Rinnovamento*, 1 (April 1907), pp. 393–414. This article is printed in its English version, with an introduction, in *S.C.*, pp. 355–86 under the title 'From Heaven, or of Men?'.   [47] *S.C.*, p. 361.
[48] Ibid.   [49] Scoppola, *Crisi*, pp. 204 f.

To the question whether Church authority comes from God or men, Tyrrell answers 'from both'. As Maude Petre remarks, this essay 'resumes . . . the conception of authority first set forth in the S.T.L. letters of 1901 on the Anglo–Roman Joint-Pastoral.'[50] There he had been concerned to criticize the sharp distinction which the Pastoral made between the 'ecclesia docens' and the 'ecclesia discens'. Here he deepens the argument and relates it to his evolved theology of transcendence and immanence. He argues that Roman authoritarianism is given theological colour by a concept of transcendence which is in effect deistic: an absent God who communicates in a 'telegraphic' manner with his vicegerents on earth.[51] Tyrrell often took a consciously dialectical position between two extreme poles which he wished to exclude. He was fond of the figure Scylla/Charybdis.[52] In the preface he wrote for the 1907 edition of *Oil and Wine* (originally written in 1900) he gives as his polar extremes deism and pantheism. He describes the 'false "transcendence" ' of scholasticism as deistic; and he develops this contention in his *Rinnovamento* article. In scholastic ecclesiology Church authority becomes 'the delegate of a purely transcendent, not of an also immanent God'.[53] 'Sacerdotalism', i.e. the clerical abuse of authority, is the direct result of the lack of a theology of immanence. Transcendence, as he never tires of emphasizing, needs symbolic expression to make it as intelligible as possible to the finite mind. In the Gospels symbolic expression takes shape in apocalyptic imagery. 'But squeeze any metaphor hard enough and it will yield poison; in this case the poison of absolutism and irresponsible government.'[54] He sets out to combat this absolutism by a theory of divine immanence, remarking that the rightful claims of immanence have made themselves felt at the same time as a growing sense of 'the authority of the general over the individual mind and conscience'.[55]

[50] *Life*, vol. ii, pp. 319 f. The reference is to letters which Tyrrell wrote to various journals criticizing the Joint Pastoral of the English Roman Catholic hierarchy of 29 December 1900 on 'The Church and Liberal Catholicism'. He signed these letters 'S.T.L.'   [51] *S.C.*, p. 360.

[52] In the book which employs the figure in its title the dialectic is between tradition and progress.

[53] *S.C.*, p. 364.   [54] Ibid., pp. 364 f.   [55] Ibid., p. 367.

Rinnovamento policy could hardly have been put more succinctly. He now goes on to argue this thesis at the two distinct but interconnected levels of metaphysics and Church government. The bearer of Church authority is, in a sense, accountable to God alone, but 'to God immanent in the collective mind and conscience of the community'.[56] Greater democratization of the Church will be the inevitable result of a 'more adequate emphasis of the Divine Immanence'.[57] To those who would object that such a concept of immanence is foreign to the mind of Jesus and the New Testament Tyrrell replies that dominical and New Testament teaching had to reflect the mind and employ the language of the age, which represented God 'as mainly transcendent, as outside and above the world and humanity'.[58] 'The underlying and complementary truth of the Divine Immanence, with all its democratic consequences, could scarcely have been grasped or formulated by the mentality to which our Lord addressed himself.'[59] Tyrrell concludes: 'If Christ spoke, and had to speak the language of pure transcendence, His whole life and teaching and spirit implied the truth of immanence.'[60] Indeed early Church government, even if it had no explicit theology of immanence, nevertheless practised it. 'The Spirit, in whose name they ruled, and ministered and taught and baptized and consecrated, was still viewed as immanent in the whole body, as audible in the collective voice.'[61] The unhappy break between a transcendently derived authority and the community over which it

---

[56] *S.C.*, p. 371.

[57] Ibid., p. 372. Giovanni Gentile, in an essay of 1908 entitled 'Il modernismo e l'enciclica "Pascendi" ' (repr. in G. Gentile, *La religione : il modernismo e i rapporti tra religione e filosofia. Discorsi di religione* (Florence, 1965), pp. 65-75), with that carefully calculated disingenuousness which infuriated Buonaiuti, attacks Tyrrell's position as destructive both of Catholicism and of humanism. A rigorous examination of the principle of divine immanence in history, claims Gentile, 'non vi dà la Chiesa democratica, ma la democrazia, senz'altro' (p. 70). He continues: 'Even in this democratic doctrine there is the same error, with the same consequences, as in the philosophy of immanence: a contradiction between method and principle: hence the scepticism and atheism alleged by the Encyclical [sc. *Pascendi*] and rejected not alone by the Pope, but also by rationalism.' (Ibid.) (The modernists, like liberal reformers in later times, were sometimes the object of an unholy alliance between ecclesiastical reactionaries and radical secularists).

[58] *S.C.*, p. 374.   [59] Ibid.

[60] Ibid., pp. 374 f.   [61] Ibid., p. 379.

was exercised came later.[62] Our forefathers 'knew nothing of that fatal discord which arises when religion is derived from outside and civilisation from inside. To their belief we must return in a better form, and derive both one and the other from God, but from God immanent in the spirit of man.'[63] Tyrrell leaves this suggestive insight undeveloped. Von Hügel, Laberthonnière, and Bremond had all made this point in their various ways: the fruit of extrinsicism is philistinism and a lack of spiritual authenticity. Tyrrell, however, hints at how this perennially relevant question might be related to the profounder question of divine immanence.

Von Hügel, having read 'Da Dio o dagli uomini?' wrote to Tyrrell that he had found it 'most striking: so strong and true, so pathetically winning in its great main contention'.[64] There followed the almost inevitable reservation: 'But I feel strongly, somehow, that your treatment of the old transcendent conception of God as requiring to be reformulated, *en toutes pièces*, by an immanental one, is somehow a bit of most tempting, yet nevertheless impoverishing, simplification.'[65] He thought that Tyrrell's 'clear-cut Immanentism' left no place for 'that noblest half of the religious experience of tip-toe expectation, of unfulfilled aspiration . . .'[66] Tyrrell may well be forgiven for feeling exasperation with this curious observation, since he was a fervent exponent of the theology of unfilfilled aspiration.[67] He had expressly stated his intention of charting a position between deism and pantheism; hence had had the right to demand that his words be read with this intention in mind.[68]

[62] Interestingly, Tyrrell traces the break back, not to Constantine, but to 13th-century Aristotelianism. It is plain, he wrote to Bailey Saunders in 1907, 'that scholastic epistemology (*nihil in intellectu nisi quod prius in sensu*) lent itself to a purely external, non-mystical view of revelation, as opposed to Protestant "illuminism" of any sort, and as such favoured the papal tendency and was favoured by it' (*G.T.L.*, pp. 53 f.).   [63] *S.C.* p. 383.

[64] B. Holland (ed.), *Baron Friedrich von Hügel: Selected Letters, 1896–1924*, p. 138.   [65] Ibid.   [66] Ibid.

[67] See, for example, *F.M.*, vol. i, p. 50. *Christianity at the Cross-Roads* had not yet been published when the Baron wrote his letter. This last of Tyrrell's works is replete with references to unsatisfied aspirations. See especially p. 125 where he dilates on this theme in one of his most beautiful passages where he says of contingent man: 'A cage-born bird, he wonders what his wings are for.'

[68] Pietro Scoppola, one should add, also finds this essay immanentist: Tyrrell's 'critique of the pictorial representation of God borders on an almost radical denial of the very transcendence of God' (*Crisi*, p. 202)

It is a matter of some interest that what are arguably the most immanentist pages in all Tyrrell's writings occur in a book he wrote in 1900 entitled *Oil and Wine* He could not get it past the diocesan censors who took issue not with what he had written about transcendence and immanence but with his treatment of faith and doctrine. *Oil and Wine* was published only in 1907, that is after he had been excommunicated. In many respects it is his most finely conceived and elegantly written work, spiritual in intent and non-polemical in execution. The book shows that, if anything, he was more immanentist in 1900 than in the full flush of his modernist period, which in turn is a warning against hasty and facile conclusions about the inevitable modernist drift towards immanentism.

In his 1907 preface Tyrrell made this highly significant judgement on his book: 'In avoiding the false "transcendence" of Deism I may have drifted too near the Charybdis of Pantheism in search of the middle course of Panentheism; in urging the unity, I may have endangered the distinctness of souls.' Since the judgement is unsolicited and uncoerced (censors being no longer a hazard and he being free to write what he pleased) it should be weighed carefully. If the charge of immanentism is to receive any support from Tyrrell's writings, the principal evidence for the prosecution will be found in Chapters 41 and 42 of *Oil and Wine* The following passage is ostensibly the most monistic of any to be found in Tyrrell's writings:

The deepest and most fundamental appetite in the soul is God's love of His own life and action, temporal and eternal. The soul is not God, yet has no reality except in conjunction with the reality of God, who is her foundation and support. Alone, she were unintelligible and incoherent, as shadow without substance, for she is essentially associated with another (namely, with her God) in the deepest springs of her conscious life. His Will is ever present to her as the will of another, however dimly that 'otherness' be apprehended. It is He who, in conjunction with her and with His whole creation — as it were, one Self, one Subject, — desires and seeks the universal good whereby all creatures enter into the eternal joy of their Lord — that joy which He finds in His inner life and action.[70]

---

[69] *Oil and Wine* p. ix.   [70] Ibid., pp. 220 f.

Monistic in language certainly; but these words were written
as a mystical meditation not as theological analysis. They
could be paralleled with quotations from many of the
classical mystics. In this context Gestalt and intent are all.
In 1907 Tyrrell the theological critic could express reservations about Tyrrell the mystical writer. He was now so familiar with von Hügel's categories that he could recognize that
he was 'in search of the middle course of Panentheism'
His position appeared to oscillate, as must that of any
religious thinker who takes seriously the problem of the relationship between transcendence and immanence. As von
Hügel noted in his *Hibbert* obituary, Tyrrell fluctuated
between an insistence on the utter transcendence and
unknowableness of God, on the one hand, and, on the other,
an emphasis on God's immanence which comes near to 'an
Anima mundi or an *Anima animarum* conception'.[71] His
emphasis on both is, as I have argued, dialectical, but in the
Kierkegaardian rather than the Hegelian sense: the truth lies
in the two extremes rather than in any higher synthesis, and
least of all in what he saw as the emasculated amalgam
produced by Liberal Protestantism. He proclaimed the cognitive limitations inherent in any approach to the otherness
of God when he contemplated, always with acute distaste,
the assurance apparently experienced by the scholastic
theologians in their statements about God. He proclaimed
immanence when he saw the ecclesiological *use* made of
Transcendence-as-externally-guaranteed-truth by the same
theologians. Both proclamations were the product of his
abhorrence of 'external religion'.

One theme pervades Tyrrell's writings during the last ten
years of his life, namely, the distinction he made between
revelation and theology. What he saw as the scholastic
identification of revelation and theology he stigmatized as
'theologism',[72] viz. 'a hybrid system which, applying logical
deduction to the inspired and largely symbolic utterances
of prophecy, imposes its conclusions in the name both of

---

[71] F. von Hügel, 'Father Tyrrell: Some Memorials of the Last Twelve Years of
His Life', in *Hibbert Journal*, 8 (1910) p. 250.

[72] *S.C.*, p. 350 n. The neologism is 'formed from *Theologia*, as sophism is from
Sophia'.

revelation and of reason, as binding at once on the conscience and on the understanding'.[73] In the earlier part of the decade he had, with Newman as his mentor, wrestled with the problem of doctrinal development. Newman's inexhaustible 'idea' seemed the only recognizably Catholic alternative to the scholastic concept of a deposit from which logical deductions might be made. Wilfrid Ward was the champion of 'Liberal Catholicism' and its espousal of Newman. Since this camp was critical of scholasticism, Tyrrell was generally considered to belong to it, till he wrote an article apparently attacking Ward's position.[74] Tyrrell's growing dissatisfaction with Newman was only marginally concerned with ecclesiology and the theology of Scripture and Tradition. It was far more radical in origin. Tyrrell was coming to the view that both the scholastics *and Newman* shared a concept of revelation which was propositional and, as such, indefensible. Newman's 'Idea' failed to reflect or preserve the mystical and experiential character of the primary prophetic vision of which the Bible is the normative and unchanging record.

Though Tyrrell recognized that Newman's 'Idea' was not an 'intellectual concept' but 'a spiritual force or impetus',[75] he nevertheless became ever more disenchanted with the possibility of its development in terms of doctrine while remaining at the same time an inexhaustible constant. In 1905 we find him working awkwardly with Newmanian categories while trying to give expression to his fresher and more radical insights. The result is not impressive 'The progressive explication of the inexhaustible significance of the Christian sentiment or spirit implies a relative truth in all symbolic constructions of the Supernatural, and a greater truth in the later than in the earlier formulations, so far as they have not been sophisticated by theology.'[76] This sentence is a kind of theological chromaticism gone wild. One is reminded of Schoenberg's realization, at this very time, that the tonal system in music would no longer bear the strain of further

[73] *S.C.*, p. 351.
[74] G Tyrrell, 'Semper Eadem' *The Month*, 103 (1904), pp. 1–17; reprinted in *S.C.* pp. 106–32 as 'Semper Eadem I' and supplemented by a second essay 'Semper Eadem II', *S C.*, pp. 133–54, originally pub. 1905 under the title 'The Limits of the Theory of Development'
[75] *C.C.* p. 33.   [76] *E.F.J.*, p. 86.

development, and that a clean break would have to be made. In this respect Newman's *Essay* is the theological analogue of Wagner's *Tristan*. Tyrrell finally realized that he would have to break completely with Newman if he were to do justice to his newer insights. What Newman meant by 'Idea' was not the same as what Tyrrell meant by 'prophetic experience', and it was idle to pretend that Newman's theory of development could be made to fit a concept of revelation which Newman would have disowned. Tyrrell did, however, give Newman the credit for separating himself from the scholastic mind. The modernists, says Tyrrell, have taken Newman's notion of an 'idea' as a spiritual force or impetus 'and turned [it] against much of that system in whose defence he had framed it'.[77] It was, he remarked, only Newman's 'own subjective and incommunicable religious experiences' that prevented him from seeing that his method 'did as much for unbelief as for belief'.[78] Tyrrell rejected, as finally self-contradictory, Newman's notion of development. Offered to the Tractarians as an *argumentum ad hominem*, it lacked universal validity and in fact raised more problems than it solved.[79]

For the last two years of his life Tyrrell therefore focused his attention ever more sharply on the nature of revelation as primary vision. In his introduction to 'Semper Eadem I' he had written: 'I had not yet [sc. in 1904] seen that Revelation is not a record, metaphorical or otherwise, of a supernatural experience, but a persistent part or element of such an experience.'[80] He was no longer prepared to say that revelation was the figurative, while theology was the exact, statement of the same truth.[81] At this point Tyrrell's thought, normally uncomplicated and expressed in limpid prose, becomes complex and not always obviously consistent.[82]

---

[77] *C.C.*, p. 33.   [78] Ibid., p. 34.   [79] *S.C.*, p. 151.
[80] Ibid., p. 107.   [81] Ibid.
[82] Though references to revelation are scattered across Tyrrell's writings, there are three sources of particular importance for an understanding of the problem as he saw it during the last two years of his life. In ascending order of importance we have his letter of 1907 to von Hügel (*G.T.L.*, pp. 56–61) in which he (1) classifies his notion of dogmas into primary and secondary, and (2) deepens still further his distinction between revelation and theology. Then there is his essay 'Revelation', in *S.C.*, pp. 264–307. Finally there is his lecture 'Revelation as Experience: A

'My own work — which I regard as done — has been to raise a question which I have failed to answer', wrote Tyrrell to Arthur Boutwood six months before his death.[83] That work, namely, the quest for 'a synthesis of Catholicism and Science — not the supremacy of the latter',[84] achieved its final focus in an analysis of the nature and scope of revelation. It was the logical conclusion to all his inquiries into the correlation of transcendence and immanence. A transcendent being is known, or experienced, only to the extent that that being operates immanently in the human spirit. Tyrrell had reiterated this contention time and again. He now restates it in terms of revelation. His last essays show that this was the area in which his primary interest and concern had always lain. The problem of transcendence and immanence receives its clearest and most daunting statement when posed as a question about the manner in which God reveals himself to man. As always, Tyrrell's attempted answer begins from his central conviction: whatever revelation is, *it is not statement.*[85] The problem was how to prevent this heartfelt negation from degenerating into 'nebulous religiosity'. Lebreton had accused Tyrrell of sentimentalism. Tyrrell replied that 'to make faith consist in an undirected, objectless, unilluminated feeling would be a shallowness that I should be sorry to attribute to any serious thinker.'[86] He had, he informed Lebreton, dwelt on 'the affective and voluntary elements of the act of faith', because scholastic rationalism had ignored them; but he had always both explicitly and implicitly 'recognised its cognitive character as involving a presentment of divine realities'.[87] Every spiritual act may be

Reply to Hakluyt Egerton', published for the first time by T. M. Loome in *H.J.*, 12 (1971), pp. 117–49. This lecture was a reply to Arthur Boutwood who, under the pseudonym 'Hakluyt Egerton', had written a book, *Father Tyrrell's Modernism: An Expository Criticism of 'Through Scylla and Charybdis' in an Open Letter to Mr Athelstan Riley* (London, 1909). Tyrrell regarded Boutwood, much as he regarded the French Jesuit, Jules Lebreton, as a constructive critic and therefore worth the effort and courtesy of a reasoned reply.

[83] *G.L.T.*, p. 119.

[84] Ibid. This quest constitutes the substance of Tyrrell's definition of modernism.

[85] Even if Mr Egerton could 'convince me that revelation were not experience, I should still refuse to believe it to be statement. I should simply say: I don't know what it is' (*R.E.*, p. 141).

[86] *S.C.*, p.. 313.   [87] Ibid.

logically analysed into knowledge, feeling, and will.[88] The response to revelation is thus susceptible to logical and psychological analysis. The term 'experience' was the best available one for describing a stimulus–response situation which includes knowledge, feeling, and will.

Tyrrell distinguishes between a 'primary' and 'derivative' sense of the term revelation.[89] In its primary sense the term means an experience, direct, existential and, normally, spontaneous. In its secondary sense it refers to the record of the experience and is therefore to a greater or less extent reflective and thus derived. Tyrrell's entire view of the revelation sequence could be represented as a terraced cone radiating outwards and downwards from the central revelatory experience and cooling in the process – in short, a kind of spiritual volcano. The crucial hiatus occurs between the primary revelatory exerience and all subsequent efforts, even by the recipient, to give it expression. The terracing and derivativeness begin as soon as the seer attempts to give halting outward expression to his inner pre-conceptual and essentially incommunicable experience. This outward expression can begin either while the seer is still under the influence of his inner experience or 'it may be the result of quiet afterthought'. It is more commonly a mixture of both.[90] The language employed to express the externalization will be symbolic, 'a translation that can never be exhaustive or adequate, but at most suggestive'.[91] The attempt to communicate the inner experience is prophecy. Prophecy is therefore the communication not of revealed statement but of vision.[92]

The aim of the prophet is to kindle in others something of the universality and intensity of his primary experience which alone is revelation in its proper sense. Prophetic language falls flat unless it encounters in the hearer 'a spirit to answer the Spirit',[93] just as the greatest love poetry will fail to stir one who has never experienced the passion of love. Revelation as such is not communicated. The prophetic vision is expressed in language (often apocalyptic) which is

---

[88] *S.C.*, p. 313 f. [89] Ibid., p. 268. [90] Ibid., p. 304.
[91] Ibid., p. 303. [92] Ibid., p. 289. [93] Ibid., p. 304.

calculated to evoke within the hearer an experience analogous to that of the prophet's own. 'It is to this evoked
revelation that we answer by the act of Faith, recognising it
as God's word in us and to us. Were it not already written in
the depths of our being, where the spirit is rooted in God,
we could not recognise it.'[94] This last sentence gives clear
expression to Tyrrell's idea of revelation as immanent and
thus comes very close to Blondel's teaching, especially as
elaborated by Laberthonnière. 'Revelation cannot be put into
us from outside, it can be occasioned, but it cannot be
caused, by instruction.'[95] All the modernists had said the
same.

Theology, as Tyrrell understands it, comes into play from
the moment reflective believers begin to speculate upon and
systematize the truths distilled from experience. But
theology is never revealed, even when theological reflection
accompanies the primary revelatory experience. Indeed, 'as
known to us, the Christian revelation is largely expressed in
the language of theology' wrote Tyrrell in 1905.[96] This
language can play its part, first in socializing the content of
revelation, i.e. in giving it an ecclesial dimension,[97] then in
helping to evoke an answering immanent response to the
original revelatory stimulus. The burden of Tyrrell's case
against scholasticism is that in construing revelation as proposition and faith as intellectual assent, it reduced itself to 'the
cold repetition of inspired utterance by uninspired lips'.[98]
Not merely did it treat the lower and outer terraces of
derived theological discourse as equal in importance to the
upper and inner, but it carried out its operations on the
slopes of an extinct volcano. Tyrrell constantly insisted that
both revelational experience and theology had their rights
and limits.[99] He also pointed out, to Lebreton and other
critics, that he fully accepted the mental element in revelation

---

[94] *S.C.*, p. 305.   [95] Ibid., p. 306.   [96] Ibid., p. 229.

[97] He makes this point at several places in 'Da Dio o dagli uomini?' In *R.E.*
(pp. 145 f.) he gives it further precision: 'Thus the creeds of the Church are
directly the creation of her collective human mind, but guided by her collective
religious experience — by the spirit of Christ that is immanent in all her members.'

[98] *S.C.*, p. 307.

[99] See 'The Rights and Limits of Theology' first publ. in *Quarterly Review*
(1905) and repr. in *S.C.*, pp. 200–41.

while insisting that this element was merely part of the total religious experience.[100]

Here we meet perhaps the most obscure area of Tyrrell's thesis. His position on derivative revelation, i.e. revelation as expression and record, is admirably clear. He is much less clear on the content and mode of the transcendental communication of the primary experience from which the derivations and records proceed. He of course insists that it must be immanent. What remains rather more obscure is the relationship between revelation and the total experience of which it is a part. Revelation

is not so much a representation of something experienced, as one of the elements of a complex spiritual experience — an experience made up of feelings and impulses and imaginings; which reverberates in every corner of the soul and leaves its impress everywhere; in the mind no less than in the heart and will — just as the impulse and sentiment of Conscience entail a complementary impression on the mind which is part and parcel of the same experience.[101]

Tyrrell is at pains to emphasize that theological analysis has as its object not simply the revelational element but the whole experience.[102] Since however 'the affective and volitional elements of the religious experience are evanescent, the mental or imaginative element abides in memory and survives as the representative of the total experience'.[103] Theology must constantly advert to the fact that, though its object is the whole experience, it has merely the mental or imaginative element to work from. If it remembers this, and avoids 'theologism', it will be ready to undertake its real task which is to re-create from the evidence of the mental and imaginative record something of the power of the original experience, just as the scientist working with fossils and partial remains attempts to reconstruct the original creature of which these are the relics.[104] The theologian must therefore be clear about his objective, namely the total experience, and the means whereby he can approach his objective, namely, the mental and imaginative element of revelation. 'Viewing that total experience as an effect, he then endeavours to divine the

---

[100] *S.C.*, p. 285.   [101] Ibid., pp. 282 f.
[102] Ibid., p. 283.   [103] Ibid., p. 283.
[104] Ibid., p. 284. Tyrrell had used the same analogy in his 1899 essay on the relation of theology to devotion.

nature of its causes and to draw certain theological and meta-physical conclusions.'[105]

Here we reach the last of the Chinese boxes within which Tyrrell deploys his argument: the 'total experience' is the im-manent effect from which the theologian infers its transcen-dent causality. Where von Hügel took up his stand against Kant by a conscious appeal to a sense of contingency which mediates transcendence, Tyrrell comes to rest, not without circumstantial irony, on what looks like the very Aristotelian, even neo-scholastic, bridge of cause and effect. 'Experience is revelational. It reveals God as every cause is revealed in and with its effects; it reveals Him not in a statement but in the moral and religious impulse that proceeds from Him.'[106]

Egerton had objected that Tyrrell assumed,where he ought to have proved, God; and that the total experience from which he inferred God could be put down to moral or ethi-cal experience.[107] In his reply Tyrrell falls back on Matthew Arnold. 'We have to analyse our spiritual experience and show that it consists in a certain converse of action and re-action between ourselves and a Power not ourselves that makes for Righteousness.'[108] To the further objection that this power is anonymous, Tyrrell replies in a louder voice rather than with a fresh argument: 'The cause is revealed by the effect in question as that to which we owe absolute obedience and unqualified worship and this is precisely what we mean, or ought to mean, by God.'[109]

Perhaps the sense of anticlimax we feel at this point is inevitable. We may indeed wonder if the ghosts of Hume and Kant have been laid. Certainly Tyrrell would protest, first, that we are here at the very heart of mystery and therefore cannot expect any adequacy of language; and, second, that he is using the correlation of cause and effect in a manner markedly different from that of the scholastics who deduce the cause from the effect and express their deduction in logical propositions. He on the contrary finds God-as-cause immanently present in experience-as-effect. The analysis he proposes is not of causality understood as an extrinsic pheno-menon but of the *fait intérieur* in which the union of God

---

[105] *S.C.*, p. 284. [106] *R.E.* p. 144. [107] Ibid., p. 143.
[108] Ibid. [109] Ibid., p. 144.

and man takes place antecedently to all analysis.

In the last months of his life Tyrrell lectured several times on the problem of evil and suffering. He called his lecture 'Divine Fecundity', and it was published under this title by Maude Petre in 1914.[110] The lecture was occasioned by the Italian religious Press's response to the appalling earthquake which, on 28 December 1908, devastated southern Calabria and eastern Sicily, killing an estimated 150,000 people. In many respects 'Divine Fecundity' is the most original of all Tyrrell's works. It is in effect an essay on divine providence without teleology, conceived under the influence of Bergson, and carried through with startling toughness of mind by a man who was at that moment suffering intensely himself. It seeks to relate divine immanence in the world to the pheno-menon of suffering and to derive from both a message of transcendental hope.[111] It is Augustinian in its pessimism and in its unsparing opposition to the 'Gospel of Progress'. The pessimism is described by Tyrrell as 'provisional'[112] in a fashion analogous to the pantheism which von Hügel described as 'preliminary' and prescribed as beneficial. 'We have been too long accustomed to a cheap eschatology . . .' Tyrrell writes,[113] with an eye upon both Liberal Protestant humanism and the scholastic treatise, *De Novissimis*, which painted the mysteries of the transcendental world to come with panache and untroubled assurance of fidelity to the facts. He rejects all attempts to identify the Kingdom of God with 'some socialist millennium'.[114] Collective humanity is not on a predetermined course for some fixed goal. 'Every future generation . . . will have tears and sorrows of its own.' The only predeterminism is to be found in the fact that we must progress in order to live at all. If we do not advance, we perish.[115] In order to impose meaning on this state of flux we either create a goal towards which it is moving in obedi-ence to an external teleology, or we find our goal in progress itself. In either case a tragedy like the Messina earthquake perplexes us. Can God be indifferent to all this? Here Tyrrell

[110] *E F.I.*, pp. 245–77.   [111] Ibid., p. 277.   [112] Ibid.
[113] Ibid., p. 270.   [114] Ibid., p. 248.
[115] Ibid., pp. 249 f. The influence of Bergson's *L'Évolution créatrice* (Paris, 1907) is particularly evident at this point in Tyrrell's argument.

provides a footnote of some importance for our present investigation.

Let me say, in passing, that in the present context I use God and Nature indifferently, i.e. I speak of God so far as God is immanent in and coincident with Nature, and not as supernatural and transcendent. Sometimes Nature sounds too inhuman for my purpose, at others God sounds too human.[116]

At first blush this looks like pure Spinozism. Spinoza, however, had spoken of *Deus sive natura* and the *sive* acted as an implicit copula of identity. Tyrrell makes it quite plain that his identification occurs only between Nature and God as immanent. He explicitly excepts God as transcendent and supernatural from this identification. This exclusion is sufficient to set Tyrrell's position apart from both Spinozism and from the more radical forms of Process Theology.[117] One has the uneasy feeling, however, that he is trying to have the best of both worlds. He saves Nature from the need for a dualistic interpretation, but only at the expense of postulating a suspiciously dualistic-seeming God. Tyrrell has nothing to say about the role of God as transcendent. He is eloquent, even lyrical, on the role of God-as-immanent-in-Nature, who, artist-like, involves himself in working out endless variations on the eternal keyboard of the universe each one of which has an eternal value in itself.[118] The core of Tyrrell's thesis is that each variation has its value totally in itself and not in the contribution it makes to some future goal. On this showing he would have little time for today's Political Theology. For him the desire for eternity has transcendent reference, or else it is an illusion. We have no clear idea of this *post mortem* state, nor do we need it. Enough to know that it is there and that our desire for it, together with the conviction of its reality, 'grows step by step with our diviner life as sons of God'.[119] The 'provisional pessimism' he prescribes is worked out in terms of man's resolution to 'atone' himself

[116] *E.F I.*, p. 250 n.
[117] There is a neo-platonist ring to some of Tyrrell's remarks in 'Divine Fecundity'. He writes for instance of the infinite 'with its centre everywhere or anywhere' (*E.F.I.* p. 264). In effect he comes near to saying that God is immanent by his power but transcendent in his essence. See David F. Wells, 'George Tyrrell: Precursor of Process Theology', in *Scottish Journal of Theology*, 26 (1973), pp. 71–84.   [118] *E.F.I.* p. 261.   [119] Ibid., p. 274.

'with the Divine Will in its endless joys and sorrows'[120] by fighting 'for victory in the face of certain eventual defeat'.[121]

It is almost impossible to summarize Tyrrell's position on transcendence and immanence. To adapt his own description of the Kingdom of God, his thought gives us a direction rather than a terminus. He leaves us very clear on what he denies but rather less clear on what he affirms. As he said himself, he pleased no one, belonged to no school, and was not an original thinker. What can be confidently said of him today is that the issues he faced with notable toughness and independence of mind are still alive. Educated in a theology which dealt in confident answers, he graduated to one which raised more questions than it could solve — which in the matter of transcendence and immanence is, or might be taken to be, a symptom of theological health.

[120] *E.F.I.*, p. 273.   [121] Ibid., p. 274.

8   The Integralist Response (1):
Prelude to the Roman
Condemnation of Modernism

In October 1903 the academic year was inaugurated at the
Milan Major Seminary with a lecture given by Father Antonio
Fumagalli in the presence of the archbishop. The lecture was
entitled 'The Snares of a New Science',[1] and it warned the
audience of young clerics about the dangers of a neo-Kantian
movement in France. Not so long ago it was possible to think
that this new-fangled immanence apologetic would be con-
fined to France. Unfortunately this is no longer true.
Attempts are being made to transplant to Italy the ill-
conceived 'neo-apologetic' which in France, while converting
no one, has shaken the faith of many Catholics. The new
school is led by Blondel, Laberthonnière, and Loisy. These
men ridicule the work done in natural theology for centuries.
Happily their neo-Kantianism is being challenged by 'a
numerous band of robust thinkers, the neo-Thomists'. The
lecturer, having exhorted his listeners to make the Vatican
Council's Constitution, *Dei Filius*, the touchstone of their
orthodoxy, concluded with a flourish. 'To the cry . . . "Back
to Kant" let us answer defiantly with the cry of Leo XIII,
repeated by Pius X, "Back to Thomas".'[2]
   It was not a particularly distinguished lecture, but it contained the sort of comment that might be heard in similar
places on similar occasions throughout Italy over the next
few years. It highlights some points which were to prove
important in determining the course and intensity of the
Roman response to modernism. Young priests and seminarists in Italy were beginning to respond to the new ideas with
an enthusiasm greater even than that of their contemporaries
in France. Indeed there was a conviction among some Italians
that Italy rather than France would be the most fruitful

---

[1] A. Fumagalli, 'Le insidie di una nuova scienza', in *La Scuola Cattolica* 31
(1903), pp. 385–400.   [2] Ibid., p. 400.

seed-bed for the new ideas.[3] There was in consequence increasing curial concern over the spread of the new ideas among the younger Italian clergy, and this concern was expressed in more restrictive measures in the organization of seminary life and studies. Fumagalli's admonitions foreshadow some of the issues which were to become central to the anti-modernist campaign. The most significant of these issues was the throwing into irreconcilable antithesis of the respective philosophies of Kant and Aquinas.

In the present chapter we shall consider, first, the build-up of the anti-Kantian campaign, then the influence and writings of some representative and key figures in the campaign, and, finally, the attempt made by Joseph Lemius to construct a coherent synthesis from the various and disparate challenges offered to scholastic integralism by the 'neo-critici'.

One of the earliest Italian responses to the new ideas came from the pen of Guido Mattiussi S.J., who shared the conviction of French scholastics like Fontaine and Schwalm that the philosophy of Immanuel Kant lay at the roots of the new and dangerous challenge to received orthodoxy. Mattiussi's chosen metaphor to describe the new threat was written into the title of his articles and book: 'Il veleno kantiano', the Kantian poison. To this poison there was but one antidote, namely, the philosophy of Thomas Aquinas. In 1902 to 1903 Mattiussi wrote a long article for *La Scuola Cattolica*, a journal published by the theological faculty of Milan, on the dangers of Kantianism.[4] In 1907 he published his book of the same title which recapitulated material from his earlier articles on Kant, Harnack, and Loisy.[5] By 1907, however, he was

---

[3] Thus Francisco Pasanisi (1852-1905), an influential civil servant in the Ministry of Foreign Affairs and a man greatly interested in religious studies, wrote to Loisy in October 1903: 'I believe that Italy is the country best fitted to give a welcome to your teachings and I would have you note that if Italy was the true homeland of Catholicism, if the Italian clergy created the existing organization of the Church at Trent, it is certainly Italy, and Italy alone, which can formulate the religion of the future and communicate it to Catholics throughout the world.' The entire letter is printed in M. Guasco, *Alfred Loisy in Italia: Con documenti inediti* (Turin, 1975), p. 217.

[4] G. Mattiussi, 'Il veleno kantiano', in *La Scuola Cattolica*, 30 (1902), pp. 52-71; 31 (1903), pp. 297-319.

[5] G. Mattiussi, *Il veleno Kantiano: Nuova ed antica critica della ragione, immanenza, filosofia dell'azione* (Monza, 1907). The *imprimatur* is dated January 1907, hence the book preceded *Lamentabili* and *Pascendi*.

concentrating his fire on Blondel and Laberthonnière.

Il veleno kantiano is a tiresome book to read. Typical of the type of anti-modernist writing to be found in *La Civiltà Cattolica*, it frequently offers a floridly expressed indignation in place of reasoned argument. Shrill in denunciation, arrogant in its assumed monopoly of truth and orthodoxy, and moralistic and hectoring in its summons to the 'neo-critici' to return to scholastic sanity, Mattiussi's book is paradigmatic of much of the anti-modernist campaign, especially in Italy. Mattiussi finds two major ideas in Kant's teaching which are particularly destructive of Christian faith. The first is subjectivism in the theory of knowledge; the second is the view that the will takes precedence over the intellect.[6] Catholic innovators such as Blondel, Laberthonnière, 'and their popularizers in Italy' have fallen under the spell of Kant in their flight from scholastic teaching on the objectivity of knowledge, on reason, on universals, and on the relationship between the act of knowing and the object known. By denying the competence of reason in religious matters the innovators demonstrate their contempt for the work of centuries, replacing it by their own new-fangled theory of immanence. Mattiussi claims that the Blondelians have taken the term 'immanence', which in scholastic usage referred to an act remaining in the subject without terminating in an external object, and have given it a new meaning. As used by the innovators the word refers to the finding of God within the soul of every right-thinking and good-living person. This is pure subjectivism, since each individual 'understands and sees according to the various dispositions immanent within himself'.[7] From this it follows that truth is relative, and, more important still, that the demonstration of truth becomes a process which is capricious and ill-determined, since it depends on such factors as the cultural differences of nations, ages, and individuals. The will replaces the intellect and, as everyone knows, the will is 'always supremely subjective'.

All thinkers since Aristotle have found it necessary to confront the knowing subject with something having real existence. Only Kant seems not to have felt this need. If, says Mattiussi, our thoughts take shape in a purely subjective

---

[6] Mattiussi, op. cit., p. 107.   [7] Ibid., p. 111.

manner, i.e., not having any relationship to real objects, there is no point looking for 'intelligible species' which conform to things.[8] Mattiussi is here merely reaffirming the basic tenets of neo-scholastic epistemology which defined truth as *adequatio intellectus et rei* achieved by means of *species intelligibiles* which represent the object in the mind. Kantianism, as he sees it, makes this correspondence between mind and object impossible. 'A Kantian can speak neither about truth nor about error.'[9]

Mattiussi goes on to discuss the consequences of the 'watered-down Kantianism' (kantismo diminuito') which he attributes to the Blondelians. (1) To distinguish between phenomena and noumena is to cast doubt upon our knowledge of the latter. (2) Truth becomes 'relative and mutable',[10] and objective certainty no longer possible. (3) Dogmas are in consequence rendered mutable. Kantianism necessarily denies revealed truth. Although these new authors do not dare to attack the divine character of revelation, they do question dogmatic definitions. Since truth depends on subjective dispositions, which are subject to change and evolution, conciliar definitions of the past will have to be adapted to the mind of our new age.[11] No one, says Mattiusi, has made this claim more shamelessly than Loisy.

All this, however, is intolerable. Since we are obliged to believe by divine faith, *cui subesse non potest falsum* (as Trent has said), the truths revealed by God and propounded by the Church, as they are contained in the clear assertions of the ordinary magisterium or of the supreme authority.[12]

To claim that these assertions are subject to alteration of meaning is to declare them false as they stand at present. Such a claim is in flat contradiction to the teaching of the Vatican Council. (4) Effective demonstration of Catholic truth is rendered impossible, since the subjectivism of the innovators rules out the possibility of universally valid argument.[13] It is thus no longer possible to establish principles which are evident in themselves and which, properly deployed, lead to conclusions which command the assent of all who are confronted by them.[14] (5) Preoccupation with

[8] Mattiussi, op. cit., p. 165.   [9] Ibid., p. 176.
[10] Ibid., p. 183.   [11] Ibid., p. 187.   [12] Ibid., p. 188.
[13] Ibid., pp. 191 f.   [14] Ibid., p. 194.

the 'modern mentality' has led the innovators to base their studies on phenomena and 'to look solely at the facts while distrusting metaphysical argument and a prioristic principles'.[15] Above all they exalt the advances made in critical history — an intellectual attitude which in a certain way chimes with Kantianism. In an excess of pride and vanity they want to reform everything: 'new philosophy, new theology, new biblical exegesis, from which will come perhaps a new kind of worship, of church order, and of the formulas proposed to faith'.[16] Failure to trust the intellect in matters of faith has led to the rejection of the wisdom of the past.

What are they going to put in the place of the scholastic philosophy of which they know nothing and which they have so unjustly ['mal'] derided? If there is in the doctrine of immanence anything which is not absurd — and there is a good deal of truth in the emphasis they lay on the influence of action over thought — it was all understood and said by the ancients with greater exactitude . . . than the new philosophers know how to do: whatever they have added can be reduced to the absurdities of Kantian idealism, to agnosticism and to scepticism.[17]

The only antidote to this 'compendium of errors' is a wholehearted return to the metaphysical wisdom of Aristotle and Aquinas standing rock-like above and beyond the sound and fury of the Kantian battlefield which strikes fear into the hearts only of the weak-minded.[18]

The primacy of will over intellect is for Mattiussi one of the most symptomatic and dangerous features of the new thinking. Here, he remarks, more than anywhere else can be found the hand of Kant, who, having shattered the intellectual order, attempted to repair the damage by his appeal to the will.[19] The innovators attempt something similar by their appeal to the freely willing and acting subject as a sufficient 'reason for affirming the *transcendent* (barbarous Kantian language)'.[20] The intellect, condemned to demolish itself, is

---

[15] Mattiussi, op. cit., p. 198: '. . . senza fidarsi delle ragioni metafisiche e dei principii a priori . . .'.
[16] Ibid., p. 199.   [17] Ibid., p. 200.   [18] Ibid., p. 205.
[19] Mattiussi's contempt for Kantian voluntarism reduces him to a patronizing pity and his prose to an indisciplined gush. The following remarks are by no means untypical of much anti-modernist apologetic: 'Lo vedete là quel povero Kant, come un polipo che stende i lunghi tentacoli, per aderire con le ventose a qualche scoglio, ma nell' immenso vuoto non trova nulla a che appigliarsi? Fa a voi compassione? A me fa ridere' (ibid., p. 208).   [20] Ibid., p. 218.

no longer a light to the heart but is itself enlightened by the heart.[21] Thus men can no longer be led to the faith by rational argument. Instead they are persuaded to find within themselves a felt need for the supernatural.[22] 'Good sense' takes over from the rationality of external proofs. Since the intellect is denied its proper powers, it cannot diagnose the presence of miracles 'those divine signs' which lead one to faith.[23] Refusal to accept the apologetic value of miracles implies a refusal to accept the necessary laws of nature, which in turn implies a rejection of physical science. (Mattiussi here takes it for granted that miracles operate on the empirical plane and as such are open to purely scientific demonstration.) It is a disgraceful confusion of ideas to claim that the act of faith cannot be built on a syllogism. Every theological novice knows that the act of faith must be directed by a good will assisted by grace; but he also knows that that act must be preceded by a rational judgement about credibility.[24] As Aquinas put it, 'non enim crederet homo nisi *sciret* esse credendum.' The function of signs such as miracles and prophecies is precisely to furnish evidence for credibility. Smart remarks about faith not proceeding from syllogisms merely confuse the issue.

The whole drive of the intellect is towards truth and away from error. Only extrinsic influences can deflect this drive. The will, however, is notoriously fickle. 'Again, we know that although original sin has indeed darkened the mind, its corrupting effect on the appetitive faculty is still greater.'[25] This fact is overlooked by the philosophers of action who place greater reliance on the will than on the intellect. Thus a bad will can effectively prevent the intellect from addressing itself to, say, the proofs for the existence of God.[26]

If Mattiussi's treatment of Blondel is cavalier and superficial, his rejection of Laberthonnière's *Dogmatisme moral* is an exercise in outrage masquerading as rational argument. Towards the end of *Il veleno kantiano* he includes Le Roy's 'Qu'est-ce qu'un dogme?' under the rubric of 'dogmatismo

[21] Mattiussi, op. cit., p. 258.   [22] Ibid., p. 260.
[23] Ibid., pp. 261 f.   [24] Ibid., p. 263.
[25] Ibid., pp. 264 f.: 'Sappiamo ancora che pel peccato originale è oscurata sì la mente, ma più corrotto è l'appetito.'   [26] Ibid., p. 267.

morale'.[27] This enables him to find new strains of the Kantian poison in the innovatory writings emanating from France.

Mattiussi's book gives evidence of an important phenomenon, characteristic of anti-modernist polemic from the start and reaching its climax in the encyclical *Pascendi*, namely, a methodological need to impose schematic unity on the new ideas coming out of France. It is important to recognize that the anti-Kant campaign, predominant feature that it was in the over-all anti-modernist strategy, was something more than theological McCarthyism. If Kant had not existed, it would have been necessary to invent someone like him. Neo-scholastic theology and philosophy formed a tightly knit schematic unit and it sought a similar cohesion in the positions of those who attacked it. The philosophy of Kant was a boon in this respect, since it provided just such a coherent philosophical system utterly antagonistic to neo-scholastic orthodoxy.

The Roman Jesuit journal *La Civiltà Cattolica*, second only to the *Osservatore Romano* as an index to curial thinking, became between 1905 and 1911 the principal counsel for the prosecution of modernism.[28] In 1905 the thirty-five year-old Father Enrico Rosa was appointed to the staff of the *Civiltà*. He was not a theologian or philosopher by choice, and it was his ability as a writer which determined his appointment.[29] He arrived in time to spearhead the literary side of the inquisition which was just then gathering pace. His output was enormous and repetitive. One reads the *Civiltà* of this period in vain for tempered criticism and the normal decencies of academic debate. A crusade had been declared and Enrico Rosa became its principal propagandist. It is impossible to synthesize his thought, which was fragmented and diffuse. He was a proficient linguist and his writings show him to have been conversant with a representative body of modernist writing. Virtually all the topics which were to appear in *Pascendi* can be found in Rosa's articles between

[27] Mattiussi, op. cit., pp. 269–74.

[28] See L. Bedeschi, *La curia romana durante la crisi modernista: Episodi e metodi di governo* (Parma, 1968), pp. 66–74.

[29] See A. M. Fiocchi, *P. Enrico Rosa S.J.: Scrittore della 'Civiltà Cattolica' (1870–1938): Il suo pensiero nelle controversie religiose e politiche del suo tempo* (Rome, 1957).

1905 and 1907. What one does not find is the systematic
unity of the encyclical. For the genesis of this unity one must
look elsewhere. Rosa's articles do, however, throw some light
on the topics which were causing greatest concern in curial
circles at the time.

As one might expect, Rosa devotes considerable attention
to the inroads made by the new thinking upon the Italian
scene and especially upon young clergy and seminarists. He
takes over in its entirety Mattiussi's thesis that the root cause
of contemporary errors in the Catholic Church is to be found
in the abandonment of scholasticism and the espousal of
Kant's philosophy.[30] He remarks that the defenders of the
philosophy of action, or moral dogmatism, of the method of
immanence, and of dogmatic pragmatism have a certain
brilliance and persuasiveness about them but lack philosophical precision and clarity.[31] They leave behind them the
shipwreck of mind ('idea'), of abstract thought, and of intellectual convictions. They abandon all possibility of demonstrating the existence and attributes of God. Faith can no
longer be for them intellectual assent 'as it must be for every
Catholic'.[32] Far more radical, however, is their denial of the
mind's natural capacity to discover reality and such matters
as the transcendentally valid relationship between cause and
effect which are indispensable to apologetics.

Rosa then attacks the new system for its psychologism.
It is dangerous to separate psychology from philosophy; it
is intolerable to reduce philosophy to the status of a branch
of psychology. The method of immanence restricts the entire
philosophical enterprise to an 'experimental perception of
consciousness'.[33] What an impoverished way of disposing of
the wisdom of centuries! This capitulation to 'the Anglo-
Saxon mentality of W. James', this 'fascination with obscure
ideas', this cult of ambiguity, all spell the death of apologetics. 'Morbid mysticism' is no useful replacement for a sound,

---

[30] Rosa devotes three articles to 'the new apologetic' all of which dwell on this
theme: 'Nuovi metodi nell' apologetica', *La Civiltà Cattolica* [*Civ. Cat.*] (1907),
vol. i, pp. 257–74; 'Illusioni del nuovi metodi di apologetica', *Civ. Cat.* (1907),
vol. ii, pp. 23–35; 'Conseguenze dei nuovi metodi di apologetica', ibid. (1907),
vol. iii, pp. 414–32.

[31] E. Rosa, 'Nuovi metodi nell' apologetica', ibid. (1907), vol. i, p. 260.

[32] Ibid., p. 264.   [33] Ibid., p. 266.

objectively based apologetic. An apologetic which is based on the subjectivism 'of religious sentiment is a contradiction in terms. What hope is there of making any impression on unbelievers by means of this new apologetic which is 'a product of sentimental mysticism, gratuitous fideism, and arbitrary ontologism'?[34] A writer in the Winter issue of *Studi Religiosi* had claimed that apologetics must begin from experimental psychology and a critique of the human cognitive faculty, not from logic. It was a carelessly made observation, and Rosa deals with it easily, pointing out that to abandon logic is to espouse irrationality, and that in order to criticize the cognitive faculty, you have to use, and therefore trust, the very faculty you are criticizing.[35] (Blondel suffered greatly from the enthusiastic simplifications of his popularizers.)

In common with all scholastics of the period Rosa laments time and again the innovators' alleged 'negation or [at least] confusion of the double order of supernatural and natural revelation'.[36] Here he does so in the context of a booklet by a certain Sostene Gelli entitled *Psicologia della religione*.[37] Rosa finds that the pamphlet is written 'con uno stile contorto ed anglosassone'.[38] This curious comment on the modernist movement's most lucid exponent is perhaps best seen as a symptom of Rosa's repugnance to Tyrrell's extreme anti-scholasticism. (It is not altogether clear what Rosa wishes to convey by the pejoratively intended 'Anglo-Saxon'. William James and Herbert Spencer are evidently in the wings of his mind.) Gelli's pamphlet, he claims, reduces to the status of an accessory what is in fact the very substance and foundation of religion, namely, the positive, supernatural, intellectual element of dogma to which the believing mind is called upon to assent. Instead we are given a definition of

---

[34] Rosa, art. cit., p. 274. The reference here is to von Hügel's article 'Experience and Transcendence', the Italian version of which had appeared in the Autumn issue of *Studi Religiosi*.

[35] E. Rosa, 'Conseguenze dei nuovi metodi di apologetica', in *Civ. Cat.* (1907), vol. ii, pp. 416–17. Rosa's prose at this point becomes less shrill and moralistic than when he is denouncing a position he dislikes but cannot refute.

[36] Ibid., p. 427.

[37] Ibid., S. Gelli, *Psicologia della religione* (Rome, 1905). 'Sostene Gelli' was one of Tyrrell's pseudonyms. The pamphlet was produced under the auspices of Murri's *Società nazionale di cultura.*   [38] Art. cit., p. 427.

religion as 'a feeling or collection of feelings determined by certain perceptions and leading to certain actions'.[39] 'In a certain sense it is possible to live religiously without any definite and concrete ('separato') act[s] of religion, internal or external, [but] solely by obeying [the dictates of] conscience and by following the interior *sense* of the absolute will.'[40] At this point Rosa's composure fails him. A pseudonymous author has produced a series of inexact and erroneous principles bearing on the most delicate matters in Christian faith, 'and a priest has printed them publicly here in Rome, together with other similar "religious pages", which have filled with doubts, and devastated the minds of, so many poor young people, clerical and lay.'[41] The theatricality of the outburst is a reminder that these passionately expressed sentiments were widely shared both in Rome and in France and that they played no small part in hastening the condemnation of modernism and in securing the advent of a regime of extreme repression. The metaphor of poison, employed by Mattiussi to characterize the alleged inroads of Kantianism into Catholic thought, suggested the need for a speedy and appropriate remedy.

The most influential theologian in Rome during the modernist period was Louis Billot S.J., Professor of Dogmatic Theology at the Gregorian University.[42] We have already seen

---

[38] Rosa, art. cit., p. 427.   [39] Ibid., pp. 427 f.   [41] Ibid., p. 428.

[42] Louis Billot, S.J. (1846–1931). There is no good biography of Billot. One might consult with much caution Henri le Floch, *Le Cardinal Billot: lumière de la théologie* (Paris, 1947), a hagiographical portrait by the influential former rector of the French Seminary in Rome who shared Billot's political as well as theological views and was forced to resign from his rectorship in the same year, 1927, and for the same reason (support for *Action Française*) as Billot's enforced resignation from the College of Cardinals. See also a somewhat more critical article written in 1911 (on the occasion of Billot's receiving the Red Hat), by J. Lebreton, 'Son Eminence le Cardinal Billot', (in *Études*, 129 (1911), pp. 514–25). If anyone could be said to have embodied the mentality of integralism it was Billot. Yet he is curiously neglected by historians of modernism. Poulat does not include him in the 'index bio-bibliographique' appended to his edition of the Houtin–Sartiaux life of Loisy. B. M. G. Reardon (*Roman Catholic Modernism* (London, 1970), p. 63 n.)) speaks of 'a certain Fr Billot'. While it is quite reasonable to regard late nineteenth- and early twentieth-century scholasticism as a very small theological tank, one should, however, recognize that Louis Billot was a very big fish in it. The condemnation of modernism ensured the theological hegemony in the Roman Catholic Church of much that Billot stood for. He taught at the Gregorian University from 1888 (when Raphael Merry del Val was in second-year

something of his theology of God, revelation, and the Church. An enemy of the Revolution and of all forms of liberalism, an admirer of Maurras and a supporter of *Action Française*, and, above all, a convinced Thomist, Billot saw in the new ideas coming from his native France all that he detested in religious, philosophical, and political thought. Even his admirers concede his defects as a scholar, most notably his lack of any historical sense or training. In fact Billot was not merely ahistorical but anti-historical in his attitude.[43] He believed that history was often invoked as a means of avoiding philosophical and theological commitment.[44] Even the most conservative commentators saw the irony (to put it at its mildest) of such a man writing a book on biblical inspiration.[45] He believed that the Bible was far too important to be left to the biblical scholars. In 1903 he defended the authenticity of the *Comma Johanneum* by syllogism and his intervention was rejected, with conscious humour also by syllogism, by the Consultors of the Biblical Commission in a statement which began 'Dissertatio Reverendissimi patris Billot supponit multa, probat nihil.'[46] By 1905 the (scholastic) theologians had effectively taken over the Biblical Commission and Billot met with no overt

theology) to 1911 when he was created a cardinal. Semeria and Murri spoke of him with respect (see L. Bedeschi, *La curia romana*, p. 67 n., and P. Scoppola, *Crisi modernista e rinnovamento cattolico in Italia* (Bologna, 1961), p. 253). Buonaiuti disliked Billot intensely, describing him as 'a bony and angular figure of a theologian, lean and dry, for whom religious and Christian life had taken on the shape of an eternal syllogism' (E. Buonaiuti, *Pelegrino di Roma* (Bari, 1964), p. 80).

[43] A. Houtin (*La Question biblique au XXe siècle* (Paris, 1906), pp. 197-8) gives Mgr. Touchet, Bishop of Orleans, as the source of the story that in 1902 Billot remarked proudly to one of his colleagues: 'Il y a vingt ans que j'enseigne; mes élèves ignorent qu'il y ait une question biblique.'

[44] Lebreton (art. cit., p. 523) said of Billot in 1911 that if he had to make a choice between metaphysics and history he would unhesitatingly choose the former, since he believed that the essence of theology consisted in the exposition of dogma and not in its history. This is a tactful understatement. In point of fact Billot threw the two into virtually irreconcilable opposition.

[45] L. Billot, *De inspiratione sacrae scripturae* (Rome, 1903). For contemporary comment see *Bulletin de littérature ecclésiastique* (1906), p. 229.

[46] F. Turvasi, *Giovanni Genocchi e la controversia modernista* (Rome, 1974), pp. 226 f. Genocchi wrote to Fracassini about Billot's method: 'Si fece un sillogismo, predendo a base la tesi di Franzelin: ogni *testo dogmatico* della volgata è autentico. Atqui. Ergo, Ma non c'e nei codici greci. Respondeo: se non c'è, deve esserci. Guardateci meglio, lo troverete' (Turvasi, op. cit., p. 222).

opposition within the Commission when he stated that the Mosaic authorship of the Pentateuch was *de fide*, if not defined, at least *proxime definibili*.[47]

In 1904 Billot published his most concentrated attack on the new ideas in a book entitled *De sacra Traditione contra novam haeresim evolutionismi*.[48] He acknowledges his debt to Mattiussi's two articles on the immutability of dogma written for *La Scuola Cattolica* in 1903. Mattiussi had traced back the notion of relative truth to Kant,[49] arguing that if dogmatic propositions are not immutable, it follows that they must be judged false in their first form and can never be said to be true as long as they are subject to change.[50] Billot takes over this thesis and restates it with even greater conviction and rigidity. The concept of relative truth is intrinsically absurd, he claims; and he will admit of no other possible definition of truth apart from the classical 'adequatio intellectus et rei'.[51] Addressing himself to Loisy's remark, 'les conceptions que l'Église présente comme des dogmes révélés ne sont pas des vérités tombées du ciel', Billot claims that Loisy's view of revelation, vitiated as it is by the philosophically absurd concept of relative truth, destroys the very possibility of faith. Billot compares the concepts used in doctrinal propositions to the letters of the alphabet which an author uses to convey his ideas when he forms words. Individual concepts such as substance, body, soul, life, spirit, cause, effect, ends, means, potency, act, all have an earthly origin, but when they are formed into doctrines proposed to faith on the authority of God who reveals, the resulting truths do indeed come from heaven. It is a calumny to say that theology has been adapted to Aristotelian philosophy.

---

[47] Turvasi, op. cit., pp. 241 f.

[48] Rome, 1904. A second edition with major changes appeared in 1907. (Le Floch omits the second edn in his bibliography, op. cit., p. 38 n.) The title of the second edn is also significantly changed to *De immutabilitate traditionis contra modernam haeresim evolutionismi* (Rome, 1907). The continuing influence of Billot's book can be gauged by the fact that two further edns. appeared in 1922 and 1929 respectively. Page references here are to the 4th edn. (Rome, 1929), which is identical with the 1907 and 1922 edns. except for pagination.

[49] G. Mattiussi, 'Dogma mutabile (Loisy ed altri)', in *La Scuola Cattolica*, 31 (1903), pp. 235-55, *passim*, but esp. pp. 239 f.

[50] Ibid., pp. 248 f.   [51] L. Billot, *De immutabilitate traditionis*, p. 101.

Philosophy does for theology what a lexicon does for exegesis. You do not say that an exegete accommodates his exposition to the lexicon he uses; neither did the scholastic doctors accommodate sacred doctrine to philosophy.[52]

Billot devotes a chapter to the refutation of Laberthonnière's *Dogmatisme moral.*[53] It is a curious fact that Laberthonnière, by no means the most radical of the modernists, drove orthodox scholastics to their most outraged reactions. He more than any other modernist, Tyrrell alone perhaps excepted, concentrated his fire on what he saw as the ravages wrought in theology by the influence of Aristotle. In attacking the system, not always temperately, he gave maximum offence to its defenders, an offence quite disproportionate to the objective reality of what he was saying. Temperamentally and spiritually, as well as philosophically, he and Billot were totally incompatible. In 1912, referring to a sarcastic letter which Billot had written to the *Bulletin de littérature ecclésiastique* about 'pauvres petits abbés immanentistes qui ont du vague à l'âme', Laberthonnière remarked to Blondel: 'Ah! lui, le card. Billot, n'a pas de vague à l'âme!'[54] Billot included under the rubric 'dogmatismus moralis' not merely Laberthonnière's theory but also the entire Blondelian concept of action, with Le Roy's interpretation of dogma thrown in for good measure. The opening sentences of his chapter on the subject are worth quoting as an indication of what tended to happen when Blondelian subtleties were translated into neo-scholastic terminology by someone convinced that the very description of these new ideas was a self-evident demonstration of their absurdity.

Moral dogmatism can be described in general terms as a system which derives the knowledge of religious truth from the prompting of the heart and the guidance of a morally good will. It retains, indeed it campaigns for, every principle of the system of immanence. It also proclaims the ruin of absolute truth, i.e. the proportioning of the intellect to external reality, which [it claims] is not possible in religious matters . . . It proposes, however, to repair the damage by reconstructing the building on the foundation[s] of morality and by bequeathing

[52] Billot, op. cit., p. 126.
[53] Ch. 3 of the 1st edn. was entitled 'De dogmatismo morali'. This becomes Ch. 5 of the 2nd edn. with the intensified heading, 'De consummatione ruinae per dogmatismum moralem'.   [54] *B.V.*, vol. ii, p. 367.

to dogmas its own notion of truth, which is not so much speculative and objective as practical and regulative of good behaviour . . . It is in morality therefore that one will find the solid basis which an exhausted intellectual dogmatism has vainly sought in an objective truth which is unknown and unknowable.[55]

Kant, from whom this new system derives, did much the same when he destroyed the entire edifice of truth, leaving not a stone upon a stone. Awestruck (*atteritus*) by the devastation he had wreaked, Kant attempted to rebuild on morality what he had destroyed in the name of reason. Today, Billot remarks, the innovators are attempting a similar operation with the help of the idea of the relative truth. The whole business goes by the name of 'philosophy of action'.[56] Billot then sets about his refutation of the new ideas.

He flatly denies that there are two notions of truth, one valid for religious, the other for non-religious, matters. There is therefore no need to call in the will to perform a task to which, in any case, the intellect, and only the intellect, is equal. Sane philosophy has long since delineated the role of the will in religious matters. (1) It stimulates and encourages the intellect in matters where the intellect is likely to take fright or grow discouraged. (2) It prompts the intellect to seek for arguments (*rationes*) which will allow truth to emerge. (3) It commands the intellect to assent to truths which are not self-evident but the acceptance of which is made rational by reason of a motivating authority.[57] The will performs all these tasks but it should never arrogate to itself the role proper to the intellect. If it were to do so, it would reduce faith to irrationality. This is precisely the role assigned to the will by the supporters of moral dogmatism.

Billot winds up his case against moral dogmatism with an attack on Le Roy's theory of dogmatic pragmatism which he describes as 'sheer somnambulism'.[58] Nowhere does he attempt a reasoned argument against the theories he attacks nor does he indicate the reservations which both Blondel and Laberthonnière had expressed about Le Roy's thesis.

---

[55] Billot, *De immutabilitate traditionis*, p. 128.   [56] Ibid., pp. 128–30.
[57] Ibid., pp. 130–2.   [58] Ibid., p. 149.

Billot's attack on Loisy in his fourth and last chapter[59] comes as something of an anticlimax in that it merely reproduces the bones of Loisy's thesis on revelation and associated questions discussed in *L'Évangile et l'Église* and *Autour d'un petit livre*.[60] Billot simply removes all the nuances of Loisy's case together with the contexts against which the main elements were set and then baldly states Loisy's main contentions in such a way as to suggest that refutation would be superfluous. 'Truly it would be impossible to think up a more radical negation of every principle and rule of Catholic Christian faith.'[61] This heresy, if indeed it can be called a heresy, has its roots in the application to Catholic tradition of the so-called *historical method* which has had the effect of reintroducing into theology the notion of dogmatic evolution sponsored by Günther, condemned by the Vatican Council, but now tricked out with the Darwinian theory of evolution helped by the concept of relative truth. From relative truth one slides easily into the denial of all objective truth. This downward journey is further aided by the Kant-inspired idea of moral dogmatism. Finally you arrive at the system proclaimed in *L'Évangile et l'Église*.

What Billot does in this book is to attempt a very rough and ready synthesis of the new ideas. There are none of the tightly knit logical sequences we find in *Pascendi*. What we do find, however, is the conviction that these new ideas are interconnected· and threaten the very foundations of the faith.

We turn now to the contribution of Joseph Lemius, at this time Procurator General of the Oblates of Mary Immaculate.[62] Lemius is today widely accepted as the principal draughtsman of the theoretical exposition of modernism given in the encyclical letter, *Pascendi dominici gregis*, issued by Pope Pius X on 8 September 1907. Although Lemius published nothing of note either during or after the modernist

---

[59] 'De fide vivente', which becomes Ch. 6 of the next 3 edns. under the title 'De cumulo omnium errorum in systemate fidei viventis' (ibid., pp. 152-68).

[60] The 1st edn. carries extensive quotations from Loisy (in French) in the footnotes. These do not appear in the three following editions, though the main body of the Latin text remains unchanged.

[61] Ibid., p. 7. [62] On Joseph Lemius see Appendix 1.

crisis, he lectured on several occasions to the Academy of St. Thomas in Rome on Loisy's thought and was respected for his mastery of that thought. There are two extant type-scripts of lectures which Lemius gave to the Academy of St. Thomas. The first, dated 14 May 1905, is entitled 'Sur les doctrines de Loisy' (the text, however, is in Italian). The second, dated 2 May 1907, is entitled 'Le basi filosofiche del sistema Loisiano'.

Though severe in his judgements on Loisy, Lemius is far less shrill in his denunciations and more reasoned in his exposition and criticism than any of the anti-modernists we have been considering. He writes as a philosopher with a flair for systematization; and it is this characteristic which provides the clearest adumbration of what was eventually to appear in *Pascendi*. He shares, it need hardly be said, a great deal of common ground with men like Schwalm, Gayraud, and Fontaine in France and with Mattiussi, Rosa, and Billot in Italy, but he evinces a stronger urge than they to connect up the disparate elements in the case he is attacking and thus to confer on those elements a logical cohesion which is academically tenuous but pedagogically satisfying. We shall concentrate here upon passages from Lemius's scripts which suggest something of the systematization to be found in *Pascendi*. It should further be noted that he is dealing expressly with Loisy and not with modernism in general.

Lemius opens his lecture of May 1905 with the blunt state-ment that Loisy is 'an intellectual atheist' who has learnt from Liberal Protestants, and especially from Auguste Sabatier,[63] the bizarre lesson of how to combine an atheistic intellect with a believing and religious heart. Lemius announces that his intention is to demonstrate that Loisy's atheism is the basic inspiration of his critical method. In Loisy's writings we find a series or chain of errors which lead logically to atheism in questions of criticism and history. 'Loisy, that is to say, is shamelessly subjectivistic and there-fore positivist; positivist, and therefore an intellectual idealist; intellectual idealist, and therefore agnostic, agnostic and

[63] Lemius would have agreed with Grandmaison's view that whatever the modernists might say, 'they sweat Sabatier from every pore' (cited in Poulat, *Histoire*, p. 100 n.).

therefore an intellectual atheist.'[64] We may wonder about the sense which Lemius intends each of his terms to carry, but the repetition of the consequential 'quindi' indicates his design of showing the causal connection between each link in the chain. Subjectivism he defines as the notion that 'all human knowledge is consciousness.' Ideas are merely pale images of subjective impressions. An idea cannot transcend the scope of the impression from which it is formed; and since impressions are caused by sensible phenomena, it follows that notions or ideas cannot transcend the phenomenal world. This, he observes, is positivism. It follows further that notions or ideas purporting to derive from beyond the phenomenal world are 'void of all reality' and thus are nothing more than logical abstractions. This is intellectual idealism. God and the transcendent order lie outside the scope of human knowledge. This is agnosticism. Loisy, Lemius claims, cannot remain in this agnosticism in respect of God's intervention in history. He therefore in effect says that God, not being a historical person, *cannot* intervene in history. This is atheism, since it denies by implication that God is God. Loisy's conception of history is atheistic precisely because it rules out, *a priori*, the *possibility* of a historical manifestation of the transcendent. Banished from the sphere of objective reality, the Transcendent becomes no more than the object ('termine') of a purely psychological phenomenon, an object, that is, externalized in sacred books and religious institutions, by means of which the psychological phenomenon can be analysed, studied, and subjected to historical examination. This phenomenon has its roots in the heart and achieves objectivity only in a mediated form, namely, in the analysis which can be made of its external manifestations. Nothing, remarks Lemius, gets on Loisy's nerves more than the notion of a revelation manifested externally by God to humanity.[65] Thus for Loisy there are two kinds of history, the one external and real, the other interior

---

[64] 'Il Loisy cioè e sfacciatamente soggettivista, quindi positivista; positivista, quindi idealista intellettuale; idealista intellettuale, quindi agnosticista; agnosticista, quindi ateo intellettuale.'

[65] 'Difatti, non vi è nulla, nel domma cattolico, quale l'intendiamo noi, che urti più i nervi del Loisy, che le rivelazione fatta esternamente da Dio all' umanità . . .'

and concerned with the transcendent.[66] Loisy gives a prioristic status to his 'atheistic principle' that every account of a
manifestation of the transcendent must be the expression of
an inner psychological state. To this principle he adds a
second: the religious mind gives birth to the transcendent
only by taking into itself real, i.e. external, phenomena,
altering and adapting them to religious needs in such a way
that while they cannot be said to belong properly to the
transcendent sphere, they nevertheless escape the limitations
of normal historicity.

Faith, then, originates in the heart and, following an instinct for self-preservation, seeks entry into the mind where a
series of judgements takes place transforming faith as religious sentiment into objectified beliefs. In this way theology
is born. 'From the moment he begins to believe, man, says
Loisy, finds it impossible not to ponder on what he believes
(here we have intellectual transposition) and then to work
further upon the fruits of his pondering, thus producing a
theology of faith.'[67] Just as faith comes to being in the
heart, so theological reflection, according to Loisy, takes
place at the heart's behest. Modern psychologists distinguish
between the logic of feeling and rational logic, the latter
being at the service of the former in religious matters. Loisy's
logical structure envisages simple beliefs proceeding through
explanation to the justification of beliefs. He describes this
process as 'idealization', in that the more abstract the treatment becomes, the more it recedes from reality. This process of idealization divides in its turn into two streams,
the one imaginative and employing symbolism and allegory,
the other speculative and employing philosophical language. The process is then historicized and given an evolutionary dynamic. 'Evolution — there in a word you have
the foundation of the philosophy of history as the neo-
critics understand it. Faith is a vital force, or in other words,

---

[66] 'Di qui due storie: l'una estrinseca cioè e reale; l'altra intrinseca o del
trascendente.'
[67] 'Dal momento che si crede, dice il Loisy, è impossibile che non si pensi
quel che si crede (ecco la trasposizione intellettiva) e che non si lavori poi su
questo pensiero e non si produca così la teologia della fede.' The reference given
by Lemius is to *Études évangéliques*, p. 171.

a seed . . .'[68] Being a vital force, or seed destined for growth, the faith will evolve not speculatively as the scholastics would have it, but 'vitally'.

Lemius then translates this process into scholastic language, laying it out according to the four classical kinds of causality, viz., efficient, material, formal, and final. The efficient cause of development is the religious impulse which battles with forces which seek to destroy faith. Evolutionists therefore speak frequently of progressive and conservative forces which come into existence by way of reaction. The material and formal causes of the evolutionary process will be expressed in dogmas and religious institutions. 'Now, those forces which the faith encounters do not leave it unaffected but transform it, transfigure it, infusing into it their own life.'[69] The final cause is embodied in the need which every living thing experiences of conserving, protecting, and propagating itself. A faith like Christianity which aspires to universality must develop in relation to a succession of environmental conditions. Without this development it will die.

Once you discover a symbolic or philosophical element in the documents, you will find it necessary to enquire, under the guidance of secular history, into the provenance of this element's ambience; then [you will have to establish] in what period the faith came into contact with this ambience.[70]

This procedure can be applied to such questions as the Logos theory in christology.

Lemius condenses his exposition of Loisy's procedure into four classes of principle: (1) the principle which eliminates the transcendent from real history. (2) The principle which reduces facts, actions, and words to the normal conditions of historicity. (3) Principles which serve to distinguish the different elements superimposed by faith on the ground of

[68] 'L'evoluzione, ecco in una parola, il fondamento della filosofia della storia, quale l'intendono i neo-critici. La fede è una forza vitale, ossia un germe . . .'.

[69] 'Orbene, quegli elementi che la fede attinge dal mezzo, non li lascia punto tali e quali, ma li trasforma, li trasfigura, infondendo loro la propria vita . . .'.

[70] 'Trovato nei documenti un' elemento simbolico o filosofico, si dovrà cercare, sotto la scorta della storia profana, a qual mezzo o ambiente questo elemento appartenga; poi, in qual epoca la fede sia entrata in contatto col medesimo mezzo o ambiente.'

reality. (4) Principles which serve to bring faith into conformity with temporal developments.[71] These principles 'in fact suppose that God never intervenes in history and that everything proceeds, both in the origin and in the development of religion, by virtue of purely natural causes'.[72]

Given his invincibly scholastic viewpoint, Lemius makes his case against Loisy with reason, moderation, and far less misrepresentation than any of the other anti-modernists we have been considering. Two years later, when he gave the second of his extant lectures, a note of urgency, not present before, has become apparent. Who can doubt, he asks, that we are now in a state of war? Under the guise of biblical criticism some of the most serious philosophical errors are being disseminated.[73] The threat can now be clearly seen to be basically philosophical. The substitution of the new philosophy for the old can result only in the destruction of dogma. We can no longer afford to remain in our ivory tower engaged in scholarly study of the issues while a war to the death is being fought in the streets below. The only answer to falsehood is truth, in this instance philosophical truth. Only Aristotelian philosophy in all its logical rigour can meet the dangers which are facing us today. 'In a system of doctrines so rigorously connected and linked as is the system of Aristotle and the Angelic Doctor, no single point can be detached from the others, [since] the light of truth which illumines each individual part is the same as that which illumines the whole.'[74] This is one of the clearest statements

[71] '1° Canone che elimina il trascendente dalla storia reale. 2° Canone che riduce i fatti, le azioni, le parole alle condizioni normali d'istoricità. 3° Canoni che servono a distinguere i diversi elementi sovvrapposti dalla fede sul fundo reale. 4° Canoni che servono ad ordinarli lungo il tempo.'

[72] 'Suppongono infatti che Iddio non intervenga mai nella storia, e che tutto proceda, anche nell'origine e nello sviluppo della religione, per pura virtù delle cause naturali.'

[73] 'Errori filosofici che, dopo girato a lungo attorno alla piazza, cercando di scagliarvi, di sopra alle mura, le loro freccie avvelenate, vi sono stati finalmente introdotti di soppiatto e sotto veste mentitrice, da chi altra incombenza non avea per contrario, che di respongerli e di farli star lontani.'

[74] '. . . in un sistema di dottrine così rigorosamente connesse e concatenate, qual'é il sistema di Aristotele e dell'Angelico, nessun punto puo andar disgiunto dagli altri, e che la vera luce che vi rischiara le singole parti è quella che va attinta dall'assieme e dal tutto.'

of philosophical integralism to be found in the Roman writings of the period.

Lemius then goes on to examine the issue of transcendence, noting that Aristotle employs the word in a manner very different from that of the moderns. According to Aristotle, being is transcendent because it exceeds in scope the limitations of individuating matter and the predicamental forms. The moderns understand the term transcendent to mean going beyond the sensible or phenomenal, and they allow the mind no direct access to it. God is therefore inaccessible to the human mind. This agnosticism is at the roots of the entire Loisian system. At this point Lemius appears to have substantially modified his approach of 1905. He is less concerned to press the charge of overt atheism. Loisy, he claims, has been driven into psychologism by his metaphysical deficiencies. In this psychological ambience he finds himself at a crossroads: he must take either the path of atheistic rationalism or that of religious immanence. In the event he takes the latter. Lemius here propounds the thesis that the doctrine of immanence (which he ascribes to Loisy) is a cover for atheism. It is, to use the language of espionage, the task of the orthodox Catholic apologist to blow this cover and reveal the agent for what he is. 'Having thus set out from agnosticism, with the intention of saving religion at all costs, Loisy was drawn inexorably to vital immanence.'[75] In consequence of this step several new possibilities open up before him. The new philosophy recognizes four human faculties: the pure intellect, the practical intellect, the faculty of feeling, and the will, or faculty of action. Therefore if you deny transcendent competence to the pure intellect, you are left with three other possibilities. With Kant you can have recourse to the practical intellect; with Sabatier you can have recourse to religious feeling; or with Blondel and Laberthonnière you can have recourse to the will and action.

But Kant's religious theory has had its day; pragmatism in the shape of the philosophy of action was not yet a live option. Be that as it may, it is only necessary to turn a few of Loisy's pages to notice that he

---

[75] 'Partito adunque dall'agnosticismo, con la volontà di salvare ad ogni costo la religione, il Loisy fu trascinato all'immanenza vitale.' This is the only instance I have found of the pre-*Pascendi* use of the precise phrase 'vital immanence'.

founds his religion on feeling, on experience, on an intuition of the heart. The heart — there you have what is for him the prime initiator of all religion.[76]

This diagnosis is particularly interesting in that it shows Lemius to have been considerably more discriminating than the other anti-modernists in not throwing together the (unacknowledged) philosophical assumptions of Loisy and the philosophical convictions of Blondel and Laberthonnière. Lemius is surely quite correct in his implication that Loisy had been far more deeply influenced by Sabatier than he was prepared to admit.[77] The progression which Lemius finds in Loisy's teaching runs from agnosticism through immanence (avoiding overt atheism), drawing close to the philosophy of action, but finally ending in religious feeling. This feeling is then, he says, analysed by Loisy, and from the analysis there result those intellectual formulas which, once they have been approved by the competent authority as responding to the social conscience of the age, are called dogmas. The intellectual validity of these formulas is non-existent apart from the sphere of religious sentiment. In every other way they are merely relative symbols fabricated by religious man to express his feeling. Such expression is necessarily controlled by the general state of human knowledge at any given time in any given place. Dogmas must therefore develop, if they are to serve their purpose.

The evolution of dogma, in the Loisian system, is the simultaneous product of three principles: Agnosticism as the negative cause; immanence as the positive cause; the relative and variable character of the intellectual formulae which serve as an envelope for religious feeling [acts] as the condition.[78]

---

[76] 'Ma la teoria religiosa del Kant aveva fatto il suo tempo; il prammatismo, ossia la filosofia dell'azione, non si era anco aperta strada. Comunque sia, basta svolgere alcune pagine del Loisy per avvertire che egli fonda la sua religione sul sentimento, su una esperienza, su un'intuizione del cuore. Il cuore, ecco per lui il primo fondatore di ogni religione.'

[77] Lemius's surviving notes show that he had read Auguste Sabatier's *Esquisse d'une philosophie de la religion d'après l'histoire et la psychologie* with great care.

[78] 'L'evoluzione del domma, nel sistema loisiano, resulte simultaneamente da tre principii: dal agnosticismo, cioè, come causa negativa; dall' immanenza, come causa positiva; dal carattere relativo e variabile delle formole intellettive, che servono d'involucro al sentimento religioso, come condizione.'

Lemius concludes his lecture by reiterating his contention that agnosticism is the root cause of all the other errors currently abroad. It is therefore upon agnosticism, he says, that we must bring our redoubled efforts to bear. We must first of all vindicate the objective validity of our mental concepts, or in scholastic language, of universals. Secondly, we must deepen our study of the principle of causality and in general of synthetic and analytic judgements. Finally, we must make it our task to demonstrate how the doctrine of analogy can chart a course between anthropomorphism on the one hand and agnosticism on the other.

The attitude manifested by the authors we have been considering in this chapter came to be described as 'integralist'.[79] The word 'integralism' has had a varied history from its origins in Spanish politics in the 1890s, through the modernist period, down to the present day when it is usually employed to describe the anti-modernist crusade launched in 1907 and lasting until the end of Pius X's pontificate. The fact that it often carried strong political overtones is a reminder of the overlap that often occurs between political and theological conservatism. (*Action Française* could count many right-wing Thomists in its membership.) The usefulness of the term integralism to describe extreme theological conservatism during the modernist period lies in its etymological suggestion of orthodoxy as devotion to an alleged 'whole' which had to be defended against the modification of any of its parts. Joseph Lemius, among the more moderate of the Roman integralists, spoke for them all when he said that in the system of doctrines comprising scholastic orthodoxy no one point could be detached from the others without endangering the whole to which they belonged. Precisely because the integralists saw this whole as transcendentally guaranteed, they insisted on its segregation from the normal commerce of critical ideas. The system was for them a faithful replica of an immutable, eternal, reality. The

---

[79] For a discussion of the term 'intégrisme' see E. Poulat, ' "Modernisme" et "Intégrisme": Du concept polémique à l'irénisme critique', in *Archives de sociologie des religions*, 27 (1969), pp. 3–28. Poulat examines the integralist movement in detail in his *Intégrisme et Catholicisme intégral: Un réseau secret international antimoderniste: La 'Sapinière', 1909–1921* (Paris, 1969).

replication was, to be sure, by way of analogy; but in the doctrine of analogy one can emphasize either the positive or the
negative content. By a theologian like Louis Billot the negative element, while theoretically affirmed, was in practice
ignored, and those who strove to affirm it in practice as well
as in theory were quickly labelled 'agnostic'. Billot could
contemplate the eternal truths with a consciousness of
absolute clarity and, what meant more to him, of absolute
logic. For all their allegiance to Aristotle, the integralists took
a Platonist view of the relationship between eternity and
time. Why should they heed the demands of science? In this
their French compeers pointed the way. Who knows, wrote
the Abbé Maignen in 1903, whether Galileo's theory will not
one day be proved false?

In response to a perpetually changing science, the Church is antecedently justified in not seeking a useless reconciliation of her dogmas
with the provisional data of the sciences. She need concern herself
only with her own teaching which relies on faith alone and with her
care for the needs of souls by defending them against the causes of
doubt and the threat of rash opinions.

Science may be constantly changing; faith, however, is immutable.[80]

The integralists saw revelation as a body of truths delivered
by God into the hands of an authoritative magisterium to be
laid before the obedient intellects of the faithful. Theology,
as Leo XIII had construed it in *Aeterni Patris*, was an exercise, partly analytic partly synthetic, in the organization of
the data of revelation as presented by the magisterium in any
age. This view of theology can be fairly described as 'dogmatic positivism'. Lucien Laberthonnière called it 'intellectualism', because it treated the speculative intellect as a
heavy-duty, omnicompetent instrument able to perform
equally well beyond as within the realm of the senses. The
integralists based their system on this omnicompetence and
stigmatized every challenge to it in religious matters as
'agnosticism'. The ferocity of their attack on Kant's philosophy is an indication of their most vulnerable areas. Their
discomfort with the post-Kantian terms 'transcendence'
and 'immanence' is evident in all they wrote. They use the
terms only under protest. 'Barbarous', said Mattiussi of the

---

[80] Cited in Poulat, *Histoire*, p. 205.

term 'transcendent'; while the term 'immanent' was for all of them redolent of 'subjectivism', with all the capricious indeterminism and instability connoted by that word. They stood for an objective order available to the intellect through the senses which provided the evidence either directly through intelligible species or indirectly through signs which pointed the mind infallibly towards the invisible and eternal. They loathed Kant with all the passion of a man who, challenged to a duel, finds that his opponent has swept from his hands the only weapon he knows how to use.

Protestant theology did what it could with the 'terms of peace' which Kant had offered;[81] scholastic orthodoxy refused to recognize that there was a case to answer, much less a peace to be negotiated. The violence of integralist polemic was to a great extent the product of fear and incomprehension. The nineteenth century had witnessed a skilfully organized Catholic retreat from the jungle of post-Enlightenment ideas to the *hortus conclusus* of an artificially constructed theology. The trouble was that at the dawn of the twentieth century some of the more adventurous of the garden-dwellers were venturing outside the walls and finding that, for all the perils and discomforts of the jungle, life was more realistic and faith more authentic there. The crisis came, however, only when they returned to the garden, leaving the gate open behind them and persuading other garden-dwellers of the excitements and challenges to be found outside. By 1910 the gate would be locked and the adventurers either excluded from the garden or persuaded to ignore the itch in their feet.

---

[81] K. Barth, *Protestant Theology in the Nineteenth Century: Its Background and History* (London, 1972), p. 278.

9 The Integralist Response (2): *Pascendi* and After

The lecture which Joseph Lemius gave to the Academy of
St. Thomas on 2 May 1907 reflected a sense of growing crisis
felt throughout Roman curial circles. A group of powerful
curial cardinals was pressing for a condemnation of the new
ideas.[1] Raphael Merry del Val, Cardinal Secretary of State,
belonged to this group and, because of the weight his
opinions carried with the Pope, was in a particularly advan-
tageous position to have something done. He and Pius shared
a pessimistic temperament, and both were becoming increasingly convinced that the Church had entered its hour of trial.
Church–State relations in France had rarely been worse.[2]
French bishops attempting to work out a *rapprochement*
with the Combes government found themselves condemned
by the Secretariat of State for faint-heartedness. Rome was
in no mood for dialogue with what it saw as the gathering
forces of darkness. Integralist orthodoxy would be proclaimed on all fronts, political, theological, philosophical,
and disciplinary. There would be no discussion, no argument,

[1] These cardinals included intransigents such as Francesco Segna, Benedetto
Lorenzelli, Gaetano De Lai, and Calesanz Vivès y Tuto (see L. Bedeschi, *La curia
romana durante la crisi modernista* (Parma, 1968), pp. 51–66). In 1906 the
Oratorian, and future Rector of the Institut Catholique of Paris, Alfred Baudrillart, visited Cardinal Vivès y Tuto in Rome to intercede for Laberthonnière.
Baudrillart was startled by the vehemence of the cardinal's outburst: 'M. Combes
has not done a hundredth part of the damage inflicted on French Catholics by the
doctrinal anarchy of your clergy . . . Philosophical liberalism, theological liberalism, biblical liberalism, spiritual ('ascétique') liberalism — it's all there and it's
killing true Catholicism. The time has come for vigorous reaction' (cited in M.-T.
Perrin, *Laberthonnière et ses amis* (Paris, 1975) p. 94).

[2] See M. Larkin, *Church and State after the Dreyfus Affair: The Separation
Issue in France* (London, 1974). This scholarly and witty study gives a valuable
picture of the political attitudes of the Vatican during the modernist period.
Merry's intransigent policy on Church–State relations in France, which brought
him into conflict with some of the French bishops, was of a piece with his theological views. 'He had an unusual capacity for lumping together those he saw as
enemies. People and groups who had little in common would suddenly find themselves thrown together in the cold embrace of one of his anathemas' (p. 197).

no compromise. 'Error has no rights' was an accepted maxim in the scholastic jurisprudence of the age, and the maxim was shortly to be put into grim practice.

On 17 April 1907 the Pope addressed some newly-created cardinals in an *Allocutio* entitled 'Contra neo-reformismum religiosum'.[3] There are rebels in the Church, Pius proclaimed, 'who profess and disseminate in a subtle form monstrous errors' on the evolution of dogma; on the need to return to the pure Gospel stripped of theological explanations, conciliar definitions, and ascetical maxims; on emancipation from the Church, though not in such an overt fashion as to court ejection; and, finally, on the need for adaptation to the times. This attack 'is not a heresy, but the compendium and poison of all the heresies'.[4] The rebels have reduced Scripture to the status of a common book, have restricted biblical inspiration to purely doctrinal matters and wish to subject Church teaching 'to the rules of so-called scientific criticism', thus enslaving Theology. They claim that tradition is relative and hence subject to change, and thereby they reduce to nothing the authority of the Holy Fathers.[5] These and a thousand other errors they publish in books, reviews, spiritual writings, and even in novels (Fogazzaro's novel *Il Santo* had been published in November 1905). They employ ambiguous terms and cloudy forms the better to sow their cockle. The Pope concluded his allocution with an appeal to the new cardinals to help him govern the Church by condemning these rebels and by denouncing their books to the Roman Congregations.

The Allocution was in effect a declaration of war in which the next shot came a month later from the other side. A group of young priests addressed the Pope in an open letter entitled *Quello che vogliamo*.[6] In general the letter deploys the Blondelian thesis of action and immanence apologetics. Since the deductive method, the authors remark, carries little

[3] *Acta Sanctae Sedis*, 40 (Rome, 1907), pp. 266-9.

[4] '. . . non è un'eresia, ma il compendio e il veleno di tutte le eresie . . .' (ibid., p. 268).   [5] Ibid., p. 268.

[6] Lorenzo Bedeschi prints the letter in full in his *Interpretazioni e sviluppo del modernismo cattolico* (Milan, 1975), pp. 150-70. It was translated by G. Tyrrell and A. L. Lilley and published under the latter's name as *What we Want: An Open Letter to Pius X from a Group of Priests* (London, 1907).

weight in the positive sciences today, man is driven to find within himself and in the dynamic circumstances and demands ('esigenze') of his life the practical reason for his own actions.[7] Defenders of the Christian faith simply betray that faith if they rely on an outdated apologetic wedded to metaphysical formulas which no longer carry meaning. Such a betrayal is all the more regrettable when we see that scholars are, by the very inadequacies of a cold science, driven to speak of an Unknown or to seek and find within themselves an inexpressible Reality which directs their lives towards the Good and the True and which they call God.[8]

Religion, if it is to be accepted, cannot be imposed by means of a syllogism, it presupposes the *rationabile obsequium* without which it lacks moral value for him who professes it. God, revelation, the Church, dogma, cannot be imposed from without by reasoned arguments. The soul must first seek them through its own free action, must find their reasons and learn their worth under the stimulus of its own religious experience, and bring this experience into relation with the religious experience of the human spirit throughout the ages.[9]

God does not offer himself to sensible experience. He manifests himself 'at first through a confused and inarticulate feeling of infinite, transcendental, incomprehensible Reality'.

Little by little this feeling, becoming more intense, invites to the act of adoration, till at last the soul feels the urgent need of entering into relations with this invisible Reality, and is led, not only to return upon itself in an act of reflection in order to investigate the origin and seek for the value of this experience, but also to review the whole history of the past and examine in it the origin and development of the relations of humanity with the supernatural world.[10]

This critical review of the past must pay special attention to Christian development with a view to discovering what belongs to the original spirit of Christian revelation, what belongs to the Old Testament, and what to Hellenistic culture. By means of such a critical inquiry the student will be able to see whether and how the Church carries on the mission of Christ and whether it meets the spiritual requirements of diverse peoples.[11]

Religions other than Christianity are also God's revelation to the human soul, however imperfect such revelation may be

[7] Bedeschi, *Interpretazioni*, p. 155.   [8] Ibid., p. 156.
[9] Ibid., p. 158.   [10] Ibid., p. 158.   [11] Ibid., p. 159.

in relation to Christianity.[12] The scholastic conception of revelation is ontological and absolute. Scholasticism sees revelation as 'a communication of the Truth made *directly* and externally by God to men, on matters which men would not otherwise have been able to know' and treats this communication as immutable. 'Certainly this conception does not respond to historico–psychological reality'.[13] Your Holiness has chosen to favour men of the syllogism over men of deep and positive science.[14]

Quello che vogliamo was an enthusiastic and somewhat eclectic document. Its importance lies in the fact that it was widely acclaimed by the younger Italian clergy; while its attempt to fuse some of the central ideas of Blondel and Laberthonnière with the more psychologically based ideas of Tyrrell and William James provided the Roman authorities with further evidence for their conviction that a concerted movement was afoot in the Church and that its object was the overthrow of Catholic tradition.[15]

The new and the old ways of thought were now committed to a collision course. By the early summer of 1907 rumours were rife in Rome that a full-scale condemnation of the new ideas, similar to that of Pius IX in 1864, was being prepared. *Quello che vogliamo* made explicit reference to this expectation. 'The publication of a Syllabus designed to arrest the modern scientific religious movement is said to be imminent'; and the authors of the letter went on to remind Pius X that he still felt the weight of his predecessor's Syllabus.[16] The new 'Syllabus' duly appeared six weeks later.

The Decree *Lamentabili sane exitu* was issued by the Holy Office on 3 July 1907.[17] It takes the form of 65 unattributed

[12] Bedeschi, *Interpretazioni*, p. 160.   [13] Ibid., pp. 160 f.   [14] Ibid., p. 167.

[15] Von Hügel was delighted with the Letter and brought it to the attention of *The Times* which published an article on it by Lilley. The Baron had some mild reservations about the Letter's anti-metaphysical bias which he attributed to 'excessive reaction' against the 'childish metaphysics of the Neo-Scholastics' (see L. F. Barmann, *Baron Friedrich von Hügel and the Modernist Crisis in England*, pp. 187–90).   [16] Bedeschi, *Interpretazioni*, p. 168.

[17] Latin text in *Acta Sanctae Sedis* 40 (1907), pp. 470–8. An English translation is conveniently available in B. M. G. Reardon, *Roman Catholic Modernism*, pp. 242–8. See also Poulat, *Histoire*, pp. 103–12. On the French origins of the Decree see P. Dudon, 'Les origines françaises du décret *Lamentabili* (1903–1907)', in *B.L.E.*, 32 (1931), pp. 73–96; and R. Aubert, 'Aux origines de la réaction

propositions which it condemned without specifying the degree of error in any case. Of these propositions 53 are derived from Loisy's writings. (The reader of *Lamentabili*, and of similar Roman condemnations, should note that teaching which is given through the medium of propositional anathemas, apart from its psychologically negative effect, raises all sorts of logical problems if one tries to extract a positive content by reversing the propositions.) The Decree was in the event eclipsed by the encyclical which was to follow it two months later. The following condemned propositions are, however, most closely relevant to our theme.

(20) Revelation could be nothing else than the conscious-ness man acquired of his relation to God.

(22) The dogmas which the Church puts forward as re-vealed are not truths fallen from heaven, but are an interpretation of religious facts which the human mind has acquired by laborious effort.

(58) Truth is no more immutable than man himself, since it evolves with him, in him, and through him.

(64) Progress in the sciences demands a reform of the con-cepts of Christian doctrine concerning God, creation, revelation, the person of the Incarnate Word, and redemption.

(65) Modern Catholicism can be reconciled with true science only if it is transformed into a non-dogmatic Christianity; that is to say, into a broad and liberal Protestantism.

Lamentabili was a singularly inept instrument for the purposes envisaged by the Pope and Curia. When the smoke of the explosion had lifted and the rubble settled, only Loisy was seen to have sustained a direct hit. Blondel was able to praise God for the decree, detracting something from the disinterested nature of the praise by adding that 'it is a great

antimoderniste: Deux documents inédits', in *Ephemerides Théologicae Lovani-enses*, 37 (1961), pp. 557–78; Aubert prints the (Latin) text of the memoir on Loisy sent by Cardinal Richard to Pius X on 1 November 1903 (art. cit., pp. 572–8).

moral victory for us, that we have not even been grazed'.[18]
He was not able to praise God with the same relief when
Pascendi was published in September, for it was to leave him
considerably more than grazed.

Although Loisy suggested that the Encyclical Letter,
Pascendi dominici gregis[19] had been long in the making,[20]
the contrary would appear to have been the case.[21] Rivière
has shown conclusively not only that Joseph Lemius was the
principal draughtsman of the doctrinal portion of the encyclical, but that Lemius produced his draft at very short notice.
Thus it may be said that although the idea and desirability
of a papal statement on modernism was in the Roman air
for some time, the document which actually appeared was
composed only shortly before its publication.[22]

The structure and aims of the encyclical are made quite
clear in two sentences at the end of the introduction.

It is one of the cleverest devices of the Modernists (as they are commonly and rightly called) to present their doctrines without order and
systematic arrangement, in a scattered and disjointed manner, so as to
make it appear as if their minds were in doubt or hesitation, whereas
in reality they are quite fixed and steadfast.[23] For this reason it will be
of advantage, Venerable Brethren, to bring their teachings together
into one group,[24] and to point out their interconnection, and thus to
pass to an examination of the sources of the errors, and to prescribe
remedies for averting the evil results.

In these highly significant and tendentious words we are
given the rationale of the exposition which follows. That exposition must be read in their light. To a man, the accused all

---

[18] *B.V.*, vol. i, p. 342. This reaction illustrates the understandable but rather
discreditable attempts by the Blondelians to detach themselves from Loisy,
Tyrrell, and Le Roy.

[19] Latin text in *Acta Sanctae Sedis*, 40 (1907), pp. 593-650. There is an
official English translation, *Encyclical Letter 'Pascendi Gregis' of Our Most Holy
Lord Pius X by Divine Providence Pope on the Doctrines of the Modernists*
(London, 1907).

[20] *Mémoires*, vol. ii, p. 580: '. . . l'encyclique est notablement plus ancienne
que sa date . . .'.

[21] J. Rivière, 'Qui rédigea l'encyclique "Pascendi"?', in *B.L.E.* (1946), pp.
143-61, presents convincing evidence that the encyclical was drafted by Joseph
Lemius O.M.I. at the specific request of the Pope through the offices of Raphael
Merry del Val.   [22] See Appendix 1.

[23] *A.S.S.* 40 (1907), p. 595. The Latin text reads '. . . firmi . . . et constantes';
Lemius's draft has 'precisi e categorici'.

[24] 'uno . . . conspectu exhibere' (ibid.).

denied the truth of the premiss stated here. They dismissed as ridiculous the idea that they formed a coherent and concerted party in the Church.[25] The accusation of conspiracy to disguise a carefully prepared brief by recourse to a fragmented presentation is refuted at every turn by all we know of the *dramatis personae*. Yet the encyclical relies heavily on this charge by undertaking to demonstrate the real nature of what it diagnoses as a fraudulently disguised case. *Pascendi* claims to unmask a system of thought, while its critics will maintain that it blatantly *creates* a system which it can then refute. Actually there is little or no speculative refutation in the document.[26] Rather, it states the alleged modernist case in such a manner as to suggest that the statement contains its own refutation.

Joseph Lemius, as we have seen, held that the twin errors of agnosticism and the doctrine of immanence lay at the roots of the new challenge to Catholic orthodoxy. This conviction forms the corner-stone of the doctrinal section of *Pascendi* which adopts the technique of identifying and labelling the various strands of modernism while knitting them into a comprehensive and wide-ranging system which the encyclical describes, in a celebrated phrase, as 'the meeting-place of all [the] heresies'.[27] Thus in the encyclical we encounter the modernist as philosopher, believer, theologian, historian and critic, apologist, and reformer. It is the modernist as philosopher who calls the tune and lays down the pattern within which the other modernist *personae* carry out their work.

---

[25] See for instance Loisy, *Simples réflexions*, pp. 151–2.

[26] J. Lebreton (*L'Encyclique et la théologie moderniste* (Paris, 1908), p. 25 n.) quotes the radical historian Alphonse Aulard, Professor of the History of the French Revolution at the Sorbonne, who wrote of *Pascendi*: 'On voit là, dans leur ampleur et leur agrément, les idées de ceux qui veulent adapter le catholicisme à l'état actuel des esprits, aux besoins actuels des societés ... Toutes les tendances novatrices des catholiques en matière de foi, d'exégèse, ou dans les questions politico-sociales sont élégamment résumées, parfois développées dans cette longue encyclique. Toutes y sont condamnées comme absurdes, après qu'on les a exposées dans ce qu'elles ont de plus séduisant, sans que jamais cette condamnation ressemble à une réfutation ...'.

[27] The fulsome passage containing the phrase 'omnium haereseon conlectum' (*A.S.S.*, p. 632), appears to have been written by someone other than Lemius. Compare with the phrase used in the *Allocutio* of 17 April, above, p. 191, n. 4.

'Modernists place the foundation of religious philosophy in
that doctrine which is commonly called Agnosticism', since
they restrict knowledge to phenomena.[28] By denying the
human mind a cognitive passage from phenomena to God,
the modernists have swept away natural theology in general
and, specifically, the motives of credibility and the possibility of external revelation. Commenting on this, Loisy
alleged that the notion of agnosticism put forward by 'the
theologians of His Holiness' cannot be found in, or deduced
from, any of his assertions. 'This, however, is the crucial
point of the doctrines ascribed to the modernists, and the
entire criticism of the system, in the Encyclical *Pascendi*,
is connected with this initial misunderstanding.'[29]

As one would expect, the encyclical cites passages from
the Vatican Council's teaching on revelation and faith and
claims that the modernists openly contravene this teaching.
Loisy's reply to this is that the Council was referring to
external proofs of revelation and said nothing about revelation itself being external. It is a legitimate question (though
one which will not be examined here) whether the Council's
teaching can be understood in a non-scholastic manner. That
teaching is reflected more faithfully, if more rigidly, in
Pascendi than in the conception of revelation formulated by
Loisy and Tyrrell. It would be a tortuous and disingenuous
exercise to attempt to distinguish the teaching of *Pascendi*
from that of Vatican I in this matter at least, just as it would
be equally tortuous to try to harmonize the teaching of
Pascendi with that of Vatican II. Given the sense in which
both Loisy and his critics used the term 'history', the encyclical singled out a point of irreconcilable opposition between
them, when it implicitly condemned the assertion that
God 'must not be considered as an historical subject'.[30]
Loisy never really tried to discuss the problems raised for

---

[28] *A.S.S.*, p. 596. Lemius's draft contains references in the margin to *Autour
d'un petit livre*, specifically to p. 10 where Loisy had written: 'Bien que Dieu
soit partout dans le monde, on peut bien dire qu'il n'est pas nulle part l'objet
propre et direct de la science.' Loisy himself recognized this as the source and he
printed the passage from *Autour* as evidence that what he had restricted to historical and scientific knowledge the encyclical had extended to cover human
knowledge in general, together with its ability to reach God (*S.R.*, pp. 156–7).
[29] *S.R.*, p. 158.   [30] *A.S.S.*, p. 596; Eng. Trans., p. 7.

traditional Catholic theology by his remark that 'Dieu n'est
plus un personnage de l'histoire humaine.'[31] Whereas *Pascendi*
found the origins of modernism in the philosophically based
notion of agnosticism, Loisy finds it in Church history and
biblical exegesis.[32] *Pascendi* gave Loisy a philosophy of which
he denied the parentage, but it was a philosophy so crudely
constructed that he was able to disown it not merely for
himself but also for any other modernist.

Agnosticism, then, is taken by *Pascendi* to be the negative
basis of modernism. This negative basis is complemented by
a positive one, namely, *vital immanence*. Here Loisy dis-
claims all responsibility for the basic term 'vital immanence',
which he attributes to Laberthonnière. In October 1907 he
wrote to the latter asking him if he recognized himself in the
opening pages of the encyclical. There is something of
Tyrrell in them, but is there something specifically yours or
Blondel's? 'I cannot believe that I have so much philosophy
in my guts . . .'[33] Laberthonnière, sensing the arrival of another Little Red Book, replied somewhat frigidly that such a
publication would do only harm. 'You ask me if I recognize
something of myself [in the encyclical]. Since my name and
Blondel's are associated with the word "immanence", there
will be no lack of those who will descry us everywhere in it.
In so far as what is termed "immanence" concerns me — in
all sincerity, I recognize the exact opposite of my thought.'[34]
Tyrrell, in his reply to Cardinal Mercier's Lenten Pastoral
Letter of 1908, averred that he 'learnt the "method of
immanentism" [*sic*], not from Kant, nor from the
Philosophy of Action, nor from Protestantism, but solely
from the Spiritual Exercises of the Founder of the Jesuits'.[35]

Since the encyclical does not name names, and since the
chief modernists fail to find their positions represented in it,
it is perhaps best to take *Pascendi*'s understanding of 'immanence' as an original creation, owing something to Loisy and
Laberthonnière, a great deal more to Auguste Sabatier, and
most of all to the genius of Joseph Lemius, who contrived

---

[31] *Autour*, p. 215. Lemius refers to this page in his marginal comments.
[32] *S.R.*, pp. 153–4.
[33] M.-T. Perrin (ed.), *Laberthonnière et ses amis* (Paris, 1975), pp. 158 f.
[34] Ibid., p. 159.   [35] G Tyrrell, *Medievalism*, pp. 111 f.

a synthesis of contemporary theological trends which would satisfy the scholastic mind. As such it can be read with compelling interest, not so much for' what it says about the modernists, as for its effect upon the following half-century of Roman Catholic theology.

The exposition of the doctrinal portion of the encyclical may be summarized as follows. Since the source of religion cannot be found outside man, it must be sought within him where it can be seen to be a form of life. It is stimulated by a need or impulse, a movement of the heart, which is called a *sense*. Man's need for the divine belongs to his subconscious and is responsible for that religious sense which the modernists call faith and which is the origin of revelation. Two conclusions follow from these premises. (1) Every religion must be considered both natural and supernatural, and (2) consciousness and revelation are seen to be synonymous.[36] A further conclusion is that even the supreme authority in the Church is subject to this religious consciousness.

The encyclical now reaches what is perhaps its most original section. The unknowable, it remarks, comes to man in close association with some natural or historical phenomenon. Faith then, enticed by the unknowable, embraces the whole phenomenon and permeates it with its own life.[37] As a result, the natural condition of the phenomenon is *transfigured* and *disfigured*. Historical criticism, already dedicated to agnosticism, derives from these principles of transfiguration and disfiguration its primary laws. The encyclical exemplifies this triple procedure by reference to the person of Christ. By virtue of its agnosticism historical inquiry can encounter only the human in Christ and must therefore reject any suggestion of the divine. Historical inquiry, however, accounts for the existence of faith in, and the attribution of divinity to, Christ by applying the principles of transfiguration and disfiguration which are manifested in the process by which Christ is seen as divine and has had attributed to him deeds and words which are out of keeping with his character, condition, education, and environment. The

---

[36] 'Hinc conscientiae ac revelationis promiscua significatio' (*A.S.S.*, p. 599).
[37] Ibid.

encyclical expresses special horror at the allegation that
Christ himself was subject to the laws of vital immanence.
It goes on to note that the intellect has not yet made its
appearance in the modernist system up to this point in the
argument.[38] The modernists do, however, give it a role. Up
to this point the religious sense has controlled events; but the
intellect now makes its contribution by analysing the generalized religious sense and expressing it first in a simple and
popular statement, then in more precise secondary propositions which, if approved by the Church, constitute dogma.
Dogmas are therefore religious formularies which mediate
the religious sense and express it symbolically. They do not
contain the truth absolutely but merely reflect it in a relative
manner. They can therefore change or, as the modernists put
it, evolve to meet man's changing religious consciousness.
In this construction of sophisms we have the destruction of
all religion.

The Leitmotifs of the encyclical are stated in the section
on the modernist as philosopher. These reappear and are
developed and applied in the subsequent sections which consider the modernist in his various *personae*. (The present
summary includes only those points which are relevant to the
basic pattern already traced out.) The modernist *believer*
bases his faith on his direct experience of divine reality.[39]
This fact, coupled with his teaching on symbols, makes it
impossible for him to distinguish between true and false
religion and is utterly destructive of the Catholic doctrine of
tradition. The reality of God is not available to the human
mind, but the idea of God is, and, as such, is subject to
philosophical and scientific investigation. The believer must
therefore subject his religious faith to the requirements of
moral and intellectual evolution.[40] The modernists would do
well to consider words addressed by Pope Gregory IX to
some theologians of his time: '. . . these men, led away by
various and strange doctrines, turn the head into the tail
and force the queen to serve the handmaid.'[41] Loisy savoured

---

[38] *A.S.S.*, pp. 600 f.; Eng. Trans., pp. 11 f.
[39] Ibid., p. 604; Eng. Trans., p. 16.
[40] Ibid., pp. 607 f.; Eng. Trans., pp. 19 f.
[41] Ibid., p. 608; Eng. Trans., p. 20.

the irony of this instance by pointing out that Gregory's words were aimed at those who were trying to introduce into theology the very Aristotelianism which now provided the yardstick for measuring the deficiencies of the modernist innovators.

The section on the modernist as theologian adds curiously little of substance to what has gone before. The assertion that God is immanent in man has three possible senses, one of which is orthodox, namely, that God is more intimately present to man than man is to himself.[42] Another interpretation of divine immanence would identify divine action with the action of nature, and this interpretation is unacceptable because it destroys the supernatural order. Finally, divine immanence can be taken in a sense redolent of pantheism. This third interpretation is most consonant with the rest of modernist doctrines.[43] (The implication here is that if the modernist does not admit to his pantheism, this is because he lacks the courage to take his principles to their logical conclusion.)

In a passage dealing with doctrinal evolution the encyclical explains what it means by the epithet 'vital' in the phrase 'vital immanence'.[44] Since every phenomenon in life is subject to evolution, faith and doctrine can be no exception. Primitive faith was rudimentary and common to all men. Vital evolution, however, produced a gradual refinement of primitive faith, negatively by the elimination of unnecessary particularisms such as nationality, and positively by intellectual and moral advance with a consequent intensification of the religious sense. Each stage of this evolution is conditioned by human needs and necessities[45] and given direction by the clash between the forces of conservation expressed by religious authority and the forces of progress to be found in the individual consciences of those especially who are in close contact with life. 'Already we observe, Venerable Brethren,

[42] In Lemius's draft, the word 'Laberthonnière' is placed in the margin opposite this sentence.

[43] *A.S.S.*, p. 610; Eng. Trans., p. 23.

[44] Ibid., pp. 617 f.; Eng. Trans., pp. 31-3.

[45] 'Hic autem, antequam procedamus, doctrina haec de *necessitatibus* seu indigentiis (vulgo *dei bisogni* significantius appellant) probe ut notetur velimus . . .' (ibid., p. 618; Eng. Trans., p. 33).

the introduction of that most pernicious doctrine which would make of the laity the factor of progress in the Church.'[46] (It was expressions such as this which alarmed Wilfrid Ward and other disciples of Newman.)

Turning to the modernist as historian and critic, *Pascendi* rehearses once again the three principles of agnosticism, transfiguration, and disfiguration. Foreseeing, perhaps, Loisy's inevitable response to this attempt to give him a philosophical position,[47] the encylical nails him down quite smartly. 'Some modernists, devoted to historical studies, seem to be deeply anxious not to be taken for philosophers . . . And yet the truth is that their history and their criticism are saturated with their philosophy, and that their historico-critical conclusions are the natural outcome of their philosophical principles.'[48] Blondel had made the point with greater subtlety; but the Roman theologians were too committed to associating the method of immanence with biblical criticism to take this opporunity of dividing their opponents. 'As history takes its conclusions from philosophy, so too criticism takes its conclusions from history.'[49] Curious reversal of roles, comments Loisy drily, going on to remark that the encyclical drives a thicker wedge than has any modernist between what it calls real history and *internal*, i.e. faith-inspired, history.[50] The encyclical in fact regards biblical criticism as the product of the philosophy of vital immanence, since it assumes that the biblical critic is committed to the principle that 'no fact can be regarded as antecedent to the need which produced it.' This a prioristic principle of the primacy of the need over the fact is extended to the history of dogma and of the Church. The philosopher intervenes again to ensure that this investigatory process remains subject to the laws of evolution. 'From beginning to end everything in [the process] is *a priori*, and an a priorism

---

[46] *A.S.S.*, p. 619; Eng. Trans., p. 33.

[47] As Loisy himself recognized, this is perhaps the most transparently anti-Loisian section of the encyclical. 'Je suis . . . peut-être le seul visé en cet endroit de l'Encyclique' (*S.R.*, p. 209).

[48] *A.S.S.*, p. 621; Eng. Trans., p. 36.

[49] Ibid., p. 623; Eng. Trans., p. 38.

[50] *S.R.*, p. 218.

that reeks of heresy.'[51] Since the controlling philosophy is agnostic and immanentist, and since the primary cause always communicates its characteristics to its secondary causes,[52] we are not surprised to find that the criticism is also agnostic and immanentist.

This becomes still clearer when we come to consider the modernist as apologist. Immanent human experience testifies to the presence of an Unknown. It is the task of the Catholic apologist, as interpreted by the modernists, to show how the kingdom preached by Christ was a germ destined for growth in and through the Church by vital assimilation to succeeding circumstances. The resulting dogmas are merely symbolic and purely relative. The subjectivity which governs the entire apologetical enterprise is common to those 'moderate modernists', who employ immanence as a method, and the radicals, who treat it as a doctrine.

'And now, with our eyes fixed upon the whole system, no one will be surprised that We should define it to be the synthesis of all [the] heresies.'[53] The modernist system lays its axe to the roots not simply of Catholicism but of all religion. With a final restatement of the two dominant motifs in full orchestration, the encyclical deplores the agnosticism of the new system and its recourse to experience as a substitute for thought. 'Take away the intelligence, and man, already inclined to follow the senses, becomes their slave.'[54] Human will and feelings are notoriously deceptive, yet modernism reduces all religion to their caprices. Sense and experience without the guidance of reason cannot reach the knowledge of God. Without this knowledge there is simple atheism from which no doctrine of symbolism can save us. If the reality of God is unknowable, there can be no guarantee that religious experience will not lead us to some such rationalist idol as the soul of the universe.

The disciplinary section of the encyclical states that scholastic philosophy, principally that of St. Thomas Aquinas,

[51] '. . . et quidem per apriorismum haeresibus scatentem' (*A.S.S.*, p. 624; Eng. Trans., p. 39.)

[52] 'Et quia primae causae hoc competit ut virtutem suam cum sequentibus communicet . . .' (*A.S.S.*, p. 626; Eng. Trans., p. 41).

[53] Ibid., p. 632; Eng. Trans., p. 48.

[54] Ibid., p. 632; Eng. Trans., p. 49.

is to be made the basis of the sacred sciences.[55] Positive theology should be held in greater esteem than it has been in the
past, but it is not to be exalted above scholastic theology.[56]
Thomism, which Leo XIII had made mandatory, was now to
be seen as the chief antidote to the Kantian poison. Anyone
not subscribing to Thomism would be automatically suspect
of modernism as defined by the encyclical.[57]

Pascendi dominici gregis gave official sanction to the terms
'modernist' and 'modernism'. It also gave them definition and
structural cohesion. What the modernists and their critics
made of the definition and the cohesion is an important part
of the history of modernism. It would be impossible to take
comprehensive cognizance of the literary response to
Pascendi, which was voluminous and, to a great extent, pre-
dictable. Selection and generalization will here be controlled
by the subject-matter of this book. We shall consider first the
modernist, then, more briefly, the anti-modernist, response.

To begin with some generalizations. All the modernists,
and some of their opponents, agreed that the encyclical
outlined a system which served the ends of ecclesiastical
teaching rather than represented the views of any actual
modernist. Tyrrell, committing ecclesiastical suicide with
characteristic and spectacular abandon in the pages of the
Giornale d'Italia and *The Times* gave his verdict in the
remark that whereas the encyclical 'tries to show the

[55] *A.S.S.*, p. 640; Eng. Trans., p. 66.
[56] Ibid., p. 641; Eng. Trans., p. 58.
[57] The disciplinary part of the encyclical was not drafted by Lemius. It finds
curiosity and pride to be the principal remote causes of modernism. It prescribed
remedies for the situation: 'In the first place, with regard to studies, We will and
strictly ordain that scholastic philosophy be made the basis of the sacred sciences'
(ibid., p. 640; Eng. Trans., p. 57). 'Anyone who in any way is found to be tainted
with modernism is to be excluded without compunction from these offices
[sc. in seminaries and universities], whether of government or of teaching, and
those who already occupy them are to be removed' (ibid., p. 642; Eng. Trans.,
p. 59). Bishops are to exercise strict censorship over all publications which smack
of modernism. Censors are to be chosen for their prudence and safety and are to
be protected by anonymity (ibid., p. 645; Eng. Trans., p. 63). Since the modernists have made use of congresses to propagate their opinions, bishops are instructed to forbid gatherings of priests except on very rare occasions and never
for the purposes of discussing matters that pertain only to bishops and the
Apostolic See. Councils of vigilance are to be set up in every diocese to 'watch
most carefully for every trace and sign of modernism' (ibid., pp. 647 f.; Eng.
Trans., p. 66).

Modernist that he is no Catholic, it mostly succeeds only in showing him that he is no scholastic'.[58] Loisy described the encyclical in a letter to von Hügel as 'un système fictif'[59] but in his *Simples réflexions* made a remark, shortly to be much quoted by conservatives, to the effect that *Pascendi* was the ineluctably logical expansion of received Catholic teaching since the end of the thirteenth century.[60] Blondel once again wrote '. . . nous ne sommes pas même effleurés',[61] but this time one senses that he is whispering and that there is a note of anxious interrogation in his voice. *Lamentabili* had kept far enough away from the sensitive area of transcendence and immanence to enable Blondel to praise God for it; not so *Pascendi*, 'cette navrante encyclique',[62] which caused him intense anguish, tempted him to doubt the goodness of the Church, and made him ask if intellectual suicide was not the only way to avoid infidelity.[63] His friends hastened to reassure him. 'You are in no way touched [by the encyclical]', wrote Mourret.[64] 'Je n'ai pas reconnu la pensée de la *Lettre* dans l'apologétique agnostique de l'encyclique', Valensin told him.[65] Bremond adopted a policy of cool detachment, deploring Tyrrell's 'furia irlandaise' and exhorting Laberthonnière not to place a tragic construction on matters.[66]

The immediate problem which faced Blondel and Laberthonnière was what line they should take in the *Annales de Philosophie Chrétienne* (of which Blondel was the owner and Laberthonnière the editor). Bremond had written to Laberthonnière that the *Annales* would head the list of dangerous

---

[58] M. D. Petre, *Life*, vol. ii, p. 337. In November Tyrrell wrote to Bremond: 'Toute notre position est que la philosophie n'a pas d'importance, que l'erreur a été de lier le catholicisme à une philosophie' (as translated by Anne Louis-David (ed.), *Lettres de George Tyrrell à Henri Bremond* (Paris, 1971), p. 271).

[59] *Mémoires*, vol. ii, p. 568.   [60] *S.R.*, p. 25.

[61] *B.L.*, p. 202.   [62] Ibid., p. 208.

[63] *B.V.*, vol. i, p. 357 n.   [64] Ibid., p. 360 n.

[65] Ibid., p. 359. In spite of these assurances Blondel knew that the encyclical would be used against him. The attacks would have to be carried out in a roundabout way. The clearest example of this tactic relevant to our theme is J. de Tonquédec, *Immanence: Essai critique sur la doctrine de M. Maurice Blondel* (2nd edn. Paris, 1913), a study which can best be described as feline; see especially Appendix III, 'L'Encyclique Pascendi et les doctrines de M. Blondel', pp. 292-6.   [66] Perrin, op. cit., p. 167.

publications and that there would be bishops eager 'for the honour of sending some corpses to the Holy Father'. He therefore advised Laberthonnière to emphasize the fact that the *Annales* was a lay publication, founded and maintained by laymen. 'It hasn't reached the age of seventy-nine in order to die of a little cold.' If necessary Laberthonnière must be ready to offer his resignation from the editorship so that the journal may not be got at through his vulnerability as a priest.[67] In the event, Blondel drafted an editorial and sent it to Laberthonnière who published it, not without considerable misgivings. It sounded a clear note of submission.[68] Signed 'La Rédaction', the editorial accepted the encyclical 'in a spirit of humility and faith'. 'But the philosophers in our readership have the right to know the reasons for our acquiescence.'[69] We have always stood out against all forms of agnosticism, naturalism, monism, fideism, and rationalism. If there is anything we have particularly repudiated, 'it is precisely that immanentism which the Encyclical condemns with such force'. Real immanentists have dismissed our philosophy as 'expressing a pure doctrine of transcendence', and we have accepted that this is our aim. The word 'immanence' is notoriously equivocal. We are therefore happy to have yet another opportunity of saying what we understand by it. The encyclical distinguishes three senses. It declares one 'irreproachable' and condemns the other two. We concur in this judgement. 'No, Christianity does not emerge out of nature by a subconscious and spontaneous evolution. No, it is not an emanation from the religious consciousness of humanity.[70] It results from a positive intervention of God, graciously, miraculously, and supernaturally. It is established by the historical fact of the Incarnation. The editorial goes on to draw a distinction between *efférence* and *afférence*. *Efférence* is the doctrine of total immanence which derives dogmas from the depths of human nature. This we repudiate. *Afférence*, on the other hand, 'affirms the specifically supernatural, free and gratuitous character of the entire Christian

---

[67] A. Blanchet (ed.), *Henri Bremond et Maurice Blondel: Correspondance*, vol. ii (Paris, 1971), p. 107.　　　　[68] *A.P.C.* 5 (1907–8), pp. 5–9.
　　　[69] Ibid., p. 6.　　　　　　　　　　[70] Ibid., p. 7.

order'.[71] The concept of *afférence* is designed to allow Blondel to accept *Pascendi*'s teaching on the external nature of revelation without having to accept the extrinsicism he had rejected in the *Letter on Apologetics*. *Afférence* might be described as the process whereby a sympathetic resonance is struck in the mind and heart of the believer when confronted with the exterior facts. *Pascendi* had condemned the contention that there is in human nature an *exigence* for the supernatural. The editorial makes its profession of faith in terms which suggest a weary capitulation.[72] 'No, human nature has no right to the supernatural, since the supernatural is a gift and a gift cannot be demanded.' One concludes a reading of the editorial wondering if Blondel and Laberthonnière have not sacrificed the controlling idea in the method of immanence. Could one accept the scholastic conception of supernature without serious qualification and still affirm an immanental apologetic of any sort whatever, however purely methodological?[73]

Tyrrell stated bluntly in *The Times* that Newman had been condemned by the encyclical. A voluminous correspondence followed in which Wilfrid Ward, Newman's biographer, took an anxious part. The fact is, of course, that nearly all the modernists referred in highly laudatory terms to Newman in their writings. Since Newman was palpably unscholastic in his, and *Pascendi* exclusively scholastic in its, thought, those admirers of Newman who accepted the encyclical had the difficult task of showing that Newman was not retrospectively attainted by this latest definition of Catholic orthodoxy. Von Hügel's immediate and uncharacteristically brash judgement was that Ward 'will be unable to evade the fact that he and such as he fare at least as badly at Pius' hands as do Tyrrell or Loisy'.[74] The Baron wrote to Ward to

---

[71] art. cit., p. 7.　　　　　　　　　[72]ibid., p. 8.

[73] Von Hügel wrote to Laberthonnière to complain that the editorial's acquiescence in *all Pascendi*'s condemnations had shocked him. '. . . comment peut-on s'incliner explicitement devant le tout d'un tel document, sans distinction, sans réserve aucune? (Perrin, pp. 171 f., original italics). Laberthonnière was inclined to blame Tyrrell for the Baron's stern verdict on the editorial; see his letter to Bremond in Blanchet, *Henri Bremond et Maurice Blondel*, p. 113 n. Von Hügel seems, however, to have been happy enough with the stance of the *Annales* on transcendence and immanence.

[74] Cited in Barmann, *Baron Friedrich von Hügel*, p. 200.

dissuade him from seeking a Roman declaration that
Newman was not envisaged in the recent condemnations.
The Roman authorities, von Hügel wrote, 'will never now put
J. H. N. on the Index nor do other suchlike things; short of
that, they will do everything to curtail and damage N's position and influence.'[75] Paul Sabatier was a great deal nearer
the mark when he claimed that Newman was not envisaged in
the encyclical, for the very good reason that its draughtsmen
did not know Newman.[76]

Among all the responses to *Pascendi* the fullest and most
closely argued was the anonymously published *Il programma
dei modernisti*.[77] Modernist commentators in their curious
anxiety to find an address for *Pascendi*-type immanentism
commonly designate Buonaiuti and the Roman modernists.
The *Programme* was of course the most influential work
produced within this circle. Professor Bedeschi describes it
as a masterpiece of Italian modernism but goes on to remark
that it made 'excessive concessions to immanentist exaggerations'.[78] This observation deserves examination.

The *Programme* opens with an orotund appeal to Pius X to
listen with open mind to what the modernists have to say, for
it is vital to the future well-being of the Church within which
the faith is beating with a new life. 'The pretended bases of

---

[75] Barmann, op. cit., p. 205.

[76] P. Sabatier, *Les Modernistes* (Paris, 1909), p. 44. This judgement is borne
out by an inspection of the Lemius papers.

[77] *Il programma dei modernisti: Risposta all' enciclica di Pio X 'Pascendi
dominici gregis'* (Rome, 1907). According to Bedeschi the *Programme* was written
in less than a month and was the work of at least four hands. The two most
important of these were Buonaiuti, who wrote the philosophical part, and
Fracassini, who wrote the biblical one. Bedeschi describes the *Programma* as 'the
most original expression of Italian modernism' (*Interpretazioni*, p. 171.) Tyrrell
was delighted with it and, encouraged by von Hügel, undertook the English translation which appeared under the name of his friend A. L. Lilley with the title
*The Programme of Modernism: A Reply to the Encyclical of Pius X, 'Pascendi
Dominici Gregis'* (London, 1908). Von Hügel exhorted Tyrrell to 'make improve-
ments and useful additions in the translation' (T. M. Loome, A Bibliography of
Published Writings of George Tyrrell (1861-1909)', *H.J.* 10 (1969), p. 294).
Tyrrell took this advice: 'I have been most free & unscrupulous, weaving little
comments of my own into the text; but with absolute fidelity, I hope, to the sense
& spirit of the writers' (T. M. Loome, 'A Bibliography of the Printed Works of
George Tyrrell: Supplement', *H.J.* 11 (1970), p. 164). References here are to the
Tyrrell-Lilley trans. (abbreviated as *Programme*).

[78] Bedeschi, *Interpretatazioni*, p. 82.

faith', however, 'haye proved themselves rotten beyond cure.'[79] *Pascendi* is wide of the mark in claiming that philosophy has dictated modernist critical method. The opposite is in fact the case. Critical study has demolished 'the tottering basis of what has proved to be an anti-critical exegesis'. Religious apologetic raised on the solid and unassailable 'basis offered by the deepest exigencies of the human soul and by those spiritual life-needs which have given birth to the whole process of Christianity'.[80]

The first section of the *Programme* comprises treatment of the biblical question[81] and questions of doctrinal and ecclesiastical history.[82] It is the second section, 'The Apologetic of the Modernists', which concerns us here. It accuses the encyclical of shuttling ambiguously between the charge of atheism and the charge of agnosticism. (This ambiguity was already noticeable in Lemius's lectures.) With what consistency, asks the *Programme*, can the encyclical reproach us with holding an agnostic philosophy and an atheistic science and history?

We accept that criticism of pure reason which Kant and Spencer have made; but far from falling back, like Kant, on the a prioristic witness of the practical reason, or from ending, like Spencer, in the affirmation of an 'Unknowable', we maintain the existence of other powers in the human spirit, every bit as reliable as the argumentative reason, for attaining to truth.[83]

What are these other powers? The *Programme* does not burke the label 'immanentist' in its answer to the question. It simply claims that the immanentism it defends is not in contradiction of the Vatican Council. In effect what the *Programme* does is to take the Council's *facta divina* and convert them into a sort of Pascalian *fait intérieur*.

It is impossible for us today to conceive a purely intellectual and speculative faculty, immune from all influence of the will and the emotions. To the latest psychology, reason seems more and more to be a sort of instrument of formulation and definition which human nature has instinctively fashioned for itself, and which it uses unconsciously in order to arrange, express and control the experiences of the more elementary and universal faculties of will and feeling and external sensation.[84]

---

[79] *Programme*, p. 8.   [80] Ibid., p. 20.   [81] Ibid., pp. 27–87.
[82] Ibid., pp. 87–110.   [83] Ibid., pp. 116 f.   [84] Ibid., pp. 126 f.

Thus Buonaiuti makes inner experience perform the role assigned by the Vatican Council to miracles and prophecies. They therefore become 'means of knowledge' which lead to 'a living certainty of the existence of God'.

And amongst these means of knowledge, taken in the widest sense, we must also set that quite indefinable experience of a divine impulse which reaches us, as members of a social organism, through past ages of collective religious life, and of an aspiration towards that fuller sense of a transcendent divinity which will be realised by the religious generations of the future.[85]

These affirmations are vulnerable to several charges, not least those of eclecticism and psychologism. They are not, however, immanentist in any monistic sense. One further quotation from an earlier passage of the *Programme* puts the matter beyond cavil.

We are therefore perfectly logical in seeking to ground our affirmation of a transcendent divinity on the immanent needs of man's conscience, and in striving to follow up the deep aspirations and ever-recurring necessities which spur the will to raise itself with all its might towards God, who, as S. Augustine says, already works in us creating this desire to seek him.[86]

Commenting on *Pascendi*'s thesis of transfiguration and disfiguration, the *Programme* draws a distinction between knowledge and ontological reality and alleges that the encyclical equivocates between the two. 'Religious facts', says the *Programme*, 'include mysterious meanings which pure science misses'. Faith penetrates and feeds on, but does not create these meanings. 'It is undeniable that an historical fact assumes ever larger proportions and ever deeper significance in the accounts of it transmitted from generation to generation of individuals interested in its ethical and religious values.'[87] Faith does indeed transfigure and disfigure facts, 'but only from the knowledge point of view and not ontologically'.[88]

The *Programme* places a heavy emphasis on subjectivity, experience, and consciousness in matters of revelation and faith. This, however, is not a denial of divine transcendence. It is symptomatic of an extreme reaction against the confident

---

[85] *Programme*, p. 128.
[87] Ibid., p. 137.

[86] Ibid., p. 120.
[88] Ibid., p. 139.

clarities of a scholastic thought which, as von Hügel saw,[89] cheapened the mystery of God and divine revelation by a rationalist system of understanding and presentation. The danger of this kind of reaction is that it may induce a rejection not merely of scholasticism but also of all metaphysics. Enthusiasts like Buonaiuti *experienced* in the new ideas a sense of release, of truth to be lived and explored and not simply registered and defended. Precisely because it was an experience and not just a set of rational data that fired them, they tended, while analysing the process whereby man becomes religiously aware, to place disproportionate emphasis on undifferentiated consciousness as distinct from the mind as an intentional faculty.

In 1908 Buonaiuti published anonymously his book, *Lettere di un prete modernista*,[90] which he later described as 'peccatum juventutis meae!'.[91] One can only agree that it is indeed an unsatisfactory work, fragmented, undeveloped, and inconsistent. It is, however, in the *Lettere* that we discover something like the immanentism which has been so universally regarded as the special threat of modernism. The context of the immanentism is epistemological, and due note must be taken of this if we are to appreciate Buonaiuti's position. He dismisses as totally outmoded the Aristotelian-Thomistic conception of truth as *adequatio intellectus et rei.* He admits that he is unsure of what to put in its place but inclines towards a 'pragmatic solution of the problem', adding that by 'pragmatic' he means a gradual assimilation of 'the abstractly formulated to the profoundly lived'.[92] The true is to be seen as 'the perfect correspondence of pure thought with sane instincts and with the more or less subconscious impulses to choose by which we are moved in our vital experiences'. This curious mixture of Bergsonian epistemology, Jamesian psychology, and Blondelian metaphysics issues in an extremely cloudy theodicy. The problem of God, says Buonaiuti, is the product of this epistemological

---

[89] See, for example, the Baron's letter to Tyrrell of 12 June 1905, in *Selected Letters*, p. 131.
[90] E. Buonaiuti, *Lettere di un prete modernista* (Rome, 1908).
[91] Idem., *Pellegrino di Roma*, p. 97.
[92] *Lettere di un prete modernista*, p. 148.

crisis. The Five Ways of St. Thomas are no longer a live
option for us, yet we seem to have nothing to put in their
place. Instead we are forced to ask 'What is the meaning of
our ephemeral lives in the maelstrom of universal life?'[93]
Is there a luminous power at work making for progress in the
world?

The solution, which will be an act of faith, true because fruitful, will
not be able to be given in terms of pure transcendence or of pure
immanence. These terms indeed reflect a metaphysical mentality still
more out of date, if they are taken in an abstract way. The divine is
perfectly immanent in and transcendent to us, in so far as it functions
as the sense of the continuity of life in the empirical universe: it is immanent through all that which is alive and holy in the consciousness of
the empirical world; it is transcendent through all which is expected
and hoped for in the psychology of humanity on the move.[94]

This *anima mundi* conception of the divine served only to
alienate moderate modernists and to convince others that the
Roman condemnation of modernism was abundantly
justified. It was not a carefully worked-out position, but
rather a reactive direction away from what Buonaiuti had
experienced as the sterile clarities of scholasticism. Towards
the end of his life he wrote that many modernists went too
far in the direction of immanentism and were thus unable
'to build solidly a faith in the Transcendent and in its revelation', but that a warning given with wisdom and breadth of
vision would have been enough to correct the deviations
which were inevitable in an age of transition.[95]
    Italian modernism expressed itself in schools, of which
Buonaiuti and the Roman radicals formed one and Murri and
the Northerners another. The ambiguities inherent in the
term 'modernism' are further complicated by the circumstances peculiar to its Italian setting. A study of Italian
modernism inevitably raises some of the wider issues of
Italian politics and culture and thus opens up the question
of how far, if at all, these should be treated within the
category of modernism. This is not a new problem. It lay at
the roots of the quarrel between the Roman and Milanese

---

[93] *Lettere di un prete modernista*, p. 149.   [94] Ibid.
[95] E. Buonaiuti, *Il modernismo cattolico* (Modena, 1943), p. 53.

schools. Buonaiuti held Murri's *Democrazia cristiana* in something like contempt. The Northerners, who included leisured laymen deeply concerned with Italian culture, saw Buonaiuti and his associates as raw enthusiasts whose radical immanentism was damaging a moderate and legitimate cause. Paul Sabatier, the Protestant apostle of Catholic modernism, sided with the Milanese, bringing to the debate what Buonaiuti peevishly refers to as his 'anachronistiche fantasie francescane'.[96] In his turn Sabatier, writing to Buonaiuti's principal colleague, Mario Rossi, expressed with nice irony the Milanese conviction that the Romans were trying to establish a modernist party-line. Proximity to the Vatican, Sabatier remarked, was having its effect upon them, for they seem to be in favour of distributing 'des brevets d'orthodoxie moderniste'.[97]

Murri stated his attitude to Buonaiuti and the *Programme* in an article he wrote for *Il Rinnovamento* on *Pascendi* and modern philosophy.[98] It is a long and at times tortuous essay written by one who felt himself untouched by the encyclical.[99] The *Programme* appeared before the publication of the second part of Murri's article. In this second part he has no hesitation in describing the *Programme* as 'immanentist'[100] in the sense condemned by *Pascendi*. He suggests that Blondel's concept of action resembled Hegel's Idea.[101] He finds Le Roy's Bergsonianism to be irreconcilable with a doctrine of transcendence,[102] but he concedes that Blondel and Laberthonnière are less radical than Le Roy. Laberthonnière is more a psychologist than a philosopher[103] and dissolves the problem of being and knowledge 'in a psychologism which has a notably apologetical and educative scope and value'. Murri goes on to observe that *Pascendi*, by failing to distinguish between the schools of Blondel and Le Roy, weakens its case. Furthermore, the encyclical bypasses the

---

[96] *Fonti e documenti*, vol. i (Urbino, 1972), p. 79.

[97] Ibid., p. 205.

[98] R. Murri, 'L'enciclica "Pascendi" e la filosofia moderna', *Il Rinnovamento*, 1 (1907), pp. 345–65, 539–65.   [99] Ibid., p. 348.

[100] Ibid., p. 548.   [101] Ibid., p. 351.   [102] Ibid., pp. 353–5.

[103] Ibid., p. 359. Later in the article Murri brings the same accusation against Tyrrell (mentioned semi-anonymously as G.T.) whom he rebukes for confusing psychology with philosophy (ibid., pp. 562–4).

problem of knowledge, so essential to an understanding of modern philosophy.[104] It adopts a position exactly inverse to that of pragmatic philosophy. by treating as final what the new apologetic regards as its point of departure.[105] The new philosophy identifies intelligibility with the possibility of being: the unknown is by definition a non-being.[106] Murri thus correctly notes that the epistemological assumptions of the modernists and those of *Pascendi* are radically different and that they are closely relevant to all the important problems concerning the philosophy of religion and dogma.[107]

As both Loisy and von Hügel observed, Murri thought in the scholastic mode, and his attempts to open himself to the influence of contemporary philosophy resulted in a neo-orthodoxy which was, as the Baron remarked to Gallarati-Scotti, a purely intellectual construction that would fall to pieces under strain.

Integralist circles in the Catholic Church received the encyclical with rapture. Books and articles emanating from these circles in the years immediately following the condemnation were triumphalist and fulsome. Enrico Rosa wrote of 'la voce del mite e soave Pio X',[108] a voice which, 'if it wounded, wounded not unto death but unto repentance, or, more truly, wounded unto death the error in order to save the erring'.[109] Rosa's book adds little of substance to what he had written before the encyclical was published, except that he now seems even more disposed to descry the influence of Liberal Protestantism on modernist thinking. A. Sabatier adopted a system of symbolistic fideism with good reason, says Rosa, since it accords well with his distinction between faith and belief and allows him to hold that we are saved by faith independently of beliefs. 'And an extremely convenient faith, this faith of the modernists, without ideas, without dogmas, and all thanks to symbolism!'[110]

Most Catholic journals and periodicals, especially in countries where modernism had been no threat, simply noted

[104] Murri, art. cit., pp. 363 f.   [105] Ibid., p. 364.
[106] Ibid., p. 365.   [107] Ibid., p. 551.
[108] E. Rosa, *L'Enciclica 'Pascendi' e il modernismo: Studii e commenti* (2nd edn., revised and enlarged, Rome, 1909), p. 4.
[109] Ibid., p. 39.   [110] Ibid., pp. 70–71 n.

that Rome had spoken, thereby once again saving the Church from perils beyond the ken of most of its members. Moderate and tempered comment was virtually impossible in the atmosphere prevailing after the condemnation and during the remainder of the pontificate. In 1908 Cardinal Mercier warned Wilfrid Ward 'to be very careful in Rome . . . they want very thorough loyalty'.[111] Such 'thorough loyalty' put an impossible strain on the consciences of many Catholic theologians, as can be seen for example in the letters of moderates like Semeria and Genocchi. In some respects the strain fell more heavily on biblical scholars than on philosophical theologians. Rome could declare one philosophy to be mandatory and others to be erroneous, and, though this might be an abuse of its authority, it was not as patently absurd as was the condemnation of critically established facts in the realm of biblical scholarship.

Authority, not reasoned argument, extinguished the crisis. Catholic theology and spirituality had been conditioned over a long period to accept this *modus operandi* as characterizing the specific difference between Catholicism and Protestantism. We have seen how and why Kantianism was so resolutely and strenuously opposed by scholastic orthodoxy. A further reason for this opposition was suggested by Jules Lebreton, Professor at the Institut Catholique in Paris, in a book written on the encyclical and modern theology in 1908. 'We must, moreover, note henceforth, how Kant's subjectivism makes adhesion to a religion of authority precarious.'[112] It is difficult to see how Kantianism could be said to have added anything in this respect not already present in classical Protestantism. The reason for Lebreton's curious remark would appear to have been that since *Pascendi* had traced back all modernist error to a philosophical foundation, itself basically Kantian, it would be more appropriate now to locate 'subjectivism' in Königsberg rather than in Wittenberg or Geneva.

Other Catholic commentators had no hestitation in linking classical Protestantism, Liberal Protestantism, Kantian and

---

[111] M. Ward, *Insurrection Versus Resurrection* (London, 1937), p. 317.
[112] J. Lebreton, *L'Encyclique et la théologie moderniste*, p. 17 n.

Spencerian philosophy, Jamesian psychology, and Darwinian evolutionism, and in claiming that the modernism condemned in the encyclical was an amalgam of all these elements. Stephane Harent, in an article on faith and experience written in the light of *Pascendi*, saw a double step in Protestantism. Luther had reduced all religion to religious experience, and Liberal Protestantism then took the reduction to its logical conclusion by separating this experience from Christian dogma.[113] Harent's article is a pointer to one of the main effects upon Roman Catholic theology of the condemnation of modernism, namely, the total outlawing of experience as a factor in religion, theology, and spirituality. The modernists had appealed to experience as the primary datum of religion. The integralist response was not merely to re-emphasize the intellectual character of faith but to repulse with vehemence, and often scorn, the notion that experience had any significant role to play in Christian faith and morals.

A useful index to the theological situation as it existed in the Roman Catholic Church after the condemnation of modernism can be found in the article A. Vermeersch wrote on modernism for *The Catholic Encyclopedia* of 1911.[114] Vermeersch makes dogma the touchstone of modernism and tells his readers that if they are in any doubt as to whether a writer or book is modernist or not, they must 'verify every statement about dogma'.

You will know whether you are dealing with a veritable modernist or not, according to the way in which the Catholic conception of dogma is travestied or respected. Dogma and supernatural knowledge are correlative terms; one implies the other as the action implies its object. In this way then we may define modernism as 'the critique of our supernatural knowledge according to the false postulates of contemporary philosophy'.[115]

---

[113] S. Harent, 'Expérience et foi à propos de la récente encyclique', in *Études*, 113 (1907), p. 248.

[114] Arthur Vermeersch, S.J., at that time teaching in Louvain, was soon to move to Rome and there to become the foremost moral theologian in the freshly centralized Catholic Church. He gave it as his view that Pius X's *Motu proprio, Sacrorum antistitum* (September, 1910) had the effect of constituting the conclusions of *Lamentabili* and *Pascendi* as infallible utterances. Vermeersch, however, conceded that this view, extreme even for its age, was not universally accepted (*The Catholic Encyclopedia* (London and New York, 1911), vol. x, p. 421).

[115] Vermeersch, art. cit., p. 416.

'Supernatural knowledge' is the defining phrase in Vermeersch's comment. It restores all to the status quo ante. Having dealt with the modernist concepts of 'intuition', 'aspiration to perfection', 'affective yearning' for God, 'gropings' of the 'soul's religious experience', together with the intellectual expression of those sentiments in symbolic form to which the modernists reduce dogma, Vermeersch proceeds by way of contrast to the 'Catholic notion of dogma'. His words are an eloquent comment on the end of an interlude.

The tradition of the Catholic Church, on the other hand, considers dogmas as in part supernatural and mysterious, proposed to our faith by a Divinely instituted authority on the ground that they are part of the general revelation which the Apostles preached in the name of Jesus Christ. This faith is an act of the intellect made under the sway of the will. By it we hold firmly what God has revealed and what the Church proposes to us to believe. For believing is holding something firmly on the authority of God's word, when such authority may be recognized by signs that are sufficient, at least with the help of grace, to create certitude.[116]

In these few sentences we have an exemplar of much that the modernists had striven to change in Catholic theology: intellectualism, extrinsicism, partition of the believer into intellect and will, dissociation of nature and grace and of knowledge and faith, and reaffirmation of authority as guarantee of truth. Vermeersch was soon to become one of the oracles of post-modernist Catholic theology, and his article, though destined for a popular readership, gives a brilliant summary of the main characteristics of that theology until the reforms of the Second Vatican Council.

[116] Vermeersch, art. cit., p. 416.

10 Modernism in Retrospect

An accurate assessment of the course of twentieth-century Roman Catholic theology depends upon an appreciation less perhaps of modernism itself than of the officially sponsored reaction it provoked within the Church. Anti-modernism became a species of ecclesiastical patriotism enforced by an oath[1] and initiated by a campaign which bore striking resemblances to the anti-communist activities of Senator Joseph McCarthy in the United States of America during the late 1940s and early 1950s. There is no need to dwell upon the disreputable tactics resorted to by the extremer elements of the victorious party. Mgr. Umberto Benigni's *Sodalitium Pianum*, the chilling parody of a secret service, set about ferreting out 'modernists' throughout the Church.[2] The cruder excesses of this movement were brought to an end by Pius X's successor, Benedict XV; but the myth of a modernist threat lingered on for two generations. The term 'modernist' remained as a convenient label for any theological initiatives in the Roman Catholic Church which appeared to deviate from the neo-scholastic norm, especially in matters of dogma, biblical criticism, and Church polity. Integralism, the frame of mind most inimical to change in the Church, achieved a position of control over Catholic theology and Church practice which was given juridical expression in the *Codex juris canonici* (1917) and executive expression in the sweeping powers exercised by the Roman dicasteries. Tyrrell had indicated the strength and significance of the link between an extrinsicist fundamental theology and the exercise of centralized authority within a pyramidal Church structure. 'Modernism' could easily be, and often was, invoked as an incantation against any attempt to provide an alternative to the neo-

[1] See Appendix 2.

[2] See E. Poulat, *Intégrisme et Catholicisme intégral: Un réseau secret international antimoderniste: La 'Sapinière', 1909–1921* (Paris, 1969).

scholastic formulation of Catholic orthodoxy or to criticize its conception and use of authority.

Critical study of modernism was, as one might expect, a major victim of the integralist hegemony. From 1907 down to the calling of the Second Vatican Council any book or article on modernism carrying an imprimatur was guaranteed in advance to be hostile in some degree to the modernists. The accepted myth of a concerted heretical movement within the Church in the first decade of the twentieth century made it incumbent upon the author of any Roman Catholic work which dealt with the period to bring in an *a priori* verdict of guilty as charged, unless he could show that his man was innocent of modernism in the sense designated by *Pascendi*. It was this deadening necessity that led to the tiresome and artificial attempts by disciples of certain modernists (Blondel and von Hügel are the paradigmatic cases) to prove that their man was not envisaged in the encyclical. This essentially sterile procedure has done much to obfuscate, if not positively to distort, the issues involved.

The change of theological and ecclesiastical climate which was brought about by the Second Vatican Council has removed the constricting and minatory atmosphere within which so much modernist research has had to be done. Much of the drama and excitement engendered by the first session of the Council stemmed from the relative suddenness of the realization that integralism was no more than a *schola* in Roman Catholic theology; whereas the basic tenets and methodology of that *schola* had been widely taken to belong more or less to the substance of Catholic faith. The experience has been both liberating and disturbing.

The Council created not a new theology but the conditions for a plurality of theologies within Catholic unity. It brought to an end the domination of Aristotle over Catholic theology. By accepting a distinction between the substance of faith and the manner of its presentation,[3] it broke with what the modernists had described as 'the cult of the formula'. Its adoption of the concept of the 'hierarchy of truths' was an implicit rejection of the integralist view of

---

[3] Vatican II, *Gaudium et spes*, art. 62.

Catholic doctrine as a body of interconnected truths the value of each of which was assessed by the status of the teaching authority which had pronounced upon them, rather than by 'their relation to the foundation of the Christian faith'.[4] The significance of these changes will be realized if one accepts that many of the questions the modernists were asking were not patient of neo-scholastic categories. Transcendence, immanence, experiential and historical models of revelation, the methodology of doctrinal formulation, symbolic communication, and other similar questions all demanded an ability and willingness to explore the central doctrines of Christian faith by means of a variety of intellectual categories, many of them uncongenial to essentialist metaphysics.

Throughout this study I have accepted the general validity of Tyrrell's observation that *Pascendi*, while seeking to show the modernist that he was no Catholic, in fact showed him that he was no scholastic. This acceptance in no way implies the view that all the modernists, in particular Loisy and Buonaiuti, were orthodox Christian theologians by all but neo-scholastic criteria of orthodoxy. It does, however, imply the view that the criteria by which their orthodoxy was judged were so narrow as to render the official condemnation nearly meaningless as a doctrinal guide today. Those criteria were the product not so much of neo-scholasticism as such as of its monopolistic imposition by authoritative decree. It was this imposition which was responsible for rigidifying mainline Catholic theology in the period between the two Vatican Councils.

The epithet 'mainline' is important here. The theology of Vatican II did not spring Athena-like from the head of the conciliar Zeus. What the Council did was to summon into the mainstream of Catholic life and theology ideas, activities, and aspirations which had, during the previous hundred years, had a suspect, and therefore precarious, existence in the Church. Most of the men who educated the Church in council in the early 1960s had been victims of the extremely narrow standards of orthodoxy which pervaded the Roman

---

[4] Vatican II, *Unitatis redintegratio*, art. 11.

dicasteries. To this fact is due, more than to any other, the intrinsic drama, undoubtedly heightened by journalistic verve, of the first session of the Council. A party in the Church had identified its tenets with those of universal Christianity. The conciliar debates demonstrated that the Roman Catholic Church now wished to break free from the control of this party. The resultant liberation ensured the reopening of questions which had been shelved as a consequence of the condemnation of modernism.

We have had occasion at several points in this study to compare and contrast the respective courses of Liberal Protestantism and Catholic modernism. One final contrast remains to be made. Liberal Protestantism ran its course untrammelled by extrinsic institutional intervention. By the end of the second decade of the twentieth century it was widely deemed to have revealed its theological and moral bankruptcy, and Karl Barth called in the official receiver with his *Römerbrief* in 1919. A theological movement had by its own dialectical momentum stimulated forces *from within* which led to the negation of its anthropocentricity and a reaffirmation of the claims of divine transcendence. Modernism, by contrast, never had the opportunity of stimulating a dialectical reaction by the inherent dynamic of ideas freely held and freely debated. Since the modernists had indulged neither in Utopianism nor in the kind of anthropocentricity associated with Liberal Protestantism, it is impossible to designate with any certainty those elements in their position which would inevitably have provoked an antithetical swing in any open exchange of freely canvassed opinions. To return sixty years later to the issues which engaged their attention is like re-boarding a *Marie Céleste* of the theological mind. One can hardly doubt that problems associated with transcendence and history would have played a crucial part in any continuing debate. Nor can one reasonably doubt that the trend towards radical immanentism would have been countered not merely by the scholastic conservatives but also within the modernist movement itself.

It was to be expected that the reforms in Catholic theology occasioned by the Second Vatican Council would reawaken interest in the modernists. Their efforts to create a relevant

and responsible Catholic theology were of course conditioned
by their age and limited by its challenges and possibilities.
Their writings must be read with a more than usually atten-
tive eye to historical context. Much that they contended for
in the realm of transcendence and immanence has now won
the right to a sympathetic and critical hearing in the Church.
The 'tyrannous transcendentalism' of which von Hügel com-
plained has given way to an apologetic of immanence. Transcendental Thomism, as found, for instance, in the writings
of Karl Rahner and Bernard Lonergan, represents an effort
to incorporate post-Enlightenment insights and convictions
within the thirteenth-century synthesis of faith and reason,
interpreted in a broad and much less doctrinaire manner.
Whether the old wineskin can continue safely to contain the
new wine remains to be seen. Since the process of fermenta-
tion is particularly violent today, any serious effort to preserve the wine must surely be welcomed, patches and all,
until more secure containers can be fashioned. It can hardly
be denied, however, that fundamental theology, once by
definition the foundation of the entire Roman Catholic
philosophico–theological system, is at the moment in some
disarray, with its basic traditional elements (revelation,
faith, history, miracle, and the nature and role of the Church)
under subjection to a series of critiques some of which are
contemporary while others are emerging from the charge-
sheet of a long-postponed day of reckoning with critical
challenges stretching back to the Enlightenment. Protestant
theologians contemplating what is happening in the Roman
Catholic Church today often have a sense of *déjà vu*, of ana-
chronism, of the fighting of yesterday's battles. Battles for
one's own soul, however, cannot be fought by proxy; and although Roman Catholics can indeed profit from Protestant
successes and failures in past efforts to relate Christian faith
to secular culture, the process has to be appropriated internally — 'recapitulated', in the Irenaean sense — by Roman
Catholics themselves.

Ecclesiology apart, the one area in which Roman Catholics
must still reckon with a continuing dialectical tension is that
of dogma, in the shape of accumulated pronouncements and
definitions of the conciliar and papal magisterium down the

ages. There are as yet no fully agreed principles for the interpretation of these pronouncements and definitions. Given the
inescapable ambiguities of the interpretative process, there
probably never will be. Although this is in the first instance
a matter of domestic concern for Roman Catholic theologians, its implications for inter-church dialogue are obvious
and serious. The attention given by the modernists to the
concept of dogma and its historical relationship with
transcendent truth is of continuing importance and relevance.

Le Roy, Tyrrell, and Laberthonnière all took their stands
against a conception of dogma which has been losing ground
steadily in Roman Catholic theology during the last twenty
years. As a consequence of the move away from the notion
of revelation as divinely communicated statements, the
notion of dogma against which the modernists were protesting has inevitably altered. Le Roy saw the problem as stemming from a failure by the neo-scholastics to appreciate the
gravamen of the Kantian critique of statements about transcendent being which purported to operate in the same
manner as statements about empirically verifiable facts.
Le Roy therefore adopted a position which has sometimes
been labelled 'pragmatic . His position, however, is pragmatic
mainly by reference to the position he was attacking. When
Catholic theologians such as Edward Schillebeeckx, speak
today of 'orthopraxis', they are adopting a line of approach
not dissimilar from Le Roy's. Le Roy's frame of reference
was Bergsonian evolutionism, and to that extent he, like
Tyrrell, appears to have anticipated some of the characteristic
concerns of Process theology. If human nature 'is more a
progression, a *becoming*, than a *thing*'[5] 'then one's apprehension of truth, including truths of transcendent reference,
must in some way correspond with this dynamic conception
of human nature. From this perspective the scholastic
dictum, 'Quidquid recipitur ad modum recipientis recipitur',
takes on a new relevance. Le Roy simply appeals to the
totality of human dynamism (for which he coined the phrase
'pensée-action') against the static view of human nature as
an abstraction and against the naïve realist understanding and
formulation of truth.

[5] *D.C.*, p. 62.

The reforms at present working themselves through contemporary Roman Catholic theology give evidence of two major concerns which exercised the modernists but which had been largely lost to sight in neo-scholastic theology and spirituality. The first is historical sensitivity. The second I shall call sensibility.

The principal consequence of the essentialism practised in the manuals was a radical disregard for the historicity of all human, including religious, thought. Laberthonnière, though not a trained historian, appreciated the implications of this consequence when he contrasted Greek 'idealism' with Christian 'realism'. As R. G. Collingwood has noted, pre-occupation with the concept of substance was the hallmark of Aristotelian metaphysics.

Now a substantialistic metaphysics implies a theory of knowledge according to which only what is unchanging is knowable. But what is unchanging is not historical. What is historical is the transitory event. The substance to which an event happens, or from whose nature it proceeds, is nothing to the historian. Hence the attempt to think historically and the attempt to think in terms of substance were incompatible.[6]

Collingwood is here reflecting on Hellenistic thought in general, but his observation has particular relevance to the problem of identity and change with which several of the modernists grappled in their different ways. The manuals of the interconciliar period were in general gravely deficient in historical sensitivity, partly because their authors genuinely feared the sense of fluidity engendered by any truly historical mode of thinking. They evaded the problem posed by Lessing's antithesis between the contingent truths of history and the necessary truths of reason. Historical thinking always imports a strain of relativity into its processes, even when these are being brought to bear on matters of transcendent reference. History is about contingencies not necessities. That is why history is the hair shirt of Christian faith. Scholastic thought has normally experienced acute discomfort with any suggestion of historical relativity. It has correctly diagnosed the threat of historicization to a theology exclusively rooted in immutable essences. Whereas Loisy removed the discomfort

---

[6] R. G. Collingwood, *The Idea of History* (Oxford, 1946), p. 42.

by jettisoning the essences, neo-scholasticism achieved its anaesthesia by contracting out of the ontological and psychological implications of a faith committed to all the consequences of its historicity. Vulnerability in principle to the insecurities of historical investigation was simply unacceptable to the scholastic mind. It was this which accounted in large measure for its hostility to critical biblical scholarship.

The neo-scholastics saw the content of Christian belief as a deposit once for all delivered to the saints to be handed on unchanged. Since the deposit was deemed to consist basically in revealed assertions about timeless truth, it was denied an *internal* history. These assertions were considered to have been transmitted from age to age in a substantially fixed and final form. Logical deductions might be made from them; but such deductions, even where they were subject to the defining activity of the magisterium, and as such were declared part of the deposit, could never be considered as new truths, only as implications hidden in the original deposit, awaiting the logical investigation of theologians and the seal of approval of the magisterium.

The neo-scholastic theologian therefore saw his task as one of justifying the doctrinal situation at any given moment in the Church's history by reference to all that had gone before. The method invoked was described, with no hint of irony or embarrassment, as the *methodus regressiva*. Sisto Cartechini, in a book designed to meet the needs of theology students and published in 1951, stated the problem thus. No post-Apostolic dogma can be totally new, since revelation is closed. Therefore all received dogmas must be justified by reference to earlier documents. But there are some dogmas which cannot be justified by historical or philosophical reference to past documents. Appeal must therefore be made to the assistance of the Holy Spirit promised to the Church not alone for conserving, but also for designating and explaining, revealed truth. If there are no documents, recourse must be had to the argument from oral transmission.[7] Cartechini was not innovating here; he was merely reproducing Bellarmine's argument for the independent existence and authority

[7] S. Cartechini, *De valore notarum theologicarum et de criteriis ad eas dignoscendas* (Rome, 1951), pp. 220–4.

of unwritten tradition (i.e. the 'two-source' theory of revelation). The 'regressive method' made use of certain historical procedures, but it did so in a manner which reflected a radically unhistorical conception of truth, dogma, faith, and Christian life.

The reforms of Vatican II, especially the quietus given to the two-source theory of revelation and the attention directed towards the process whereby Christian revelation has been transmitted across the ages, have been instrumental in promoting a genuinely historical mode of approach to doctrine and tradition. Nicholas Lash, in a chapter entitled 'The Recovery of History',[8] points to the work of several Roman Catholic theologians in recent years in which he detects a move away not merely from logical theories of development — the conciliar abandonment of the notion of revelation as assertion ensured the demise of such theories — but also from the 'cumulative', 'homogeneously evolutionary' perspective. These theories are being replaced by a more 'situational' approach which brings 'catholic studies of doctrinal change and continuity into a discernibly closer relationship to protestant studies of "hermeneutics" '. In short, Catholic and Protestant theologians are now conscious of facing the same basic problems in this field.

'Ultimately', wrote Tyrrell, 'the question resolves itself into this: Does thought grow architecturally or biologically?'[9] and he freely admitted that he had no cogent answer to his question. His achievement was to draw attention to the problem of methodology in all theological discussion of identity and change. One might, however, today wish to criticize the implication in his question that one has to choose between two, and only two, models, or, indeed, that the notion of growth is the most suitable one for representing diversity and unity deployed on a time-scale. Catholic and Protestant theologians increasingly recognize that no one model can make more than a partial and inherently defective contribution to any problem, including that of identity and change, in Christian doctrine, and that this situation is to be found in Scripture itself.

[8] N. Lash, *Change in Focus: A Study of Doctrinal Change and Continuity* (London, 1973), pp. 128–40.　　　　　　　　　　　[9] *S.C.*, p. 153.

Maurice Wiles, reflecting on the limits of the notion of development, has written of his willingness to discuss the problem of doctrine as 'change through alteration of perspective'.[10] Substantial identity survives the featural change which results from an altered perspective. Jaroslav Pelikan sees the problem as the need to chart a course between doctrinal positivism and historical relativism. He suggests that such a course might be described as 'confessional', namely, 'an attempt to go beyond the antithesis between historical relativism and the claim to absolute truth'.[11] G. A. Lindbeck, in his important article, 'The Problem of Doctrinal Development and Contemporary Protestant Theology',[12] employs the term 'historical situationalism' to combat both the view that doctrines are the result of 'continuous and cumulative growth' and the view that they remain 'fixed at some primitive stage'. Instead, they should be thought of 'as the products of the dialogue in history between God and his people, as the historically conditioned and relative responses, interpretations and testimonies to the Word which addresses man through the scriptural witness'. Avery Dulles accepts Lindbeck's situational theory as enabling a faithful Christian to question a previous 'canonized formulation of faith'.[13]

Historical perspective is rapidly becoming a normal characteristic of contemporary Roman Catholic theology. The abandonment of 'non-historical orthodoxy' is leading to a reckoning with problems to which that orthodoxy was impervious. The admission of a historical dimension raises the spectre of 'relativism', with which the integralists charged the modernists; but the traditionally strong ontological vein in Catholic theology shows all the signs of remaining a powerful antidote to any kind of radical relativism.[14] Catholic theology

---

[10] M. Wiles, *The Remaking of Christian Doctrine* (London, 1974), p. 7.

[11] J. Pelikan, *Historical Theology: Continuity and Change in Christian Doctrine* (London, 1970), p. 159.

[12] *Concilium*, 1 (1967), pp. 64–72.

[13] A. Dulles, *The Resilient Church: The Necessity and Limits of Adaptation* (Dublin, 1978), p. 52.

[14] Thus Bernard Lonergan, the Canadian Jesuit theologian, has an influential following among Roman Catholic theologians and philosophers today, some of whom see his thought as a check to the dangers of relativism in post-conciliar theology.

is coming to accept the inevitability and fruitfulness of what von Hügel called 'friction', especially the friction between the eternal and the historical. There is no escaping 'the sting of contingency' in either prayer or theology. The ability to register and respond creatively to this sting might well be called 'sensibility'.

We have seen more than once in the course of this study that the modernists employed the term 'mystical' to designate a mode of thought which they believed to be most appropriate for responding to transcendent truth. It is an unsatisfactory term, lacking, as it does, the properties of an agreed intellectual currency. The modernists for the most part used it loosely to describe a mode of thought antithetical to scholasticism. It is thus not the word itself which matters here but the circumstances which led to its being invoked. Neo-scholasticism treated the speculative intellect as the only faculty capable of responding with reliable objectivity to revealed truth. It tended to regard the conative and affective processes as capricious and unreliable, and therefore as fundamentally unfitted to the reception of religious truth. When the modernists spoke of scholastic 'intellectualism', they were referring to what they saw as the spiritual impoverishment which results from the heavy, indeed virtually exclusive, emphasis laid by Catholic theology of the period upon the role of the intellect in the things of faith. Seeking to heal the serious breach between reason and feeling which neo-scholasticism had relentlessly widened, they emphasized the non-speculative aspects of religious faith and life. Tyrrell and Loisy appealed to experience as the basic mode of religious apprehension. Von Hügel explored the epistemological implications of this appeal. Under the rubric of 'action', Blondel and Laberthonnière examined the metaphysical character and implications of total involvement in the dynamism of human existence. All of them were trying to repatriate for Roman Catholicism that stream of thought which went back to St. Augustine but which had been driven underground by Aristotelianized Christianity. Blondel and Laberthonnière were especially responsive to Pascal and the logic of the heart. Von Hügel, Tyrrell, and Loisy were influenced by Newman's appeal to the non-discursive function of

the mind for which he had coined the term 'illative sense'.
Bremond was particularly alive to the consequences of the
condemnation of Quietism in 1699, which he described as
'the rout of the mystics'.

The condemnation of modernism not merely restored the
status quo, it reinforced the alienation of feeling from reason
which was always present, at least implicitly, in neo-
scholasticism and which had been intensified by the condemnation of Quietism. Paul Claudel (no friend of modernism) was to describe this alienation as a crisis caused by the
contempt in which Catholic theology held 'the noble
faculties of imagination and sensibility'. The crisis, which
reached its most acute phase in the nineteenth century, was
not primarily an intellectual crisis '. . . I would prefer to say
it was the tragedy of a starved imagination.'[15] The fear of
Quietism led to the externalization of devotion, 'and the
emphasis was placed on outward expressions of religion'.[16]

Claudel's use of the word 'sensibility' prompts one to
wonder whether it might not be a more appropriate word
than 'mysticism' to describe the spiritual quality for which
the modernists were questing and which was the principal
casualty of so many Roman condemnations since the end of
the seventeenth century. Raymond Williams describes 'sensibility' as a word which denotes 'a particular area of interest
and response which could be distinguished not only from
rationality or *intellectuality* but also . . . from morality'.[17]
Williams's interesting discrimination of 'sensibility' from both
intellectuality *and* morality would exactly represent Tyrrell's
reaction against both scholasticism and Liberal Protestantism
— a reaction which William Inge found so hard to understand.
Williams points out that the word 'sensibility' acquired a
particularly well-defined meaning in the eighteenth century.
It could be related to 'taste', 'criticism', and 'culture'. It took
in awareness ('not only *consciousness* but *conscience*').[18]
It survived its obvious and vulnerable association with 'sentiment' when the latter became tainted by 'sentimentality'.
Eventually, however, it too became subject to the iconoclastic

---

[15] Cited in *Dru*, p. 21.   [16] Ibid., p. 23.
[17] R. Williams, *Keywords: A Vocabulary of Culture and Society* (London,
1976), p. 237.   [18] Ibid., p. 236.

process which seems to overtake all terms that seek to conceptualize the experiential, non-discursive, operations of the human spirit, whether in thought or art. Perhaps the paradox of using a word associated so closely with eighteenth-century classicism to replace a word with strong romanticist associations might be taken to symbolize the will to heal the breach between reason and feeling which has marked so much Catholic theology and spirituality since the seventeenth century.

Religious sensibility, already stunned by previous condemnations, received a particularly crippling blow from the condemnation of modernism. The victory of integralism resulted in the virtual exclusion of the term 'experience' from the Roman Catholic theological vocabulary. Deep distrust of the affective processes, coupled with an intellectual regimen which cultivated system at the expense of imagination, had the inevitable effect of inhibiting emotional and aesthetic growth, especially in priests, seminarians, and members of religious congregations. As several of the modernists had pointed out, lack of an immanent dimension in theology and spirituality inevitably produces a coarsening of religious outlook. It is only when we have appreciated the implications of this spiritual malnutrition that we are in a position to evaluate much that is happening by way of reaction in the Roman Catholic Church of today.

The relatively sudden pursuit of relevance in a Church which has for long fostered 'otherworldliness' as an ecclesiastical virtue was bound to be traumatic. The intellectual implications of seeking a synthesis between the essential truth of religion and the essential truth of modernity (Tyrrell's definition of modernism) are hardly less traumatic. One cannot with spiritual and intellectual impunity exchange a thirteenth-century synthesis for a twentieth-century one, bypassing the developments which intervened between the two. There is circumstantial irony in the fact that the Roman Catholic Church has come to belated and reluctant terms with secular culture just at the moment when that culture is undergoing a major crisis of its own. The battle for an immanent *point de départ* in fundamental theology has been won just at the moment when man has never been less sure of what it means to be human. Credible Christian theology can no longer take its stand upon a rigid dichotomy between transcendence and immanence. Events, however, have committed it to a search for transcendence within total human experience just at the moment when that experience is revealing further, unsuspected, and bewildering depths.

Laberthonnière had seen the challenging and disturbing implications of this never-ending search. The Jewish convert, he remarked in his book, *Le Réalisme chrétien et l'idéalisme grec*, found in Christianity the fulfilment of prophecy, the realization of promise. The Greek convert found in it the revelation of truth. But whence, he asks, came this promise and this aspiration towards truth?

Because Christianity responded to both and was welcomed for its ability to do so, we have concluded that it had its roots in humanity and is consequently human. Ah yes; it had its roots in humanity. But where does humanity have its roots? It is human, profoundly human, more human than we could ever say. But is this not so, precisely because there is in humanity something of the divine? And if there is something divine in humanity, under what conditions and in what manner is it to be found there? There you have the question that must never be lost to sight.[10]

That question will always be the most insistent one to which theologians can address themselves. When believers and churches become dogmatic in the assurance of their ability to answer it once and for all, events may occur which destroy the power of the traditional answer to satisfy and thus force them to ask the question anew in a spirit chastened by adversity. The modernists saw and accepted the consequences of professing an historical faith. In this they saw further and deeper than their scholastic opponents; for they appreciated, in a way their opponents did not, the specific challenge and asceticism of a faith which places at least as much emphasis on the quest for further meaning and relevance as it does on the assured possession of inherited truth.

[19] *R.C.I.G.*, p. 244.

Appendix 1
Joseph Lemius (1860–1923),
Draughtsman of *Pascendi*

Papal encyclicals, like many other public documents issued over the signatures of the leaders of men, are normally drafted by 'experts'. It is not always easy to determine who these experts were; and until quite recently the matter was considered theologically unimportant. Once the Pope had signed a document, it was as if he had personally conceived and executed it from the beginning. Draughtsmen may not be sworn to secrecy, but convention has decreed their practical anonymity. The drafting of papal documents has been merely one of the many arcane procedures associated with Roman curial activity.

Since it is hard to think of a papal document which has had more far-reaching and dramatic repercussions throughout the Roman Catholic Church in any age than the encyclical *Pascendi dominici gregis*, interest in its origins and draughtsmanship is something more than a matter of ephemeral curiosity. The disciplinary portion of *Pascendi*, with its Draconian measures, could have been drawn up by many figures of the period, including the Pope himself. Its severe and constricting injunctions were the fruit of intense fear, resentment, and anxiety coupled with a single-minded determination to rid the Church of modernism root and branch. Cardinal Calasanz Vivès y Tuto possessed and indulged all these emotions to the full, and it is to this Spanish Capuchin that Father Jean-Baptiste Lemius (Joseph's brother and, like him, a member of the Oblates of Mary Immaculate) attributes 'the moral part' of the encyclical (see J. Rivière, 'Qui rédigea l'encyclique "Pascendi"?', in *B.L.E.*, 47 (1946), pp. 154 f.).

Authorship of the doctrinal section has been a much more problematical business. Patently neo-scholastic in conception and language, the systematic exposition which forms the most substantial part of the encyclical has nevertheless an originality about it for which there were no clear precedents in the published anti-modernist writings which preceded it.

The modernists themselves were widely disparate in their speculations about its authorship. Wilfrid Ward thought it was probably written by 'one of those *Civiltà* Jesuits' (Letter to Lord Halifax cited in Barmann, *Baron Friedrich von Hügel*, p. 200). Houtin ascribed it to 'numerous theologians, notably Fr Billot and Mgr Benigni' (Rivière, art. cit., pp. 144 f.). Bremond had heard it said that Dom Laurent Janssens, the Belgian Abbot Primate of the Benedictines, was the author of the 'intellectual' part (*Bremond–Blondel Correspondance*, vol. 2, p. 105). Buonaiuti attributed it to Billot (*Pellegrino di Roma*,

p. 80); *La Croix*, to Mgr. Sardi, Secretary of Letters to Princes (Sabatier, *Les Modernistes*, p. 66 n).

None of the modernists mentioned the name of Joseph Lemius, O.M.I. (1860–1923), Procurator General of the Oblates of Mary Immaculate and a Vatican curial consultor. In point of fact he was probably unknown to most of them. His writings consisted of a booklet, catalogued in the library of the Oblate General House of Studies in Rome as 'P. Giuseppe Lemius, O.M.I. (Socio dell'Academia Romana di S. Tommaso, Consultore della S.C. degli Studi): *Saggio sintetico della metafisica di S. Tommaso d'Aquino* (Rome, 1895)'.

In 1946 Jean Rivière published an article which established beyond reasonable doubt Lemius's authorship of the theoretical portion of the encyclical (art. cit., pp. 143–61. The principal evidence is discussed in pp. 149–56). The then Superior General of the Oblates, Father Théodore Labouré, had sent Rivière a copy of two unpublished lectures given by Joseph Lemius to the Academy of St. Thomas in Rome (ibid., p. 157). Rivière gives the titles of these lectures as 'Le dottrine del Loisy' (14 May 1905) and 'Le basi filosofiche della critica biblica moderna' (2 May 1907). Thanks to the kindness of the General Archivist of the Oblates I was allowed to consult the originals of these lectures, together with other Lemius papers. The titles as given by Rivière differ from the titles to be found on the originals. The lecture of 14 May 1905 is entitled by Lemius himself 'Sur les doctrines de Loisy' (the text of the lecture is, however, in Italian). The lecture of 2 May 1907 is entitled, again in Lemius's hand, 'Le basi filosofiche del sistema Loisiano'. Rivière noted the close similarity between the method of approach of these lectures and that of *Pascendi*, together with the controlling conviction that modernist philosophy was rooted in 'agnosticism' and 'vital immanence' (ibid., p. 159).

There is, however, among the Lemius papers far more striking evidence of the Oblate Procurator General's involvement in the production of *Pascendi*. This is a sixty-two-page typescript inscribed at the beginning 'Lemius Joseph' 'Modernisme: Theorie'. A later hand has added 'Texte préparé par le R. P. Lemius Joseph, 1905–1907'. The dating here is clearly inaccurate and conflicts with what we know from other sources about Lemius's part in the encyclical. One can only speculate on the precise nature of this document. It is written in Italian and is very similar to the official Italian translation of the encyclical. The principal differences between the Lemius document and the published encyclical are stylistic and editorial. Some passages are extended, others contracted. The changes leave the main argument unaffected. The document is almost certainly the Italian version made at the Vatican from Lemius's original French draft. What I have been unable to determine is whether, and to what extent, there have been further substantial editorial changes made in Lemius's French original (a copy of which was not among the papers I inspected), and whether the document in the Oblate General Archives is the first Italian draft or a subsequent one. The document has marginal comments in Lemius's hand which are mainly references to, and occasionally quotations from, Loisy's writings. Other names mentioned in the margin are: Laberthonnière, W. James, Kant, and Le Roy. Neither Tyrrell (of whose writings Lemius seems completely unaware) nor Blondel appear. The only Italian reference is to *Quello che vogliamo*.

Also included among the Lemius papers is a wad of typed notes which may have served as a quarry for his final draft. These notes contain many long quotations from Loisy and Sabatier, but they also show Lemius's concern to systematize the case he is attacking. It is almost certainly these notes, and not the draft of *Pascendi*, which should be dated 1905–1907.

As we have seen in Chapter 8, Lemius's prose is less shrill and self-indulgent than that of most other anti-modernists. (There are signs in *Pascendi* of considerable intensification of such invective as appears in Lemius's work.) He is not, however, above an occasional excursion into rhetoric. The following sample comes from the general notes referred to in the preceding paragraph.

Certes, on ne peut les [sc. the modernists] accuser de manquer de logique. Leurs principes posés, ils en font une application rigoureuse, impitoyable, et il n'est conclusion, si téméraire qu'elle soit, qui les puisse arrêter. Ils vont, la tête haute et le pas assuré, satisfaits d'eux-mêmes et dédaigneux des autres, renversant tout sur leur passage, et faisant de la tradition catholique un champs désolé, où l'oeil attristé ne rencntre [sic] plus que des ruines. Véritablement, où ils ont passé, il ne reste plus rien. C'est scientifiauement [sic] et historiquement, le nivellement total du surnaturel, ou, pour parler plus exactement du divin, en y comprenant l'existence même de Dieu, et tout ce que les catholiques ont toujours tenu comme légitime objet de la théologie naturelle. Nous démontrerons plus bas que la foi, dans les conditions d'isolement qui lui sont faites, dans la volonté et le sentiment, est incapable, quoiqu'ils en disent, de relever une seule de ces ruines.

This is one of the better pieces of rhetoric to be found in anti-modernist writing. The indignation is honest and reflects the feelings of a man utterly devoted to the Thomistic synthesis. It was indeed with a 'saddened eye' that Joseph Lemius contemplated the desolation which Loisy had wreaked on the neo-scholastic environment that Lemius, and those who thought as he did, identified with the pastures of perennial Catholic truth.

Appendix 2
The Anti-Modernist Oath

Although *Lamentabili* and *Pascendi* constitute the doctrinal substance of the Roman condemnation of modernism, the coping-stone of the anti-modernist programme was an oath prescribed by the *motu proprio, Sacrorum Antistitum* (1 September 1910) (*Acta Apostolicae Sedis*, 2 (1910), pp. 655–80. The formula for the oath is printed in Denzinger–Schönmetzer *Enchiridion*, nos. 3537–50). This oath was to be taken by clerics on the reception of Major Orders, and by other office-holders in the Church on the occasion of their taking up office. (Persons and occasions covered by the *motu proprio* are listed in *A.A.S.*, loc. cit., p. 669.) Its historical importance lies in the fact that it was treated as a formulary of faith by the clerical Church at large and as a *locus theologicus* by teachers of dogmatic theology. It, more than any other document, kept alive the memory of modernism in the Roman Catholic Church long after modernism had ceased to be seen as an actual threat. It remains a useful summary of the doctrinal position struck by the magisterium of the Church as a direct response to the modernist challenge.

I, NN, firmly embrace and accept as a whole and severally all that has been defined, asserted, and declared by the inerrant magisterium of the Church, especially those principal dogmatic truths (*ea doctrinae capita*) which are directly opposed to the errors of this time. And first of all I profess that God, the beginning and end of all things, can be known with certainty and demonstrated by the natural light of reason from the things that have been made, that is, from the *visible* [original italics, not included in Denzinger] works of creation, as a cause known from its effects. Secondly, I accept and willingly recognize the external proofs of revelation, that is, the divine facts, in the first instance miracles and prophecies, as most certain signs of the divine origin of the Christian religion, and I hold that they are valid in the highest degree (*maxime accommodata*) for the intelligences of all men, in every age, including those of the present time. Thirdly, I believe with equally firm faith that the Church, the guardian and teacher of the revealed word was immediately (*proxime*) and directly instituted by the true and historical Christ himself while he lived among us, and that this Church has been built upon Peter, the prince of the apostolic hierarchy, and upon his successors down the ages. Fourthly, I sincerely accept the doctrine of the faith which has been transmitted to us in the same sense and meaning from the apostles through the orthodox Fathers; therefore I altogether reject the heretical theory (*commentum*) of the evolution of dogmas, that is, that they pass from one meaning to another different from that which the Church first held; I also condemn every error which, in place of the divine deposit given by Christ to his Spouse the Church to be faithfully guarded, is satisfied with a philosophical foundling (*philosophicum inventum*), or creature of human consciousness, a product of human effort destined for indefinite progress towards perfection. Fifthly, I hold as certain and sincerely profess that faith is not a blind religious sense (*caecum sensum religionis*) welling up from the recesses of the *subconscious* under the impulse of the heart and at the bidding* of a morally-informed will, but a genuine assent of the intellect to a truth received extrinsically by hearing, by an assent, namely, based on the authority of an all-truthful God, and given to a truth that has been revealed and attested by a personal God, our creator and Lord.

With like respect I submit and adhere whole-heartedly to the condemnations, declarations, and all the prescriptions which are contained in the encyclical letter 'Pascendi' and in the decree 'Lamentabili' especially those which bear on what is called history of dogma. Likewise I repudiate the error of those who claim that the faith proposed by the Church is open to falsification by history and that Catholic dogmas, in the sense in which they are now understood, cannot be reconciled with the origins of the Christian religion as they really were. I also condemn and repudiate the opinion of those who say that the more learned Christian man puts on a double persona, the one of a believer, the other of an historian, as though an historian could legitimately maintain things which contradicted the faith of the believer, or set up premises from which it followed that dogmas are either false or dubious, as long as these were not directly denied. Equally I repudiate the method for judging and interpreting holy Scripture which discounts the Church's tradition, the analogy of faith, and the norms of the Apostolic See, and which enthusiastically adopts *rationalist* procedures, illegitimately and rashly embracing textual criticism as the one and only rule. Furthermore I reject the thesis of those who hold that the teacher or writer in the field of historical theology must from the start set aside all preconceived ideas, whether about the supernaural origin of Catholic tradition, or about the promise of divine help in the enduring preservation of each revealed truth. [I also reject the view] that the writings of each of the Fathers should be interpreted by scientific principles alone to the exclusion of all sacred authority and with the same freedom of enquiry with which any profane document is normally examined. Finally, I express my vehement opposition to the error of the *modernists* who hold that there is nothing of a divine character to be found in sacred tradition, or – what is far worse – who take it in a pantheistic sense, in such a manner that nothing is left but a bare and simple fact on a par with the common facts of history, in short, [the fact that] men by their own effort, care, and genius fostered through subsequent ages the school founded by Christ and his apostles. Hence I hold most firmly and will continue to hold until my last breath, the faith of the Fathers in the *certain* charism of *truth* that exists, has existed, and always will exist in the *episcopal succession from the Apostles*, so that not what might seem better suited to the culture of each age should be held, rather that the absolute and immutable truth first preached by the Apostles *should never be believed* or understood *in a different manner*.

I promise that I shall observe all these things faithfully, sincerely and in their entirety, protecting their inviolability and never deviating from them whether by teaching or by any word or writing whatsoever. Thus I promise, thus I swear, so [help me] God etc.

---

*Denzinger–Schönmetzer, *Enchiridion*, no. 3542, note, suggests that *inflexionis* should read *inflexione*.

Bibliography

BOOKS

Alberigo, J., *et al.* (eds.), *Conciliorum oecumenicorum decreta* (2nd edn., Bologna, 1962).

Arnold, M., *Literature and Dogma: An Essay towards a Better Apprehension of the Bible* (Popular Edn., London, 1884).

Aubert, R., *Le Problème de l'acte de foi: Données traditionelles et résultats des controverses récentes* (4th edn., Louvain and Paris, 1969).

Barmann, L. F., *Baron Friedrich von Hügel and the Modernist Crisis in England* (Cambridge, 1972).

Barth, K., *Protestant Theology in the Nineteenth Century: Its Background and History* (London, 1972).

Baum, G., *Man Becoming: God in Secular Experience* (New York, 1971).

Bedeschi, L., *La curia Romana durante la crisi modernista: Episodi e metodi di governo* (Rome, 1968).

—— *Lineamenti dell'antimodernismo: Il caso Lanzoni* (Parma, 1970).

—— *Interpretazioni e sviluppo del modernismo cattolico* (Milan, 1975).

Beillevert, P., *Laberthonnière: L'Homme et l'œuvre* (Paris, 1972).

Bellamy, J., *La Théologie catholique au XIXe siècle* (3rd edn., Paris, 1904).

Bergson, H., *L'Évolution créatrice* (Paris, 1907).

Billot, L., *De Deo uno. De Deo trino* (Rome 1895).

—— *De ecclesia Christi* (Vol. i, 1898, vol. 2, Rome, 1910).

—— *De inspiratione sacrae scripturae* (Rome, 1903).

—— *De immutabilitate traditionis contra modernam haeresim evolutionismi* (Rome, 1907).

Blanchet, A. (ed.), *Henri Bremond et Maurice Blondel: Correspondance* (Vols. i and ii, Paris, 1970–1).

Blondel, M., *Les Premiers Écrits de Maurice Blondel*, vol. i (Paris, 1950); vol. ii (Paris, 1956).

—— *Lettres philosophiques de Maurice Blondel* (Paris, 1961).

—— *Carnets intimes, 1883–1894* (Paris, 1961).

Boedder, B., *Natural Theology* (London, 1891).

Boegner, M., *The Long Road to Unity: Memories and Anticipations* (London, 1970).

Bouillard, H., *Blondel et le christianisme* (Paris, 1961).

de Boyer de Sainte Suzanne, R., *Alfred Loisy: Entre la foi et l'incroyance* (Paris, 1968).

Briggs, C. A., and F. von Hügel, *The Papal Commission and The Penta-teuch* (London, 1906).

Buonaiuti, E., *Lettere di un prete modernista* (Rome, 1908).

—— *Il modernismo cattolico* (Modena, 1943).

—— *Pellegrino di Roma: La generazione dell'esodo* (Bari, 1964).

Butler, C., *The Vatican Council, 1860–1870* (Fontana Library, London, 1962).

Castelli, E., *Laberthonnière*. Traduit de l'Italian par Louis Canet. (Paris, 1931).

Catalogus professorum et alumnorum Pontificiae Universitatis Gregori-anae (Rome, 1888).

Chadwick, O. W., *From Bossuet to Newman: The Idea of Doctrinal Development* (Cambridge, 1957).

Chevalier, J., *Pascal* (London, 1930).

Collingwood, R. G., *The Idea of History* (Oxford, 1946).

Congar, Y. M.-J., *Tradition and Traditions: A Historical and a Theologi-cal Essay* (London, 1966).

—— *A History of Theology* (New York, 1968).

Copleston, F., *A History of Philosophy*, vol. ix, *Maine de Biran to Sartre* (London, 1975).

Coulson, J., *Newman and the Common Tradition: A Study in the Language of Church and Society* (Oxford, 1970).

—— and A. M. Allchin (eds.), *The Rediscovery of Newman: An Oxford Symposium* (London, 1967).

Dakin, A. H., Jr., *Von Hügel and the Supernatural* (London, 1934).

Dansette, A., *Religious History of Modern France*, vol. ii (Edinburgh and London, 1961).

de la Bedoyère, M., *The Life of Baron von Hügel* (London, 1951).

Denzinger, H. and A. Schönmetzer (eds.), *Enchiridion symbolorum definitionum et declarationum de rebus fidei et morum* (34th edn. Barcelona *et alibi*, 1967).

Dru, A. and I. Trethowan (eds.), *Maurice Blondel: The Letter on Apolo-getics and History and Dogma* (London, 1964).

Dulles, A., *A History of Apologetics* (London, 1971).

—— *The Resilient Church: The Necessity and Limits of Adaptation* (London, 1975).

Duméry, H., *Blondel et la religion: Essai critique sur la 'Lettre' de 1896* (Paris, 1954).

Eastwood, D. M., *The Revival of Pascal: A Study of His Relation to Modern French Thought* (Oxford, 1936).

Études blondéliennes, vol. i (Paris, 1951), vol. ii (Paris, 1952).

Feuerbach, L., *The Essence of Christianity*. Trans. George Eliot (Harper Torchbook edn., New York, 1957).

Fiocchi, A. M., *P. Enrico Rosa, S.J.: Scrittore della 'Civiltà Cattolica' (1870–1938): Il suo pensiero nelle controversie religiose e politiche del suo tempo* Rome, 1957).

Fontaine, J., *Étude comparative des deux synthèses catholique & moderniste d'après le Concile du Vatican et l'encyclique 'Pascendi'*

(Paris, 1914).

Foucher, L., *La Philosophie catholique en France au XIX siècle avant la renaissance thomiste et dans son rapport avec elle (1800-1880)* (Paris, 1955).

Franzelin, J. B., *De divina traditione et scriptura* (Rome, 1870).

Gelli, S. [Tyrrell], *Psicologia della religione* (Rome, 1905).

Gentile, G., *La religione: Il modernismo e i rapporti tra religione e filosofia: Discorsi di religione* (Florence, 1965).

Gilson, E., *Introduction à l'étude de Saint Augustin* (3rd edn., Paris, 1949).

— *Being and Some philosophers* (2nd edn., Toronto, 1952).

Guasco, M., *Alfred Loisy in Italia. Con documenti inediti* (Turin, 1975).

von Harnack, A., *What Is Christianity?* Trans. T. B. Saunders (London, 1901).

Harvey, V. A., *The Historian and the Believer* (London, 1967).

Hastings, A. (ed.), *Bishops and Writers: Aspects of the Evolution of Modern English Catholicism* (Wheathampstead, Hertfordshire, 1977).

Heaney, J. J., *The Modernist Crisis: von Hügel* (London, 1969).

Hébert, M., *Souvenirs d'Assise* (Paris, 1899).

Heer, F., *The Intellectual History of Europe* (London, 1966).

Hocedez, E., *Histoire de la théologie au XIXe siècle*, 3 vols. (Brussels and Paris, 1947-52).

Holland, B. (ed.), *Baron Friedrich von Hügel: Selected Letters, 1896-1924* (London, 1928).

Houtin, A., *La Question biblique au XXe siècle* (Paris, 1906).

— *Histoire du modernisme catholique* (Paris, 1913).

— *Un prêtre symboliste: Marcel Hébert, 1851-1916* (Paris, 1925).

von Hügel, F., *Eternal Life: A Study of Its Implications and Applications* (Edinburgh, 1912).

— *The Mystical Element of Religion: As Studied in Saint Catherine of Genoa and Her Friends.* 2 vols. (2nd edn., London, 1923).

— *Essays and Addresses on the Philosophy of Religion.* 1st Series (London, 1921); 2nd Series (London, 1926).

— *Letters from Baron Friedrich von Hügel to a Niece.* Edited with an Introduction by Gwendolen Greene (London, 1928).

Hurter, H., *Theologiae dogmaticae compendium in usum studiosorum theologiae*, vol. i (12th edn., Innsbruck, 1909).

Krailsheimer, A. J. (ed.), *Pascal: Pensées* (Penguin Books, Harmondsworth, 1966).

Laberthonnière, L., *Essais de philosophie religieuse* (Paris, 1903).

— *Le Réalisme chrétien et l'idéalisme grec* (Paris, 1904).

— *Positivisme et catholicisme: A propos de 'L'Action française'* (Paris, 1911).

— *Les Fruits de L'Esprit.* Instructions pour une retraite. Publié par les soins et avec une préface de M.-M. d'Hendecourt (Paris, 1961).

Lacroix, J., *Maurice Blondel: An Introduction to the Man and His Philosophy* (New York, 1968).

Larkin, M., *Church and State after the Dreyfus Affair: The Separation

Issue in France (London, 1974).

Lash, N., *Change in Focus: A Study of Doctrinal Change and Continuity* (London, 1973).

—— *Newman on Development: The Search for an Explanation in History* (London, 1975).

Latourelle, R., *Theology of Revelation* (New York, 1966).

Lebreton, J., *L'Encyclique et la théologie moderniste* (Paris, 1908).

Lecanuet, R. P., *La Vie de l'Église sous Léon XIII* (Paris, 1930).

Le Floch, H., *Le Cardinal Billot: Lumière de la théologie* (Paris, 1947).

Le Roy, E., *Dogme et critique* (Paris, 1907).

—— *Le Problème de Dieu* (Paris, 1930).

Lilley, A. L. (ed.), *What We Want: An Open Letter to Pius X from a Group of Priests* (London, 1907).

—— *The programme of Modernism: A Reply to the Encyclical of Pius X, 'Pascendi Dominici Gregis'* (London, 1908).

Loisy, A., *L'Évangile et L'Église* (Paris, 1902).

—— *Autour d'un petit livre* (Paris, 1903).

—— *Quelques lettres sur des questions actuelles et sur des événements récents* (Ceffonds, 1908).

—— *Simples réflexions sur le décret du saint-office Lamentabili sane exitu et sur l'encyclique Pascendi dominici gregis* (Ceffonds, 1908).

—— *Choses passées* (Paris, 1913).

—— *La Religion* (Paris, 1917).

—— *Mémoires pour servir à l'histoire religieuse de notre temps*, 3 vols. (Paris, 1930-1).

—— *La Crise morale du temps présent et l'éducation humaine* (Paris, 1937).

Louis-David, A. (ed.), *Lettres de George Tyrrell à Henri Bremond* (Paris, 1971).

de Lubac, H. (ed.), *Maurice Blondel et Auguste Valensin: Correspondance, 1899-1947*, 3 vols. (Paris, 1957-65).

—— *The Mystery of the Supernatural* (London, 1967).

Marlé, R., *Au cœur de la crise moderniste: Le dossier inédit d'une controverse* (Paris, 1960).

Mattiussi, G., *Il veleno kantiano: Nuova ed antica critica della ragione, immanenza, filosofia dell'azione* (Monza, 1907).

McNeill, J. J., *The Blondelian Synthesis: A Study of the Influence of German Philosophical Sources on the Formation of Blondel's Method and Thought* (Leiden, 1966).

Mercier, D., *Le Modernisme* (Brussels, 1908).

Nédoncelle, M., *Baron Friedrich von Hügel: A Study of His Life and Thought* (London, 1937).

Ott, L., *Fundamentals of Catholic Dogma*. English edn. by James Canon Bastible D.D. Trans. from German by Patrick Lynch Ph.D. (Cork, 1962).

Palmer, J., *Hermeneutics: Interpretation Theory in Schleiermacher, Dilthey, Heidegger, and Gadamer* (Evanston, 1969).

Pelikan, J., *Historical Theology: Continuity and Change in Christian*

Doctrine (London, 1970).

Perrin, M.-T. (ed.), *Laberthonnière et ses amis* (Paris, 1975).

Perrone, J., *Praelectiones theologicae*, 4 vols. (Paris, 1883).

Petre, M. D., *Autobiography and Life of George Tyrrell*, 2 vols. (London, 1912).

—— (ed.), *George Tyrrell's Letters* (London, 1920).

—— *Von Hügel and Tyrrell: The Story of a Friendship* (London, 1937).

—— *Alfred Loisy: His Religious Significance* (Cambridge, 1944).

Poulat, E. (ed.), *Alfred Loisy: Sa vie – son œuvre*. Par Albert Houtin et Félix Sartiaux. Manuscrit annoté et publié avec une Bibliographie Loisy et un Index Bio-Bibliographique (Paris, 1960).

—— *Histoire, dogme et critique dans la crise moderniste* (Paris, 1962).

—— *Intégrisme et Catholicisme intégral: Un réseau secret international antimoderniste: La 'Sapinière', 1909-1921* (Paris, 1969).

—— *Une œuvre clandestine d'Henri Bremond: Sylvain Leblanc: Un clerc qui n'a pas trahi: Alfred Loisy d'après ses Mémoires, 1931*. Édition critique et dossier historique (Rome, 1972).

Il programma dei modernisti: Risposta all'enciclica di Pio X 'Pascendi dominici gregis' (Rome, 1907).

Rahner, K. and H. Vorgrimler, *Concise Theological Dictionary*. Ed. C. Ernst. Trans. R. Strachan (London, 1965).

Ranchetti, M., *The Catholic Modernists: A Study of the Religious Reform Movement, 1864-1907*. Trans. I. Quigly (Oxford, 1969).

Ratté, J., *Three Modernists: Alfred Loisy, George Tyrrell, William J. Sullivan* (London, 1968).

Reardon, B. M. G., *Liberal Protestantism* (London, 1968).

—— *Roman Catholic Modernism* (London, 1970).

—— *Liberalism and Tradition: Aspects of Catholic Thought in Nineteenth-Century France* (Cambridge, 1975).

Richardson, A., *The Bible in the Age of Science* (London, 1961).

—— *History Sacred and Profane* (London, 1964).

Rivière, J., *Le Modernisme dans l'Église: Étude d'histoire religieuse contemporaine* (Paris, 1929).

Rodé, F., *Le Miracle dans la controverse moderniste* (Paris, 1965).

Rosa, E., *L'Enclica 'Pascendi' e il modernismo: Studii e commenti* (2nd edn., Rome, 1909).

Sabatier, A., *Outlines of a Philosophy of Religion Based on Psychology and History* (London and New York, 1902).

Sabatier, P., *Les Modernistes: Notes d'histoire contemporaine* (Paris, 1909).

Saint-Jean, R., *L'Apologétique philosophique: Blondel, 1893-1913* (Paris, 1966).

Schoof, M., *Breakthrough: Beginnings of the New Catholic Theology*. With an introduction by E. Schillebeeckx. Trans. N. D. Smith (Dublin, 1970).

Sciacca, M. F. (ed.), *Les Grands Courants de la pensée mondiale contemporaine: Les tendances principales*, vol. i (Milan, 1961).

Scoppola, P., *Crisi modernista e rinnovamento cattolico in Italia*

(Bologna, 1961).

Somerville, J. M., *Total Commitment: Blondel's L'Action* (Washington, 1968).

Taymans D'Eypernon, F., *Le Blondélisme* (Louvain, 1933).

de Tonquédec, J., *Immanence: Essai critique sur la doctrine de M. Maurice Blondel* (2nd edn., Paris, 1913).

Tresmontant, C. (ed.), *Maurice Blondel — Lucien Laberthonnière: Correspondance philosophique* (Paris, 1961).

—— (ed.), Lucien Laberthonnière, *Le Réalisme chrétien: précédé de: Essais de philosophie religieuse*. Publié par les soins et avec une préface de C. Tresmontant (Paris, 1966).

Turvasi, F., *Giovanni Genocchi e la controversia modernista* (Rome, 1974).

Tyrrell, G., *External Religion: Its Use and Abuse* (2nd edn., London, 1900).

—— *The Faith of the Millions: A Selection of Past Essays*. 1st Series (2nd edn., London, 1902); 2nd Series (London, 1901).

—— *Lex Orandi: Or, Prayer and Creed* (London, 1903).

—— *Nova et Vetera: Informal Meditations for Times of Spiritual Dryness* (4th edn., London, 1905).

—— *A Much-Abused Letter* (London, 1906).

—— *Through Scylla and Charybdis; Or, The Old Theology and the New* (London, 1907).

—— *Oil and Wine* (London, 1907).

—— *Medievalism: A Reply to Cardinal Mercier* (London, 1908).

—— *Christianity at the Cross-Roads* (London, 1909).

—— *Essays on Faith and Immortality*. Arranged by M. D. Petre (London, 1914).

L'Università Gregoriana del Collegio Romano nel primo secolo della restituzione (Rome, [1925]).

Van Riet, G., *Thomistic Epistemology: Studies Concerning the Problem of Cognition in the Contemporary Thomistic School*, 2 vols. (St. Louis and London, 1963).

Vidler, A. R., *The Modernist Movement in the Roman Church: Its Origin and Outcome* (Cambridge, 1934).

—— *The Church in an Age of Revolution: 1789 to the Present Day* (Penguin Books, Harmondsworth, 1961).

—— *A Variety of Catholic Modernists* (Cambridge, 1970).

Virgoulay, R. and C. Troisfontaines, *Maurice Blondel: Bibliographie analytique et critique*, vol. 1, *Œuvres de Maurice Blondel, 1880–1973*; vol. 2, *Études sur Maurice Blondel, 1893–1975* (Louvain, 1975-6).

Vorgrimler, H. (ed.), *Commentary on the Documents of Vatican II*, 5 vols. (New York and London, 1967-9).

Ward, M., *The Wilfrid Wards and the Transition* (London, 1934).

—— *Insurrection versus Resurrection* (London, 1937).

Ward, W., *The Life of John Henry Cardinal Newman: Based on His Private Journals and Correspondence*, 2 vols. (London, 1912).

Whelan, J. P., *The Spirituality of Friedrich von Hügel* (London, 1971).
Wiles, M., *The Remaking of Christian Doctrine* (London, 1974).
Wilhelm, J. and T. B. Scannell, *A Manual of Catholic Theology Based on Scheeben's 'Dogmatik'*, 2 vols. (London, 1890).
Williams, R., *Culture and Society, 1780-1950* (Penguin Books, Harmondsworth, 1961).
— Keywords: *A Vocabulary of Culture and Society* (London, 1976).

ARTICLES

Aimant, B. [Blondel], 'Une des sources de la penseé moderne: l'Évolution du Spinozisme', *A.P.C.* 54 (1894), pp. 260-75, 324-41.
Allo, M.-B., 'Extrinsécisme et historicisme', in *Revue thomiste*, 12 (1904), pp. 437-65.
Aubert, R., 'Aspects divers du néo-thomisme sous le pontificat de Léon XIII', *Aspetti della cultura cattolica nell'età di Leone XIII* (Rome, 1961).
— 'Aux origines de la réaction antimoderniste: Deux documents inédits', *Ephemerides Theologicae Lovanienses*, 37 (1961), pp. 557-78.
— 'Recent Publications on the Modernist Movement', *Concilium*, 7 (1966), pp. 47-55.
Aufieri, R., 'Baron Friedrich von Hügel: A Doctrine of God', *Dunwoodie Review*, 14 (1974), pp. 3-21.
Ballard, R., 'George Tyrrell and the Apocalyptic Vision of Christ', *Theology*, 78 (1975), pp. 459-67.
Barmann, L. F., 'The Heresy of Orthodoxy', *Theology*, 71 (1968), pp. 456-62.
Beatie, J. W., 'Von Hügel's "Sense of the Infinite" ', *H.J.* 16 (1975), pp. 149-73.
Bécamel, M., 'Lettres de Loisy à Mgr. Mignot: À propos de la crise moderniste', *B.L.E.* 67 (1966), pp. 3-44, 81-114, 170-94, 257-86.
— 'Autres lettres de Loisy à Mgr. Mignot', *B.L.E.* 69 (1968), pp. 241-68.
Bernard-Maitre, H., 'Lettres d'Henri Bremond à Alfred Loisy', *B.L.E.* 69 (1968), pp. 3-24, 161-84, 269-89; 70 (1969), pp. 44-56.
— 'Un épisode significatif du modernisme: "Histoire et dogme" de Maurice Blondel d'après les papiers inédits d'Alfred Loisy, 1897-1905', *R.S.R.* 57 (1969), pp. 49-74.
Browne, R. K., 'Newman and von Hügel: A Record of an Early Meeting', *The Month*, 26 (1969), pp. 24-33.
Cartechini, S., *De Valore notarum theologicarum et de criteriis ad eas dignoscendas* (Rome, 1951).
Chapman, R., 'The Thought of George Tyrrell', in W. W. Robson (ed.), *Essays and Poems Presented to Lord David Cecil* (London, 1970), pp. 140-68.
Chenu, M. D., 'Vérité évangélique et métaphysique Wolffienne à Vatican II', *Revue des sciences philosophiques et théologiques*, 57 (1973),

pp. 632–40.

Crehan, J. H., 'Tyrrell in His Workshop', *The Month*, 231 (1971), pp. 111–15, 119.

Daly, G., 'Some Reflections on the Character of George Tyrrell', *H.J.* 10 (1969), pp. 256–74.

—— 'Tyrrell's "Medievalism" ', *The Month*, New Series, 42 (1969), pp. 15–22.

Dimnet, E., 'Une meilleure voie', *R.C.F.* 31 (1902), pp. 5–23, 129–49, 351–72.

Dudon, P., 'Les Origines françaises du décret *Lamentabili*, 1903–1907', *B.L.E.* 32 (1931), pp. 73–96.

Firmin, A. [Loisy], 'Le Développement chrétien d'après le Cardinal Newman', *R.C.F.* 17 (1898–9), pp. 5–20.

—— 'La théorie individualiste de la religion', *R.C.F.* 17 (1899), pp. 202–15.

—— 'La Définition de la religion', *R.C.F.* 18 (1899), pp. 193–209.

—— 'L'Idée de la révélation', *R.C.F.* 21 (1900), pp. 250–71.

—— 'Les Preuves et l'économie de la révélation', *R.C.F.* 22 (1900), pp. 126–53.

Fontan, P., 'Maurice Blondel et la crise moderniste (années 1902–1903) d'après la correspondance du philosophe', *B.L.E.* 78 (1977), pp. 103–34.

Fumagalli, A., 'Le insidie di una nuova scienza', *La Scuola Cattolica*, 31 (1903), pp. 385–400.

Gardeil, A., 'La Reforme de la théologie catholique: Idée d'une méthode régressive', *Revue thomiste*, 11 (1903), pp. 5–19.

Garrigou-Lagrange, R., 'Les Preuves thomistes de l'existence de Dieu critiquées par M. Le Roy', *Revue thomiste*, 15 (1907), pp. 313–31.

Gayraud, H., 'Une nouvelle apologétique chrétienne', *A.P.C.* 133 (1896–1897), pp. 253–73, 400–8.

—— 'Le problème de la certitude religieuse', *R.C.F.* 30 (1902), pp. 113–30.

Goichot, E., 'En marge de la crise moderniste: La correspondance Bremond–von Hügel', *Revue des sciences religieuses*, 48 (1974), pp. 209–34.

Haight, R., 'The Unfolding of Modernism in France: Blondel, Laberthonnière, Le Roy', *Theological Studies*, 35 (1974), pp. 632–66.

Harent, S., 'Expérience et foi à propos de la récente encyclique', *Études*, 113 (1907), pp. 221–50.

Heaney, J. J., 'The Enigma of the Later von Hügel', *H.J.* 6 (1965), pp. 145–59.

Hébert, M., 'La Dernière Idole: Étude sur la "personnalité divine" ', *Revue de métaphysique et de morale*, 10 (1902), pp. 397–408.

von Hügel, F., 'Du Christ éternel et de nos christologies successives', *La Quinzaine*, 58 (1904), pp. 285–312.

—— 'Experience and Transcendence', *Dublin Review*, 138 (1906), pp. 357–79.

—— 'Father Tyrrell: Some Memorials of the Last Twelve Years of His Life', *Hibbert Journal*, 8 (1910), pp. 233–52.

— 'Petite consultation sur les difficultés concernant Dieu', in P. Scoppola, *Crisi modernista e rinnovamento cattolico in Italia* (Bologna, 1961), pp. 368–92.

Inge, W. R., Review of G. Tyrrell, *Christianity at the Cross-Roads, Hibbert Journal*, 8 (1910), pp. 434–8.

Kelly, J. J. (ed.), 'Von Hügel on Religion: An Unpublished Paper', *The Month*, 236 (1975), pp. 212–15.

— 'Von Hügel on Authority', *The Tablet*, 6 May 1978, pp. 445 f.

Laberthonnière, L., 'Notre programme', *A.P.C.* 1 (1905), pp. 5–31.

— 'Réponse à Mgr Turinaz', *A.P.C.* 1 (1906), pp. 398–477.

— 'Dogme et théologie', *A.P.C.* 4 (1907), pp. 561–601; 5 (1907), pp. 10–65; 5 (1908), pp. 479–521; 7 (1908), pp. 5–79; 9 (1909), pp. 279–313.

— 'Discussion − Réponse à M. Rousselot', *A.P.C.* 9 (1910), pp. 397–420, 527–35.

Lebreton, J., 'La Connaissance de foi', *Études*, 117 (1908), pp. 731–57.

— 'Son Eminence le Cardinal Billot', *Études*, 129 (1911), pp. 514–25.

Leclère, A., 'Le Mouvement catholique kantien en France à l'heure présente', *Kantstudien*, 7 (1902), pp. 300–63.

Le Roy, E., 'Comment se pose le problème de Dieu', *Revue de métaphysique et de morale*, 15 (1907), pp. 129–70, 470–513.

Lindbeck, G., 'The problem of Doctrinal Development and Contemporary Protestant Theology', *Concilium*, 1 (1967), pp. 64–72.

Loome, T. M., 'A Bibliography of the Published Writings of George Tyrrell' (1861–1909)', *H.J.* 10 (1969), pp. 280–314.

— 'A Bibliography of the Printed Works of George Tyrrell: Supplement', *H.J.* 11 (1970), pp. 161–9.

— (ed.), ' "Revelation as Experience": An Unpublished Lecture of George Tyrrell'. Ed. with notes and historical introduction, *H.J.*, 12 (1971), pp. 117–49.

— 'The Enigma of Baron Friedrich von Hügel − As Modernist', *Downside Review*, 91 (1973), pp. 13–34, 123–40, 204–30.

de Lubac, H., 'Sur la philosophie chrétienne: Réflexions à la suite d'un débat', *Nouvelle revue théologique*, 63 (1936) pp. 225–53.

Lynch, T. (ed.), 'The Newman–Perrone Paper on Development', *Gregorianum*, 16 (1935), pp. 402–47.

Macpherson, D., 'Von Hügel on George Tyrrell', *The Month*, 232 (1971), pp. 178–80.

Mattiussi, G., 'Il veleno kantiano', *La Scuola Cattolica*, 30 (1902), pp. 52–71; 31 (1903), pp. 297–319.

— 'Dogma mutabile (Loisy ed altri)', *La Scuola Cattolica*, 31 (1903), pp. 235–55.

Mercier, D., 'La philosophie néo-scholastique', *Revue néo-scholastique*, 1 (1894), pp. 5–18.

Méry, M., 'Immanence et religion: Un critique italien du modernisme: Giovanni Gentile', *R.S.R.* 61 (1973), pp. 187–215.

Michel, A., 'Intégrisme', *Dictionnaire de théologie catholique. Tables Générales*, Part 2 (Paris, 1967), cols. 2294–2303.

Murri, R., 'L'Enciclica "Pascendi" e la filosofia moderna', *Il Rinno-*

vamento, 1 (1907), pp. 345–65, 539–65.

Nédoncelle, M., 'A Recently Discovered Study of von Hügel on God', *International Philosophical Quarterly*, 2 (1962), pp. 5–24.

O'Connor, F. M., 'George Tyrrell and Dogma', *Downside Review*, 85 (1967), pp. 16–34, 160–82.

Pégues, T.-M., 'Le livre de M. L'Abbé Loisy', *Revue thomiste*, 11 (1903), pp. 70–88.

—— 'Les explications de M. L'Abbé Loisy', *Revue thomiste*, 11 (1903), pp. 593–612.

Poulat, E., ' "Modernisme" et "Intégrisme": Du concept polémique à l'irénisme critique', *Archives de sociologie des religions*, 27 (1969), pp. 3–28.

—— 'Critique historique et théologie dans la crise moderniste', *R.S.R.* 58 (1970), pp. 535–50.

Rivière, J., 'Modernisme', in *Dictionnaire de théologie catholique*, vol. X, Part 2 (Paris, 1929), cols. 2009–2047.

—— 'Qui rédigea l'encyclique "Pascendi"?', *B.L.E.* 47 (1946), pp. 143–61.

Rosa, E., 'Nuovi metodi nell'apologetica', *Civ. Cat.* (1907), pp. 257–74.

—— 'Illusioni dei nuovi metodi di apologetica', *Civ. Cat.* (1907), pp. 23–35.

—— 'Conseguenze dei nuovi metodi di apologetica', *Civ. Cat.* (1907), vol. ii, pp. 414–32.

Schoenl, W. J., 'George Tyrrell and the English Liberal Catholic Crisis, 1900–1901', *Downside Review*, 92 (1974), pp. 171–84.

Schwalm, M. B., 'Les Illusions de l'idéalisme et leurs dangers pour la foi', *Revue thomiste*, 4 (1896), pp. 413–41.

—— 'L'Apologétique contemporaine: Doit-elle adopter une méthode nouvelle?', *Revue thomiste*, 5 (1897), pp. 62–94.

—— 'La Crise de l'apologétique', *Revue thomiste*, 5 (1897), pp. 338–70.

—— 'Le Dogmatisme du cœur et celui de l'esprit', *Revue thomiste*, 6 (1898), pp. 578–619.

Scott, W. A., 'The Notion of Tradition in Maurice Blondel', *Theological Studies*, 27 (1966), pp. 384–400.

Venard, L., 'La Valeur historique du dogme: A propos d'une controverse récent', *B.L.E.* 9–10 (1904), pp. 338–57.

Vermeersch, A., 'Modernism', *The Catholic Encyclopedia* (London and New York, 1911), vol. X, pp. 415–21.

Virgoulay, R., 'Note d'exégèse blondélienne de L'Action à la Lettre de 1896', *R.S.R.* 57 (1969), pp. 205–19.

—— 'La Méthode d'immanence et l'encyclique Pascendi: Incidences de la crise moderniste sur la pensée Blondélienne', *R.S.R.* 58 (1970), pp. 429–54.

Wells, D. F., 'George Tyrrell: Precursor of Process Theology', *Scottish Journal of Theology*, 26 (1973), pp. 71–84.

Wernz, W. J., 'Loisy's "Modernist" Writings', *Downside Review*, 92 (1974), pp. 25–45.

Whelan, J., 'Friedrich von Hügel's Letters to Martin d'Arcy', *The Month*, 42 (1969), pp. 23–36.

Index

Academy of St. Thomas (Rome), 180
action, philosophy of, 29–34 *passim*,
    39–40, 42, 103, 111, 177, 198,
    228
L'Action (Blondel), 6, 31, 34, 35, 36,
    41n., 48, 71
Action Française, 93, 174n., 175
Aeterni Patris (Leo XIII), 9, 188
afférence
    Blondel on, 206–7
agnosticism, 1, 2, 114, 197, 198, 199,
    209
    Lemius on, 181, 185–8 *passim*
    and symbolism, 145
analogy (of Being), 18, 187, 188
Annales de philosophie chrétienne, 44,
    93, 98, 113, 205–7
    editorial on *Pascendi*, 206–7
apologetics, 14, 17, 107, 165, 173,
    192, 209, 222
Aristotelianism, 18, 20, 24, 30, 46, 92,
    126n., 152n., 169, 176, 184,
    201, 211, 219
Aristotle, 31, 185, 188
Arnold, M., 147, 161
atheism, 180, 209
Aubert, R., 10, 17 and n., 32, 92, 106,
    113
Aufieri, R., 139n.
Augustine, St., 24, 33, 210
Augustinianism, 10, 22, 145–6n., 162,
    228
    of Laberthonnière, 92, 93, 98,
    101n., 103, 108, 115
Aulard, A., 196n.
Autour d'un petit livre (Loisy), 55, 61,
    66, 67, 77–8, 179, 197n.

Barmann, L. F., 118n.
Barth, K., 139
'Le basi filosofiche del sistema Loisi-
    ano' (Lemius), 180–4, 233
Battifol, P., 55, 74n.
Baudrillart, A., 190n.

Bedeschi, L., 208 and n.
Being, 101, 103n.
    Laberthonnière on, 98, 100 and n.,
    103, 104, 105
Bellarmine, R., 225
Benedict XV, 218
Benigni, U., 218
Bergson, H., 47, 76n., 162n.
Bernard, St., 48
Bible, 69, 73, 99, 155, 175, 191, 236
Biblical Commission, 175
biblical criticism, 99, 119, 136, 184,
    202, 215, 218, 225, 236
biblicism, 100
Billot, L., 15–17, 105, 124, 174–9,
    188, 232
    and Laberthonnière, 17, 177
    Tyrrell on, 15n.
Blake, W., 115
Blondel, M., 2, 19, 26–50, 56, 62, 93,
    96, 97, 109, 117n., 121, 128,
    136, 165, 167, 173, 178, 185,
    186, 193, 194–5, 198, 202,
    205, 206, 207, 213, 219, 228,
    234
    and contemporary French philoso-
        phy, 29–30
    and Dechamps, 21n., 22
    and von Hügel, 72, 78, 87, 88
    and Kant, 30, 40
    and Laberthonnière, 91 and n.,
        95, 100n., 107
    and Le Roy, 109
    and Loisy, 69–90
    and *Pascendi*, 27–8
    'Tetralogy' of, 27
    as theologian, 28–9
Boegner, M., 93
Bourne, F., 145
Boutroux, E., 30, 43
Boutwood, A., 157
de Boyer de Sainte Suzanne, R., 52,
    54, 57
Bremond, H., 51, 92, 97, 98n., 105n.,

Bremond, H. (*cont.*)
147, 152, 205, 229, 232
on Loisy's 'foi mystique', 52
Browne, R. K., 129n.
Brunschvicg, L., 41n
Bulletin de littérature ecclésiastique, 82, 177
Bultmann, R., 100n.
Buonaiuti, E., 151n., 208, 210–13, 220, 232

Cartechini, S., 225
Castelli, E., 91, 104
The Catholic Encyclopedia (1911), 216–17
causality, 187
de Caussade, J. P., 64
Chapman, R., 141
Chenu, M.-D., 100n.
'Du Christ éternel' (von Hügel), 78–9
Christianity
Blondel's two methods of approach to, 76–7
Christianity at the Cross-Roads (Tyrrell), 144n., 146
christology, 87, 183, 199–200
and Loisy, 72
and von Hügel, 136
Church, R. W., 98
La Civiltà Cattolica, 167, 171–4
Claudel, P., 229
Cock, A., 140n.
Codex juris canonici, 218
Coleridge, S. T., 117n
Collingwood, R. G., 224
Combes, E., 190
Comma Johanneum
Billot on, 175
Comte, A., 57
conscience
Loisy on, 63
Tyrrell on, 160
Constantine, Emperor, 152n.
contingency, 224
Von Hügel on, 122, 123, 126, 137
conversion
Laberthonnière on, 102
Coulson, J., 117, 129n.
Crespi, A., 124n.
La Croix, 233

Dechamps, V., 21–2, 125–6n.
Blondel on, 21n., 22

Dei Filius (Vat. I), 8
Dei Verbum (Vat. II), 14
deism, 150, 153
De Lai, G., 190n.
de la Bedoyère, M., 120
Denis, C., 35
Descartes, R., 10, 31, 48, 104
'Da Dio o dagli uomini?' (Tyrrell), 135, 149, 152
'disfiguration', 210
Pascendi on, 199, 202
'Divine Fecundity' (Tyrrell), 162–4
doctrine, *see* dogma
'Sur les doctrines de Loisy' (Lemius), 180, 184–7, 233
dogma, 20, 109, 114, 115, 168, 175n., 176, 187, 192, 194, 202, 222–3, 235
Blondel on, 81, 82
Le Roy on, 110–12
Loisy on, 59, 67–8
Pascendi on, 200, 201, 203
Vermeersch on, 216–17
and history, 57, 69–90
dogma, development of, 155, 183, 186, 201, 235
Laberthonnière on, 98 and n., 99
Tyrrell on, 155–6
'dogmatism'
Laberthonnière on, 98, 100
'Le dogmatisme moral' (Laberthonnière), 98, 102, 103, 106, 170
Billot on, 177
'Dogme et critique' (Le Roy), 109n.
'Dogme et théologie' (Laberthonnière), 113–15
Dulles, A., 227
Dupuy, B. D., 97n.

Eastwood, D. M., 103n.
efférence
Blondel on, 206–7
episcopal succession, 236
epistemology
Von Hügel on Kant's, 124
Loisy's, 81
eschatology, 135–6
Tyrrell on, 148–9
l'esprit de finesse, 23
l'esprit de géométrie, 22, 23
essentialism, 100
Eternal Life (von Hügel), 119

Eucharist, 110
Eucken, R., 45, 137
L'Évangile et l'Église (Loisy), 43, 55,
61, 66, 67, 69, 71, 72, 74, 77,
179
existentialists, 100
experience, 101, 102, 117–39 *passim*,
192, 217, 231
von Hügel on, 117–39 *passim*
Laberthonnière on, 113
Le Roy on, 113
Tyrrell on, 140–64 *passim*
'Experience and Transcendence' (von
Hügel), 121–3
extrinsicism, 9, 38, 75, 217
of Billot, 16–17
Laberthonnière on, 106, 114

facta externa, 19
fait extérieur, 20, 21, 84
fait intérieur, 20–4, 32, 84, 108, 161,
209
faith, 8, 40, 105, 113, 172, 235
Billot on, 15–16
Blondel on, 87
von Hügel on, 128
Laberthonnière on, 96, 101
Loisy on, 182–3
Pascendi on, 199
Programme of Modernism on, 210
and history, 70
and knowledge, 106
and reason, 9
preliminaries to, 8, 15
Feuerbach, L., 124, 144
Ficino, M., 45
fideism, 84, 105, 134, 173
Fogazzaro, A., 191
Fonsgrive, G., 35
Fontaine, J., 97, 166
'friction'
von Hügel on, 136, 228
Froude, H., 132
Fumagalli, A., 165
fundamental theology, 7–25 *passim*,
222, 230
defined by Hurter, 9n.
and scholasticism, 19–20

Gardeil, A., 48
Gayraud, H., 22, 44, 46, 94, 97
Gelli, S. (Tyrrell), 173
Genocchi, G., 175n., 215

Gentile, G., 151n.
Gilson, E., 100n., 101n., 106
Giornale d'Italia, 76, 130
Gnosticism, 76, 130
God
Loisy's idea of, 58
Goichot, E., 98n.
Gombault, 45
Grammar of Assent (Newman), 129n.
Grandmaison L. de, 180n.
Gregorian University (Rome), 10, 174
Gregory IX, 200
Guisan, R., 139n.

Haight, R., 56n.
Harent, S., 216
Harnack, A. von, 67–8, 146, 166
Blondel on, 72
and Loisy, 55, 62, 63
Tyrrell on, 148
Harvey, V. A., 70
Hébert, M., 128 and n., 130n.
Hegel, G. W. F., 132
Heidegger, M., 102
Hellenism, 192, 224
von Hügel on, 130, 134
hermeneutics, 87, 102 and n., 226
Laberthonnière on, 99–104
Herrmann, W., 69, 133, 136
heteronomy
Laberthonnière on, 108
'Histoire et dogme' (Blondel), 27, 40n.,
72, 73–7
historical sensitivity, 224–8
historicism, 70, 75, 76, 77, 82, 84
history, 86, 183–4, 197, 199, 236
and dogma, 57, 58, 69–90
von Hügel on, 136
Pascendi on, 202
and scholasticism, 20
holiness
von Hügel on, 136
Houtin, A., 51, 71, 128n., 175n., 232
Von Hügel, F., 2, 58, 74n., 97, 98n.,
117–39, 146, 152, 161, 193n.,
207 and n., 214, 219, 228
and Blondel, 72, 78, 87, 88
on Kant, 122–5, 138
on Kierkegaard, 132–3
and Laberthonnière, 88
and Loisy, 51, 58, 78–9, 87–90
passim, 119n., 120, 134n.
and Newman, 129n., 131n.

Von Hügel, F. (*cont.*)
  and *Pascendi*, 138, 139
  and Tyrrell, 120n., 126n., 140 and
    n., 146, 152, 154
Von Hügel, G., 120n.
Hume, D., 101n., 161
Hurter, H., 9n., 111n., 124

idealism, 99
Ignatius Loyola, St., 198
immanence apologetics, 165, 222;
  see also apologetics
immanence, doctrine of, 26, 185
  Blondel distinguishes from principle
    and method of, 39n.
  von Hügel rejects, 118
immanence, method of, 39, 50, 73, 89,
    139n., 172
  Blondel on, 26, 34n., 41
  Laberthonnière on, 101, 106
  Le Roy on, 111
immanence, philosophy of, 46-7
immanence, principle of, 39 and n.
  Le Roy on, 112
immanentism, 1, 49, 77, 84, 203, 208
  and Blondel, 206
  and Buonaiuti, 208, 212, 213
  and von Hügel, 120-1, 124, 133,
    137-8
  Le Roy on, 111
  of Loisy, 53, 59, 120
  and *The Programme of Modernism*,
    209
  and scholasticism, 49
  and Tyrrell, 141, 152-3
Index of Prohibited Books, 60, 109n.
Inge, W., 229
integralism, 7, 187, 218, 219, 230
  of Billot, 16 and n., 174n.
integralist response to modernism
  before *Pascendi*, 165-89
  after *Pascendi*, 190-217
intellectualism, 92, 109
Institut Catholique
  (Paris), 44, 45, 215
  (Toulouse), 29n.
interpretation, *see* hermeneutics
intuition, 23-5
  von Hügel on, 122
  and Laberthonnière, 106, 113, 116
Italian modernism, 212-13

Jansenism, 23

Janssens, L., 232

Kant, I., 8, 101 and n., 112, 124, 138,
    161, 185, 198, 209, 234
  Billot on, 178
  Blondel on, 30, 40
  von Hügel on, 122-5, 138
  Mattiussi on, 166-71
  scholastics on, 189
Kantianism, 2, 18, 26, 30, 43, 45-9,
    104, 165, 215, 223
  scholastics on, 45
Keats, J., 127n.
Kierkegaard, S., 69
  von Hügel on, 132-3
Kingdom of God
  Tyrrell on, 162, 164
Klein, F., 60

Laberthonnière, L., 35, 38, 42, 43, 44,
    47 and n., 50, 62, 71, 74n.,
    75, 77, 91-116, 128, 145-6n.,
    152, 165, 167, 178, 185, 186,
    188, 193, 201n., 213, 224, 228
  and Billot, 17, 177
  and Blondel, 91 and n., 95, 100n.,
    107
  character of, 91-2
  and von Hügel, 88
  and Loisy, 198
  on mandatory Thomism, 11
  and Newman, 97
  and Pascal, 23, 92, 103n., 108, 125
  on *Pascendi*, 205-7
Labouré, T., 233
Lachelier, J., 43
Lacroix, J., 42, 78n, 91n.
Lagrange, M.-J., 74n.
Lamentabili sane exitu, 193-5, 205, 235
Larkin, M., 190n.
Lash, N., 226
Lebreton, J., 106, 113, 114, 115, 157,
    175, 196n., 215
Leclère, A.,
  on Kantianism in France, 46-7
Le Floch, H., 174n.
Leibniz, G. W., 100n., 122
Lemius, J., 166, 179-87, 195, 196,
    197n., 198-9, 209
  on Loisy, 179-87
  draughtsman of *Pascendi*, 232-4
  on the modernists, 234
  and A. Sabatier, 185, 186n.

Lemius, J. B., 232
Leo XIII, 18–19, 97, 165
  and mandatory Thomism, 9–10
Le Roy, E., 47, 52, **109–13**, 170–1,
    178, 213, 223, 234
  and Blondel, 109
  and Laberthonnière, 108, 114–15
Lessing, G. E., 57, 69, 121
Letter on Apologetics (Blondel), 26,
    27, 34, 35–6, **36–43**, 45, 71,
    207
Lettere di un prete modernista
    (Buonaiuti), 211–12
Liberal Catholicism, 4, 155
Liberal Protestantism, 56, 115, 141,
    149, 154, 162, 180, 194, 214,
    215, 229
  compared with modernism, 221–2
  Tyrrell on, 146–8
Lilley, A. L., 191n., 193n., 208n.
Lindbeck, G. A., 227
Livre inédit (Loisy), 44–5
Loisy, A., 51–68, 99, 128, 141, 146,
    165, 166, 214, 220, 224–5,
    228, 234
  Billot on, 176, 179
  and Blondel, 69–90
  claim of to be only an historian,
    54
  'Firmin' articles of, 62–6
  and von Hügel, 51, 58, 78–9,
    87–90 *passim*, 119n., 120,
    134n.
  and Laberthonnière, 198
  and *Lamentabili*, 194
  Lemius on, 179–187
  and Newman, 61–2
  and *Pascendi*, 197–8, 202, 205, 207
  personal faith of, 51
  as undisclosed philosopher, 57
London Society for the Study of
    Religion, 89, 118
Loome, T. M., 118n., 140n.
Louvain, Catholic University of, 10
Lonergan, B., 222, 227n.
Lossky, W., 95n.
de Lubac, H., 42, 45, 95n.
Luther, M., 216

McCarthy, J., 218
McNeill, J. J., 31n., 48
Maignen, C., 188
Maine de Biran, F., 32, 33, 92

manuals (neo-scholastic), 11–13, 224
  and the Catholic priesthood, 13
Maritain, J., 42
Marlé, R., 71n.
Maubec, E.,
  Loisy's letter to, 59–60
Mauras, C., 175
Maurice, F. D., 117n.
Mattiussi, G., 166–71, 172, 174, 176
Mercier, D., 10, 11, 198, 215
Merry del Val, R., 174n., 190 and n.
Messina earthquake, 162
methodus regressiva, 225
Mignot, E.-J., 63n.
miracle, 44, 210, 235
  Billot on, 17
  Blondel on, 37
  Gayraud on, 46
  Mattiussi on, 170
modernism
  towards a definition of, 1–16
  events surrounding the condemna-
    tion of, 165–217
  effect of condemnation on subse-
    quent Catholic theology, 218–
    231
Möhler, J. A., 117n.
'morcelage'
  Le Roy on, 109
Mourret, F., 205
Murri, R., 173, 175n., 212
  on *Pascendi*, 213
The Mystical Element of Religion
    (von Hügel), 119, 122, 124,
    129n., 130
mysticism, 127–8, 173, 228
  von Hügel on, 117–39 *passim*
  Tyrrell on, 147–8

Nédoncelle, M., 119, 137, 138 and n.
'Negative Capability', 127n.
neo-scholasticism, *see* Scholasticism
Newman, J. H., 23, 98, 117n., 149,
    228–9
  and Laberthonnière, 97
  and von Hügel, 129n., 131n.
  and Loisy, 61–2
  and Tyrrell, 155–6, 207
  and *Pascendi*, 207–8

Oath against Modernism, 218, 235–6
Oblates of Mary Immaculate, 179,
    232, 233

O'Connor, F. M., 142n.
Oil and Wine (Tyrrell), 150, 153
Ollé-Laprune, L., 32, 35, 66
Ontologism, 173
  and Laberthonnière, 104, 105n., 108
Osservatore Romano, 171
Ott, L., 1
Oxford Movement, 97-8

Palmer, R. E., 102n.
'panchristisme'
  of Blondel, 72, 136
panentheism
  von Hügel on, 135
  Tyrrell on, 153, 154
pantheism, 133-4, 135, 162, 201
  and von Hügel, 133-4
  and Tyrrell, 150, 153
papal infallibility, 21
Parousia
  Blondel on, 85
Pasanisi, F., 166n.
Pascal, B., 22-5, 32, 33, 47, 107, 132, 228
  and the *fait intérieur*, 22, 24
  and modernism, 25
  ordre du cœur of, 24
  and Vat. II, 24
  and Laberthonnière, 92, 103n., 108, 125
Pascendi dominici gregis, 1, 45, 77, 114, 149, 151n., 171, 179, 180, 190, 195-204, 219, 232-4, 236
  and Blondel, 27-8
  disciplinary section, 204n.
  Laberthonnière on, 205-7
  and von Hügel, 138, 139
  Murri on, 213-14
  and Newman, 207-8
  response to, 204-17
  Tyrrell on, 4, 204-5, 220
Pattison, M., 98n.
Pégues, T.-M., 55
Pelikan, J., 227
Pentateuch, 176
'pensée-action'
  Le Roy on, 111, 223
Perrone, G., 13-14
  on Latin, 12n.
Pesch, C., 124
Petite consultation (von Hügel), 138, 139

Petre, M. D., 57, 119, 137, 140, 145, 146n., 150
philosophy
  Blondel on autonomy and insufficiency of, 42-3
  Lemius on, 184
  of Loisy, 80-1
Plotinus, 130
Political Theology, 163
Portalié, E., 28-9, 74n.
positivism, 77, 93, 181
Poulat, E., 4, 55, 60, 78, 187
prayer
  von Hügel on, 119, 128, 129n.
Le Problème de la philosophie catholique (Blondel), 36
'Le Problème religieux' (Laberthonnière), 94
Process Theology, 112, 163, 223
Proclus, 130
Programme of Modernism, 208-11
  Tyrrell on, 208n.
proofs for the existence of God
  Buonaiuti on, 212
  von Hügel on, 125
  Laberthonnière on, 105
  Le Roy on, 112
  Loisy on, 58
  Sacrorum antistum on, 235
prophecy, 210, 235
  Tyrrell on, 158-9
Protestantism, 40, 47, 70-1, 189, 215; *see also* Liberal Protestantism
'provisional pessimism'
  Tyrrell on, 162-4
Pius X, 165, 190, 108, 214, 218
  Allocutio of (1907), 191

Quello che vogliamo, 191-3, 234
'Qu'est-ce qu'un dogme?' (Le Roy), 59, 109 and n.
Quietism, 32, 229
La Quinzaine, 59, 74, 78, 109

Rahner, K., 222
rationalism, 21
Le Réalisme chrétien (Laberthonnière), 94n., 102, 104n., 231
Reardon, B. M. G., 174n.
'The Relation of Theology to Devotion' (Tyrrell), 142

relativism, 227 and n.
religion, 79, 186
  von Hügel on, 88, 127n., 129, 131-3, 137n.
  Laberthonnière on, 107
  Loisy on, 58, 60, 63-4
  Quello che vogliamo on, 192
religious sense, 32, 63, 186, 236
  Lemius on, 185-6
  Loisy on, 65
  Rosa on, 174
  Pascendi on, 199-200
Renan, E., 61
Renouvier, C., 43
resurrection of Christ, 110
  Blondel on, 85
revelation, 29, 113, 114, 176, 192, 194, 199, 217, 226, 235
  Blondel on, 36, 39, 41
  von Hügel on, 126, 136
  Loisy on, 64-8
  Perrone on, 14
  Tyrrell on, 140-64 *passim*
  Vat. I on, 8
Revue du clergé français, 46, 54, 83
Revue d'histoire et de littérature religieuse, 71
Revue de métaphysique et de morale, 112
Revue Thomiste, 43 and n.
Richard, F., 194n.
Richardson, A., 86
Il Rinnovamento, 213, 149, 151
Ritschl, A., 69
Rivière, J., 195, 232, 233
Rosa, E., 171-4, 214
Rossi, M., 213

Sabatier, A., 146, 180, 198, 214, 234
  Catholic influence upon, 66n.
  and Lemius, 185, 186n.
  and Loisy, 62-6 *passim*
  Tyrrell on, 142
Sabatier, P., 208, 213
De sacra traditione (Billot), 176
Sacrorum antistitum (1910), 216n., 235-6
Sagnier, M., 93
Saint-Jean, R., 78n.
de Sales, St. François, 64
Sardi, V., 233
Sartiaux, F., 51, 53
Schillebeeckx, E., 223

Schleiermacher, F., 32, 64, 69
  von Hügel on, 136
Schoenberg, A., 155
Scholasticism, 7-25 *passim*, 32, 46, 47, 49, 97, 114, 141, 169, 171, 172, 193 and n., 204, 210-11, 218-19, 220, 224-5, 228, 229
  and von Hügel, 118, 128 and n., 130n., 137
  and Laberthonnière, 106-7
  on supernature, 40
  Tyrrell on, 11n., 145, 148-52, 157, 159, 162
Scholastics, 75, 112
  on Kantianism, 45, 189
Schwalm, M.-B., 22, 43 and n., 44, 94, 97, 166
Schweitzer, A., 56, 141
scepticism
  Laberthonnière on, 98
science, 157, 170, 188, 194, 210
  Blondel on, 36
  von Hügel on, 134
  Tyrrell on, 157
Scoppola, P., 152n.
La Scuola Cattolica, 166, 176
Segna, F., 190n.
Semeria, G., 175n., 215
  Loisy's letter to, 58-9
'Semper Eadem' (Tyrrell), 156
sensibility, 229-30
Simples réflexions (Loisy), 205
Societé Française de Philosophie, 41n.
sociology, 75n., 125
'Socratic determinism'
  Laberthonnière on, 96, 101
Sodalitium pianum, 218
Sorbonne, 29
Spencer, H., 173, 209
Spinoza, B., 48-9, 163
Strauss, D. F., 69
Suarez, F., 10, 100n.
subjectivism, 47, 181
suffering
  von Hügel on, 129n.
  Tyrrell on, 162-4
supernatural, *see* supernature
supernature, 35, 50, 94, 114, 115, 236
  Blondel discusses, 36, 76; relates to transcendence, 38-9; postulates human exigence for, 41, 44
  central place of in Catholic theology, 94-5

supernature (*cont.*)
    Laberthonnière on, 93; criticizes role of in Catholic theology, 94-7 *passim*; relates to method of immanence, 107-8
    Le Roy on, 112
superstition, 107
symbol
    Loisy on, 59, 66, 82
    Tyrrell on, 145
symbolism, 77, 182, 203, 214
    Laberthonnière on, 99
    Pascendi on, 200

Talbot, G., 13n.
'theologism'
    Tyrrell on, 154-5, 160
theology, 69, 182
    von Hügel on, 129
    Tyrrell on, 142-3, 159-60
Thomas Aquinas, St., 137, 138, 165, 166, 169, 170, 184
    and *Pascendi*, 203-4
Thomism, 39, 40n., 92, 93, 95
    restoration of, 9-11
    see also Scholasticism
The Times, 204, 207
de Tonquédec, J., 205n.
tradition, 83, 155, 191, 236
    Blondel on, 81, 84, 85
traditionalism, 105n.
transcendental Thomism, 222
'transfiguration', 89n., 210
    Pascendi on, 199, 202
Trent, Council of, 102
Troeltsch, E., 68, 137
truth (epistemology), 96, 168, 194, 236
    Blondel on, 31, and religious truth, 84
    Laberthonnière and, 94, 108, 231
    Loisy on, 80-1
    relativity of, 178, 179
'tyrannous Transcendentalism'
    von Hügel on, 120, 121, 124, 135, 122
    related by Tyrrell to Church government, 150-2

Tyrrell, G., 4, 45, 55, 113n., 128 and n., 140-64, 191n., 193, 198, 213n., 218, 220, 226, 228, 229, 230, 234
    and Blondel, 84n.
    and von Hügel, 120n., 126n., 140 and n., 146, 152, 154
    and Laberthonnière, 92-3, 98, 99, 105n.
    and Newman, 155-6, 207
    and *Pascendi*, 4, 204-5, 220
    on A. Sabatier, 142

Underhill, E., 136
universals, 187

Valensin, A., 205
Vatican I, 8, 15, 44, 113, 165, 168, 179, 197, 209, 210
    on rationalism, 21
    on revelation and faith, 8
Vatican II, 100, 197, 217, 219, 220-1, 226
    on 'hierarchy of truths', 219-20
Il veleno Kantiano (Mattiussi), 166-71
Venard, L., 83, 84n., 85
Vermeersch, A., 5
    on modernism, 216-17
Vidler, A. R., 52n., 127n.
'vital immanence'
    Lemius on, 185
    Pascendi on, 198, 201
Vivès y Tuto, C., 190n., 232
volonté voulante
    Blondel on, 33-4, 40
volonté voulue
    Blondel on, 33-4, 40
Voltaire, F., 22

Ward, W., 126, 202, 207, 215, 232
Webb, C. C. J., 120
Wehrlé, J., 54, 72n., 73, 87, 88, 111
Weiss, J., 56, 141
Whelan, J. P., 130n.
Wiles, M., 227
Williams, R., 127n., 229
Wolff, C., 100n.